STUDIES IN MODERNITY AND NATIONAL IDENTITY

Sibel Bozdoğan and Reşat Kasaba, Series Editors

STUDIES IN MODERNITY AND NATIONAL IDENTITY

Studies in Modernity and National Identity examine the relationships among modernity, the nation-state, and nationalism as these have evolved in the nineteenth and twentieth centuries. Titles in this interdisciplinary and transregional series also illuminate how the nation-state is being undermined by the forces of globalization, international migration, and electronic information flows, as well as resurgent ethnic and religious affiliations. These books highlight historical parallels and continuities while documenting the social, cultural, and spatial expressions through which modern national identities have been constructed, contested, and reinvented.

Modernism and Nation Building: Turkish Architectural Culture in the Early Republic by Sibel Bozdoğan

Chandigarh's Le Corbusier: The Struggle for Modernity in Postcolonial India by Vikramaditya Prakash

Islamist Mobilization in Turkey: A Study in Vernacular Politics by Jenny B. White

The Landscape of Stalinism: The Art and Ideology of Soviet Space, edited by Evgeny Dobrenko and Eric Naiman

Architecture and Tourism in Italian Colonial Libya: An Ambivalent Modernism by Brian L. McLaren

Everyday Modernity in China, edited by Madeleine Yue Dong and Joshua L. Goldstein

Nationalizing Iran: Culture, Power, and the State, 1870–1940 by Afshin Marashi

NATIONALIZING IRAN

Culture, Power, and the State, 1870–1940

AFSHIN MARASHI

UNIVERSITY OF WASHINGTON PRESS   Seattle and London

THIS PUBLICATION WAS SUPPORTED IN PART BY THE DONALD R.
ELLEGOOD INTERNATIONAL PUBLICATIONS ENDOWMENT.

University of Washington Press
P.O. Box 50096, Seattle, WA 98145 U.S.A.
www.washington.edu/uwpress

Library of Congress Cataloging-in-Publication Data

Marashi, Afshin.
    Nationalizing Iran : culture, power, and the state, 1870–1940 / Afshin
Marashi. — 1st ed.
        p.   cm. — (Studies in modernity and national identity)
    Includes bibliographical references and index.
    ISBN 978–0–295–98799–6 (hardback : alk. paper)
    1. Iran—History—Pahlavi dynasty, 1925–1979.   2. Nationalism—Iran.
    3. Education and state—Iran—History.   4. Iran—Civilization.   I. Title.
DS316.32. M37   2008
955'.04—dc22   2007038561

The paper used in this publication is acid-free and 90 percent recycled from
at least 50 percent post-consumer waste. It meets the minimum requirements
of American National Standard for Information Sciences—Permanence of
Paper for Printed Library Materials, ANSI Z39.48–1984.

For my mother and for my family in Iran and America

CONTENTS

ACKNOWLEDGMENTS

THIS BOOK BEGAN ITS LIFE SO LONG AGO THAT IT IS DIFFICULT NOW TO remember exactly when and where it originated. Perhaps it began during my years as a graduate student in the history department at UCLA, where it took shape as my PhD dissertation. Perhaps it started during my undergraduate years at Berkeley, conjured up somewhere in the cafes and bookstores along Telegraph Avenue. Going back even further, perhaps it first stirred during a childhood and adolescence lived—like those of so many other Iranians of my generation—in the shadow of the Islamic revolution. Wherever and whenever it started, this work is the record not only of an intellectual inquiry but also of a personal odyssey. I must therefore acknowledge the many teachers, mentors, friends, family members, and colleagues who helped and encouraged me along the way.

I owe the greatest debt to my teachers. Nikki Keddie, as my PhD advisor, shaped my understanding of Iranian history in too many ways to count. It was her stern hand that led me through these pages as I made the many changes and revisions to the manuscript, first as a dissertation and later as a book. I thank her for all she has taught me, as well as for her tireless and generous support in other matters. Also at UCLA, I thank Jim Gelvin for challenging me and pointing me in directions in which I would not otherwise have ventured. I would like to think that those thick wafts of smoke coming from his Cuban cigars inspired at least some of the ideas in this book.

At Berkeley I was fortunate to meet Kiren Chaudhry, the first person to encourage me to think of myself as an academic. Also at Berkeley, I thank Hamid Algar, from whom I learned the art of historiographic iconoclasm, and Ira Lapidus, from whom I learned the virtue of tempered, reasoned judgment. I believe there are traces of both in this book. I also thank Eric Hooglund for his support and for sharing with me his infectious enthusiasm for Iranian history and politics. Houchang Chehabi was in many ways the role model for whom I had always looked. For young Iranians growing up outside of Iran since the revolution, I can think of no better role model than Houchang.

I received generous financial support from a number of institutions during the research and writing of this book, including UCLA's Gustave Von Grunebaum Center for Near Eastern Studies, the UCLA Center for Social Theory and Comparative History, the Andrew Mellon Foundation, the UCLA Department of History, and the California State University, Sacramento, Office of Research and Sponsored Projects. This work could not have been completed without their help. I also thank Michael Duckworth, of the University of Washington Press, for ably shepherding this project from manuscript to book.

I am grateful to the many friends and colleagues whose encouragement, patience, and inspiration made the challenges posed by such an undertaking easier to bear. At UCLA I was fortunate to be part of a thriving community of history and Middle Eastern studies graduate students, including Touraj Daryaee, Mitch Numark, Reza Mehdizadeh, John Eskander, Maya Yazigi, Magdy Al-Shama, Patricia Singleton, Seth Jameson, Lars Schumacher, Maher Mamerzadeh, Ali Anoushahr, Maziar Behrooz, Houri Berberian, Keith Watenpaugh, Heghnar Watenpaugh, Nancy Um, Wendy Shaw, Howard Eissenstat, and Edgar Francis. I especially thank Sandra Campbell for being a great friend, a wonderful teacher, and a genuine *hoca* all rolled into one. At Berkeley I learned a great deal from friends and fellow travelers such as Mike Berk, Elizabeth Lobb, Tony Ro, Clementine Oliver, Thaddeaus Bordofsky, Lisa Bass, Phil Lowenthal, Greg Battersby, Donald Frades, Kevin Walsh, Adam Marsh, Rafael Simon, and Rob Perez. Karen Lottman and Sohaib Kureshi have been my dear friends since I was knee-high to a stack of overdue library books. They both inspired the budding historian in me.

In Sacramento I have received great support from the history department at California State University, Sacramento. Chris Castaneda, chair of the history department, and Bahman Fozouni, director of the Iranian and Middle Eastern Studies program, have been sources of great encouragement, as has Suad Joseph of UC Davis's Middle East and South Asian Studies program. Special thanks go to my friend Erin Stiles, who stands out among a group of already exceptionally supportive colleagues at Sacramento State. Students Malina Dunk, Alma Shaykhani, and others in my Modern Middle Eastern History courses also helped shape many of the ideas in this book. Special thanks go to Kathleen Kelly for her support as this adventure comes to an end. I look forward to all the other adventures we have yet to share.

Most importantly, I thank my parents. I am aware that in a work in which my subject matter is the world into which my parents were born and which my grandparents helped to create, I am in a sense embedded in my own narrative. I will say only that I am aware of this embeddedness and leave it to others to derive its implications. Because of the circumstances of history, I was never able to know my grandparents, but through the writing of this book I feel I have drawn closer to them. From my mother I learned everything that is good about Iranian modernity; her support and love have been the most important guiding forces in my life. The greatest satisfaction I receive in completing this work is in knowing that she is here to witness its conclusion. I thank my father, too, through whom I lived the revolution and everything that followed. From his life I have learned more about the wages of history than anything mere books can teach.

I also acknowledge my uncle Mehdi Marashi, whose career as an academic, I am proud to say, paved the way for my own. I thank my uncle Ahmad, aunt Joy, and cousin Jaleh, who were always powerful exemplars of the idea that there is no contradiction between being an Iranian and an American. I thank my sister for allowing me to indulge my prodigal interests, even if it has meant shirking my other responsibilities. I promise I will make it up to her in other ways. Finally, I also dedicate this book to my niece and nephew. As they grow older and begin to ask the same questions I asked in my adolescence, I hope they will not feel burdened by their history but that they might look to this book and see themselves as part of the story. I hope they will take comfort in knowing that their uncle has already sifted through the rubble of their past so that they can spend their lives looking forward.

NATIONALIZING IRAN

INTRODUCTION

IN OCTOBER 1971, MOHAMMAD REZA SHAH PAHLAVI—THE SHAH OF IRAN, "LIGHT of the Aryans"—staged an official celebration marking the twenty-five-hundredth anniversary of the founding of the Persian Empire.[1] Seven days of commemorative ceremonies were held in the windswept desert oasis of Persepolis, in southwestern Iran, amid the ruins of the ancient imperial capital. What was most remarkable about the spectacle was not the parade of foot soldiers and cavalrymen dressed in the garb of the Achaemenid, Parthian, and Sassanian armies marching in sequence past the shah, against the backdrop of the archaeological remains; nor was it the nine kings, five queens, thirteen princes, eight princesses, sixteen presidents, three premiers, four vice presidents, two governors general, two foreign ministers, nine sheikhs, and two sultans who attended the gala affair as the shah's honored guests; nor was it the twenty-five thousand bottles of wine, eight thousand pounds of lamb, and like quantities of caviar, quail eggs, and roasted peacock stuffed with foie gras that were served to those in attendance. Rather, what was most noteworthy about the spectacle at Persepolis was the speech the shah made to launch the celebration. Standing before the unadorned stone tomb of Cyrus the Great, founder of the Persian Empire some two and a half millennia before, the shah offered salutations to his ancient predecessor and declared before his assembled guests, and to his countrymen via radio and television, "Rest in peace, Cyrus, for we are awake and we will always stay awake."[2]

Implicit in the shah's words was a set of assumptions grounded in the social, cultural, and political coordinates of nationalism—assumptions that became possible only as a result of modernizing transformations that had taken place in Iran since the late nineteenth century. These transformations included the creation of a national infrastructure and bureaucracy, a national army, a nationwide system of communication, a permanent and regularized system of revenue gathering, a modern national system of education, and a uniform system of law. They also involved the quelling of corporate or subnational sources of authority such as tribal, linguistic, and sectarian identifications and the promotion of a uniform sense of national memory, culture, and identity.[3]

It was this work of state-building and cultural production, going back to the late nineteenth century, that gave meaning and coherence to the words the shah spoke before Cyrus's tomb. He sought to affirm the existence of an Iranian nation characterized by a congruence of state institutions, social structures, and cultural forms—a congruence that was the defining characteristic of modern nations. The shah was thus conjuring up, in what Benedict Anderson called "the magic of nationalism," an intangible yet vivid abstraction, linking together a set of implicit social, cultural, and political assumptions.[4]

What exactly was the nature of this symbolic invocation? First, the shah's words affirmed the existence of the state not merely as a set of impersonal governmental institutions but also as something infused with identity and a sense of history. The tomb of Cyrus symbolized the Iranian state's point of origin, and the shah himself represented its contemporary embodiment. His words assumed continuity between Cyrus and himself. Second, beyond invoking the vivid abstraction of the state, the shah's words presumed an equally vivid and abstract notion of collectivity. This was represented in his choice of the pronoun "we" as he made his declaration before the cold stone of Cyrus's tomb. "We are awake and we will always stay awake," he affirmed, presenting himself not only as the embodiment of the state but also as the spokesman for the collectivity. The shah was thus first among Iranians—not above and beyond the collectivity, basking in the halo of monarchical sacrality, but a member of a uniform collectivity sharing common characteristics.

Finally, the spectacle at the tomb invoked a particular form of historical memory. The shah's referencing of ancient Iranian culture implied a return to a primary authenticity associated with that period. As he spoke in the name of the state and the nation, he asserted them to encompass a unique memory and culture that all members of the collectivity could understand and to which they could feel a sense of belonging. The choreography of the ceremony amid the ancient ruins, the parade of foot soldiers dressed in the replica garb of ancient armies, and the invocation of Cyrus all assumed that the state and the nation could claim the right to speak in the name of a particular notion of authenticity. The entire series of ceremonies associated with the anniversary vividly illustrates the convergence of state, society, and historical memory that had been achieved by the time of the Pahlavi monarchy's political apex.

STATE, SOCIETY, AND CLAIMS OF POLITICAL AUTHORITY

The ceremonies of 1971 were not the beginning of this convergence of state, nation, and historical memory in Iran. Rather, they were made possible as a consequence of a century of social, cultural, and political transformation. Clearly, a transformation had taken place from the time Naser al-Din Shah (r. 1848–96) claimed the titles "Shadow of God on Earth" and "Pivot of the Universe" to the time Mohammad Reza Shah Pahlavi (r. 1941–79) proclaimed himself "Shah of Iran" and "Light of the Aryans." The former's claims of authority were tied to premodern conceptions of sacred kingship, whereas the language of modern nationalism infused the latter's. Underlying this change in formal claims of political authority were more important transformations in the social, cultural, and political assumptions that animated Iranian consciousness.

The most fundamental transformation took place in the idea of the state vis-à-vis society. At the beginning of Naser al-Din Shah's reign, his claims of authority were tied to cosmic and sacred sources of power. The category "the state" had premodern roots in Iranian history, as is clear from the court rituals of pomp and circumstance detailed in the travel writings of myriad European scholars, adventurers, and fortune seekers who came to see the proverbial peacock throne in all its ceremonial grandeur.[5] But despite its existence in premodern Iranian history, the state was also to a great extent characterized by a political solipsism, remaining largely self-referential, or more concerned with linking its authority to external, cosmic, and sacred points of reference than with any awareness of its relationship to "society."[6] Society, in turn, was atomized and segmented through vertical lines of authority linked to regional, tribal, sectarian, and linguistic loyalties, poorly integrated beyond a conception of certain basic yet highly fluid, overlapping, and evolving geographic parameters.[7] Prior to the transformations of the late nineteenth and early twentieth centuries, "state" and "society" were thus only partially actualized as social categories and were at best parallel and incongruous.

By the mid-twentieth century, a fundamental change had taken place in state-society relations. The state was now externally robust and internally more integrated, capable of projecting its will across society. Under the influence of the state's new power, society itself was reimagined as a single cloth. Mohammad Reza Shah Pahlavi's claims of authority, as Shah *of Iran* and Light *of the Aryans,* thus were not tied to sources of power above or outside the nation but rather were grounded in the fabric of society itself. This transformation was based on the premise that state and society were tied together by a common culture and that the role of the state was now to be the representative and agent of that common and sharply delineated culture. The ideological details or contents of that culture became, as we know, the source of dramatic contestation. But the form of the conceptualization itself—the notion of a social abstraction characterized by a congruence of state, society, and culture—presumed a novel set of institutional and cultural arrangements that became feasible only as a result of the changes that took place in the late nineteenth and early twentieth centuries. This realignment of state-society relations marks the fundamental transformative experience of modern Iranian history.

IRANIAN HISTORIOGRAPHY

In the rest of this book I examine this transformation by considering the evolution of the Iranian state during the late nineteenth and early twentieth centuries. The state's evolving role vis-à-vis society and culture suggests that a new framework of political community emerged in Iranian society during this period. Chiefly through the encounter with European models of political community, state structures and cultural forms began to change during the course of the nineteenth century. By the 1920s and 1930s, the adoption of those models had led to the establishment of a modern nation-state in Iran. The years from 1870 to 1940 are those in which the social, cultural, and political convergence identified here can be isolated.

Although the late nineteenth and early twentieth centuries hold a significant place in most important works of modern Iranian historiography, the period has rarely been isolated for consideration of its social, cultural, and political continuities. With few exceptions, the common conventions of periodization in Iranian historiography correspond closely to the major political epochs of the modern period. They focus, for example, on Qajar politics, the constitutional revolution, the emergence of the Pahlavi state, and the Islamic revolution as distinct historical moments juxtaposed and often opposed to previous periods. The utility of this approach, on the one hand, is self-apparent; the major political milestones of modern Iran are the most obvious parameters within which to frame Iranian historiography. On the other hand, these parameters, also work to obscure more deeply rooted and fundamental social and cultural changes.

The history of Iranian nationalism and the Reza Shah period illustrates the point. The conventions of Iranian historiography consider nationalism in either of two ways: it is something natural and primordial to Iranian consciousness from the earliest times or it is tied narrowly to the state-building efforts of Reza Shah between 1921 and 1941. The first argument stems from the influence of philological science on the development of Iranian historiography and fails to understand nationalism according to its modern definition.[8] It is flawed because it places the origin of Iranian nationalism too far back in time.

The second argument is also flawed, because it locates Iranian nationalism in the too-recent past. Associating Iranian nationalism narrowly with the Reza Shah period stems from the convention of following the political narrative of modern Iranian historiography. The Reza Shah period was the first political era in which the state self-consciously used nationalism as its ideology. Yet the emergence of the state-led project of nation-building at that time cannot be fully understood without considering the larger social and cultural processes of the late nineteenth and early twentieth centuries, which cumulatively led to the formation of the modern Iranian nation-state. In this book I want in part to reframe Iranian historiography by situating the nationalism of the Reza Shah period within a larger process of *nationalization* that cuts across the conventions of political periodization.

In order to demonstrate this process, I have isolated continuities in the formation of state institutions, social structures, and cultural forms that crosscut the political boundaries of the period under review. The political narrative of modern Iran is ultimately congruent with the social and cultural narrative of modern Iran, but in order to see this congruence, the political changes must be placed against a backdrop of the more deeply rooted transformations that cross imposed historiographic boundaries. To do otherwise would be to miss the forest for the trees.

What ties the history of the period 1870–1940 together, despite its political discontinuities, is the fundamental realignment of state-society relations and the convergence of state, society, and culture that took place during those years. This book is therefore intended to be not a political history of the Iranian state but rather a social and cultural history of the Iranian state as it evolved from a traditional monarchical state into a modern national one. How did notions of statehood evolve in the Iranian context during the modern period? How did the Iranian state see itself in relation to society? How did this conception change during the late nineteenth and early twentieth centuries? How did new notions of national culture complicate these understandings and help shape the changing relationship between state and society?

Ultimately, answering these questions suggests that it was between 1870 and 1940 that the convergence between state, society, and culture made it possible for social actors to make political claims to speak on behalf of the nation. Such actors might include a constitutionalist activist in 1906 invoking "the nation" in the newly emergent radical press, Mohammad Mosaddeq in his attempt, from the bully pulpit of the premiership, to nationalize "Iranian oil" in the early 1950s, and Mohammad Reza Shah, with his 1971 pretensions at the tomb of Cyrus. They might also include Ayatollah Khomeini, claiming to speak on behalf of both God and the nation during the revolution of 1978–79 and, more recently, President Ahmadinejad, asserting that developing a nuclear program was rooted in Iran's "national rights." None of these political claims could have been made without the social, cultural, and political realignments that took place between 1870 and 1940, realignments that were prerequisites for nationalism. More broadly, this is the period in which we can identify the emergence of modern politics in Iran, a politics that takes as its basic assumption the existence of the social abstraction known as the nation.

NATIONS AND NATIONALISM IN IRANIAN HISTORIOGRAPHY

Two interrelated yet distinct phenomena are central to the argument made in this book: *the nation* and *nationalism*. For *nationalism* I have in mind the definition used by John Breuilly, Elie Kedourie, and others, in which nationalism is primarily a political movement. Breuilly, for example, wrote that nationalism "is, above and beyond all else, about politics and that politics is about power. Power, in the modern world, is principally about control of the state."[9] Nationalist claims and the ideology associated with them were therefore principally associated with the "objectives of obtaining and using state power."[10] Breuilly then isolated the dynamics of political mobilization as it varied across types of nationalist movements and state formations. It was the instrumentality of nationalist claims within the arena of political contestation, rather than anything else, that unified the phenomenon of nationalism across the comparative typology Breuilly presented.

Elie Kedourie not only presaged Breuilly's instrumentalist reading of nationalism but also emphasized nationalism as a political ideology, or a program of doctrine and ideas, by which political aims might be achieved. Ideological nationalism, Kedourie and others have argued, normally makes use of symbols tied to language, race, ethnicity, and geography to achieve primarily political ends. The nationalisms of Asia and Africa had in common a "doctrinal system [having] affinity with certain strands in the political and intellectual tradition of Europe."[11] These doctrines, however, should be considered not on their own terms but as political instruments; they were "not spoken with their own spontaneous and unquestioning conviction, but used in an operational and, so to speak, Pavlovian mode, to elicit and arouse emotions of solidarity and group loyalty."[12] Viewed in this Pavlovian sense, nationalism is again a phenomenon tied to the domain of ideas and political contestation; its historical significance is limited merely to the arena of those vying for state power.

The strength of Kedourie's and Breuilly's definition of nationalism lies precisely in the skepticism it shows toward its object of analysis. Their skepticism works to demystify the phenomenon and free it of the exotic and menacing sheen it had accumulated as a result of the experience of interwar European fascism.[13] In this sense the political definition of nationalism articulated by Kedourie was the first to question, in a proto-deconstructionist mode, the organic and perennialist definitions of nationalism that preceded it and that still circulate, though with considerably less resonance, today.

The weakness of Breuilly's and Kedourie's definition is that it presumes the existence of the political arena in which nationalism, as an instrument of political contestation, comes into play. If defined as a form of politics, nationalism itself does not account for the historical conditions underlying the moment when nationalist claims achieve viability as political claims. Significantly, while acknowledging the instrumentality of the claims of nationalists, the political definition of nationalism as posed by Breuilly, Kedourie, and others also suggests that such claims have a transhistorical political viability. This definition does not address the historical crystallization of the political arena itself, within which nationalism comes to circulate. Without the emergence of this arena—or field of contestation—nationalist claims would go unheard, be irrelevant, and remain apolitical. The task of the historian of nationalism is thus in part to take into account the emergence of the political arena, which has been described as the "domain of formal politics" and as "a bounded and relatively homogeneous transactional and communicative space."[14] Any historical appreciation of the phenomenon of nationalism would be incomplete without a consideration of the social-structural apparatus within which nationalism, as politics, comes to circulate.

The concept of *the nation* comes closer to achieving this focus on the social and cultural environment within which nationalism operates. The nation can be understood as an abstract social category or framework tying together state, society, and culture. It is not a phenomenon defined by its political nature or ideological content but rather a historical artifact defined by its institutional dimensions and representational form.

Benedict Anderson's now famous use of the term "imagined communities" to describe this artifact has been praised and criticized as being both elegant and elliptical. Just as often, it has been misunderstood to suggest a definition of the nation as something fake, false, or fabricated. To the contrary, Anderson went to great pains to distinguish his reading of the phenomenon from the more skeptical readings of Kedourie and Breuilly and, for that matter, of Eric Hobsbawm and Ernest Gellner.[15] To Anderson, nationalism was no mere matter of "Machiavellian hocus-pocus" but something "deeper and more interesting."[16] He wrote: "Communities are to be distinguished, not by their falsity/genuineness, but by the style in which they are imagined."[17] This style of imagination is characterized by implicit social and cultural assumptions, shared by all members of the collectivity, that their community is "inherently limited and sovereign."[18] Anderson called this "deep, horizontal comradeship" *imagined* because, in communities beyond the size of small villages, most members of the community never come into face-to-face contact with their fellow members, and yet all share a similar abstraction of community that is maintained in their collective imaginations.

What makes this style of imagination possible, he goes on to illustrate, is large-scale historical transformations at the level of society and culture that have had profound effects on the way individual social actors perceive themselves and their surroundings. This definition of the phenomenon is thus not tied narrowly to politics but rather tied to changes in metahistorical structures—what Anderson described as "the spontaneous distillation of a complex 'crossing' of discrete historical forces"—that in turn produced profound alterations in social and cultural consciousness.[19] The nation is thus much more than yet another political ideology in the tradition of communism and fascism; it is a social-cultural artifact linked to the monumental historical ruptures and resulting epistemic realignments of the modern world.

The novelty of Anderson's analysis was precisely the "anthropological spirit" with which he approached questions of modern history.[20] Viewed in this broader context, the politics of nationalism—or the more mundane contestation for state power—is but a symptom or a reflection of a much more fundamental transformation at the level of society and culture. Movements of nationalism are thus *made possible by,* and premised upon, the emergence of the nation as a conceptual category and the more profound structural transformations at the level of state, society, and culture which that new category signifies.

This distinction is important for the argument made in this book. The history of Iranian nationalism is not at issue here. I am not concerned with Iranian nationalism as a political movement, or merely as a set of ideas, or even as a set of "narratives" disconnected from their historical contexts. To some extent that work has already been accomplished.[21] What is of central concern is the structural transformations that took place during the late nineteenth and early twentieth centuries, which in turn made the category "the nation" a viable and tangible social abstraction. The emergence of this abstraction resulted from the convergence of state, society, and culture into an integrated political-cultural category. Thus, the political discontinuities that characterized the period from 1870 to 1940, and the symbols and rhetorical forms that distinguished the myriad ideological tendencies of Iran's twentieth-century history, are of less concern to me than are the form and style in which political and ideological claims were made. What form and style identify is a unique mode of consciousness that characterized the modern nation, a mode of consciousness that assumed the congruence of state, society, and culture in a uniform set of institutional arrangements and as a coherent system of representation. This congruence and its attendant mode of consciousness began to crystallize in the late nineteenth century and became permanent and formalized in the Reza Shah period.

THE CHANGING ROLE OF THE IRANIAN STATE

Analyzing the changing role of the Iranian state vis-à-vis society and culture illustrates this transformation. As state structures evolved from the late nineteenth century onward, the state began to experiment with new ways of defining and legitimating itself. In chapter 1, I examine this experimentation during the reign of Naser al-Din Shah. Under the influence of internal social and economic changes and external ideological models, the political elites of the Qajar state sought to reinvent the notion of the state. Borrowing extensively from the model of late imperial systems of authority as imposed by nineteenth-century European monarchs, Naser al-Din Shah sought to project a new public image of monarchy in Iran. His new style of politics made use of public ceremonies, rituals, and festivals, all designed to take place in newly reconstructed urban settings in order to present a public image of the state to the increasingly socially mobilized urban masses. The shah's 1873 tour of Europe was key in his learning about this new model of public monarchy, which he imported into Iran upon his return. The new model of legitimacy was premised on a new set of assumptions that saw a much closer and more intimate relationship between state and society than existed under premodern legitimation practices. *Nationalism* was never an ideological claim made by the late Qajar shahs to authorize their rule, but the new set of assumptions on which their reinvention of the Iranian state stood was crucial in laying the framework within which *the nation* could be imagined.

Although the late Qajar state posed a new model of state-society relations, ethno-national identity was never part of its new mixture of legitimation practices. The reinvention of the Qajar state by Naser al-Din Shah remained focused primarily on the person of the shah as the sole unifying symbol linking state and society. In this way, too, Naser al-Din Shah's reinvention of the public image of the Iranian monarchy paralleled European late imperial styles of rule, in which dynastic loyalty played the surrogate for national solidarity.

Yet the late Qajar period also witnessed a discovery, by people outside official state structures, of national identity and historical memory as the bases for a possible new form of identification mediating the relationship between state and society. Just as late imperial models of monarchical authority were posing one way of realigning the relationship between state and society, other models were being posed as well—models that substituted notions of national culture and historical memory for loyalty to the monarch.

As I demonstrate in chapter 2, intellectuals carried out the work of constructing this sense of cultural and historical memory during the late nineteenth and early twentieth centuries. Many of their ideas were influenced by their discovery of nineteenth-century European historical and philological scholarship, an encounter that had a profound effect on Iranian national consciousness. The intellectual movements performed a twofold function. First, they carried out the philosophical labor of reconciling Iranian culture with the demands of modernity. The "discovery" of modern values in the legacy of the ancient past was the philosophical sleight of hand needed to reconstruct Iranian culture in terms of now universalized values of modernity.

Second, this new notion of Iranian history and culture, grounded in ancient, pre-Islamic authenticity, performed an important social function. The reconstruction of national memory during the late nineteenth and early twentieth centuries produced a new repertoire of symbols and memories to which all Iranians could make equal claim. The reconstruction of Iranian history and memory was carried out in a secular and antisectarian spirit, designed not only to reconcile Iran to modernity but also to provide a new uniformity of memory and identity that could be applied evenly across society. It was the secularism of the historical memory being excavated and reconstructed by late-nineteenth- and early-twentieth-century Iranian intellectuals which gave that historical memory the ability to function as a national culture, transcending ethnic, linguistic, tribal, and religious divisions.

In chapters 3 and 4, I illustrate just how this new sense of national identity came to play its social role during the 1920s and 1930s. In chapter 3, I analyze the expansion of the state's role in education during the reign of Reza Shah. Foremost among Reza Shah's policies was to nationalize the system of education and make it the instrument through which national culture would become uniform across society. The state became chief national pedagogue, responsible for educating the nation. This role, novel in Iranian history, was premised on the assumption of congruence between state, society, and culture.

In chapter 4, I show how public ceremonies and commemorations were used during the Reza Shah period to promote a unique notion of official national memory. The contrast between the ceremonies and festivities of the Qajar period and these new Pahlavi ceremonies is significant. Whereas the ceremonies of Naser al-Din Shah invoked the legitimacy of the shah, the commemorative ceremonies held under Reza Shah in the 1920s and 1930s marked something decidedly new. They emphasized secular national symbols—usually newly built tombs dedicated to long-dead poets—as objects of veneration. The symbolic shift between the uses of ceremony in the late Qajar and early Pahlavi periods is subtle but significant. Pahlavi commemoration presumed the existence of an abstract category of nationhood to which symbols could refer. Both late Qajar and early Pahlavi ceremonies were premised on a common conception of state-society relations, but only in the Pahlavi period did this conception come to be mediated by a notion of national culture. What an analysis of the continuities of the late Qajar and early Pahlavi periods suggests is a process of crystallization by which the international model of the nation form entered into Iranian history. This crystallization meant that a new model of political community would come to define the relationship between state, society, and culture in Iran.

Whereas the institutional apparatus tying state and society together would be successfully consolidated in Iran, the dilemma of culture would ultimately remain unresolved in Iran's appropriation of the nation form. The institutional and conceptual framework of the Iranian nation became successfully established by the early twentieth century, but the question of which culture should animate the new national framework went unanswered. The "dual society" or "two cultures" phenomenon—in which a secular, pre-Islamic-based nationalism became the official culture of the state and elite classes while Islam became the basis of an increasingly politicized popular identity among the urban and rural masses—is therefore a phenomenon not only of the period preceding the revolution of 1979.[22] The emergence of the dual society was implicit in the nation-building efforts that unfolded in the late nineteenth and early twentieth centuries.

Although unique circumstances of the post–World War II era contributed to the ultimate demise of Iran's secular nationalist project, underlying contradictions existed within Iranian nationalism going back to the decades of its modern inception. These contradictions eventually became crystallized as cultural fault lines that led to the dual society of the immediate pre-revolutionary period. Thus, while the years under review here are important for identifying the state-society relationship that gave birth to Iran as a modern nation, they are equally important for identifying the roots of the two-cultures phenomenon in modern Iran—a phenomenon that became the central drama of Iran's modern history.

1 STAGING THE NATION

City, Ceremony, and Legitimation in Late Qajar Iran

ON MAY 1, 1896, NASER AL-DIN SHAH (R. 1848–96), FOURTH MONARCH OF THE Qajar dynasty of Iran, was assassinated while making a pilgrimage to the shrine of 'Abdolazim, a popular gathering place for urban worshipers just outside Tehran.[1] Eyewitness accounts estimated that as many as two thousand people had gathered on the sanctuary grounds during the shah's visit.[2] Both contemporary and later observers conceded that it was unusual for the shah to visit a public site where he would come into direct contact with so large a crowd of his subjects. Members of the shah's staff and others recalled that they had assumed the shrine would be cleared in preparation for the shah's arrival, as was the usual practice. On this occasion, however, the shah rebuffed his attendants and insisted on worshiping among his subjects as a common pilgrim.[3]

As the shah entered the sanctuary and performed the customary prayers, a crowd of fellow worshipers surrounded him. When he finished the prayers and rose to leave, one of his subjects approached him, bearing a petition. The petitioner was Mirza Reza Kermani, a sometime peddler and itinerant radical with ties to the Istanbul-based opposition figure Jamal al-Din al-Afghani.[4] As accounts of the event indicate, when Naser al-Din Shah stepped forward to receive the petition, Mirza Reza Kermani drew a revolver and fired into the shah's chest, killing the monarch. In the following commotion, a quick-thinking Amin al-Soltan, the main minister accompanying the shah during the pilgrimage, hastily retrieved the royal carriage and helped move the shah's body into it. Amin al-Soltan, keenly aware of the public's presence at the shrine and the ability of news of the shah's death to circulate quickly in the newly modernized and increasingly bustling capital, told bystanders that the shah had received only minor injuries to the leg.

Inside the royal carriage, the drama continued. Amin al-Soltan saw the carriage ride back to the palace as an opportunity to slow the inevitable circulation of rumors of the shah's assassination by stage-managing a public image of the shah alive and well. In a scene reminiscent of the story of El Cid, he ordered the attendants to position the shah's corpse in a seated posture and carefully manipulate his arms to wave at the crowds who lined the streets as the carriage made its way back to the royal compound.[5]

The circumstances surrounding the shah's assassination, along with the drama inside the carriage, are suggestive of changes that had taken place in Iran by the end of the nineteenth century. At the end of Naser al-Din Shah's reign, the public presence of the shah in the urban life of the capital was no longer uncommon, and the distance that traditionally separated the monarch from the populace was gradually narrowing. Indeed, the encounter between Naser al-Din Shah and Mirza Reza Kermani at the shrine of 'Abdolazim can be read as a metaphor for the troubled history to follow, in which an increasingly socially and politically mobilized urban populace would become tied ever more closely to a visible and omnipresent state. Gone were the days when the monarch could remain remote and distant from the population, rooting his authority in sacral sources. Largely because of changes he himself had introduced, Naser al-Din Shah recognized that cultivating a public image was a prerequisite for effective rule. This image was cultivated through a new style of politics borrowed from an increasingly available model of state authority as practiced by the imperial monarchies of Europe. Such politics made use of spectacles, celebrations, ceremonies, parades, and commemorations to break down the barriers separating the monarch from the masses and to circulate symbols tying state and society together.

Naser al-Din Shah's public visit to the shrine of 'Abdolazim was in keeping with this new style of politics. The visit was scheduled as the first public event initiating a week of jubilee celebrations marking the triumphal fiftieth lunar year of Naser al-Din Shah's reign. The jubilee had been meticulously planned to include all the public pomp and ceremony characteristic of the royal houses of Europe—from the flags and decorations adorning the public spaces of the city to the extravagant fireworks displays, the singing of odes commemorating "fifty years of justice," and the minstrels and bards who had been specially commissioned to stage productions for the amusement of the shah and his guests.[6] The jubilee celebrations scheduled for May 1896 were a classic example of ceremonies choreographed in the new political style, reflecting the importance of public perception as the basis of political legitimacy and for cultivating loyalty to the monarch.

Although the new style of ceremony became increasingly common during the reign of Naser al-Din Shah, it was not a development peculiar to nineteenth-century Iran. As Eric Hobsbawm and Benedict Anderson both noted, by the late nineteenth century this style of politics had become a global imperative, as common in Britain, France, and Austria as it was in the Ottoman Empire and Japan.[7] In Europe especially, ceremony and spectacle were instruments wielded by conservative dynastic states to maintain the loyalty of the newly mobilized urban masses and to quell the emergence of rival loyalties percolating up from below. Hobsbawm noted: "After 1870, therefore, and almost certainly in connection with the emergence of mass-politics, rulers and middle-class observers rediscovered the importance of 'irrational' elements in the maintenance of the social fabric and social order."[8] What Hobsbawm called "irrational elements" were precisely those new practices—spectacles, ceremonies, commemorations, and so forth—that had come to preoccupy much of European public life by the end of the nineteenth century. The frequent staging of public ceremonial events during the late imperial period was intended to promote the increasingly intimate communion between state and society in a shared set of symbolic associations.

Outside Europe, the appropriation of this new style of politics followed the broader European pattern of legitimating conservative dynastic states in the face of increasingly mobilized urban populations. Certain unique circumstances made the use of these new methods of legitimation attractive to non-Western elites. The integration of non-Western states into the world economy produced social dislocations analogous to those of the early stages of European modernization. Moreover, an increasingly accessible transnational print culture, along with growing opportunities for travel abroad, made the European style of politics a universal model capable, as Anderson noted, of being "pirated."

In semicolonial zones that had escaped direct colonization but where sovereignty remained precarious—such as the Ottoman Empire and Iran—the new style of legitimation was an especially attractive model to appropriate. Spectacles, parades, and commemorations elevated the ceremonial status of these weak modernizing states, adorning them with the trappings of the advanced states of Europe while cultivating the loyalty of their masses. Outside Europe, the appropriation of this model of legitimation was thus staged for two audiences, one international and one domestic. For the international audience it was intended to convey the equal status of the semicolonial states and thus discourage further imperial encroachments. For the domestic audience the new ceremonies and public spectacles enhanced the position of the state as the main focus of domestic loyalty, providing a basis of modern identity in an age when social forces were producing rival and centrifugal identifications.

The jubilee celebrations of Naser al-Din Shah's reign and his public visit to the shrine of 'Abdolazim should be understood within this global context of the appropriation of new methods of legitimation during a time of internal social transformation and external political confrontation. The origin of this process can be traced to the early encounter with this model of legitimation by members of the Iranian diplomatic corps abroad. Letters, reports, and dispatches sent back to Iran described the urban environments and ceremonial cultures of the cities in which the diplomats were stationed. Most important for the transmission of the model was Naser al-Din Shah's official tour of Europe in 1873. A seminal cultural moment in the history of Iranian state-building, the tour marked the shah's first direct encounter with the urban model of ceremonial practice (figure 1).

The changes in ceremonial practices, in both Europe and Iran, were closely connected to changes in urban form. As the shah experienced during his European tour, the relationship between urban form and ceremonial activity was central to the new style of politics. The rebuilding of Tehran into an appropriately national capital, with broad boulevards and centralized open spaces in the European style, became a prerequisite for the effective use of legitimating ceremonial activity. Although the project of redesigning and modernizing the capital had begun as early as the 1860s, Naser al-Din threw his full weight behind it after returning from Europe in 1873.

Changes in forms of ceremonial activity mark the late Qajar era as a transitional period, a midpoint between the remote and sacral status of the traditional monarchy and the intrusiveness and omnipresence of the later nationalizing Pahlavi state. Despite the gradualism, the new public presence of the state in late Qajar urban culture was notable in the Takyeh Dowlat, the twenty-thousand-seat royal amphitheater built by Naser al-Din Shah in the center of the redesigned capital. As I describe later, the Takyeh Dowlat was the Qajar state's most creative effort in building places of public gathering where mass ceremonies could be managed from above. The original use of the site was for the staging of the *ta'ziyeh*, the so-called passion play commemorating the martyrdom of Imam Hoseyn (626–680), the grand-

FIGURE 1. *Sketch of Naser al-Din Shah and his entourage during one of his tours of Europe.*

son of the Prophet Muhammad and the third Imam of Shiʻa Islam. The staging of the taʻziyeh at the Takyeh Dowlat during the reign of Naser al-Din Shah suggests a unique synthesis of traditional ritual and novel, legitimating ceremonial practice designed to cultivate political-religious loyalty on the part of the masses.

Ultimately, however, the appropriation of the new model of urban ceremony remained partial in the late Qajar period. Although the rudiments of a new urban ceremonial form were adopted during the reign of Naser al-Din Shah, the cultural and symbolic content of the new ceremonies remained tied to what might be termed a "royalist Shiʻism" characterized by simultaneous monarchical and religious symbolism and grounded in traditional notions of political authority. The use of national symbolism as the basis of ceremonial legitimating practices would require the discovery of national culture as an appropriate basis for mass identity. That discovery, too, as I show in the next chapter, was taking place during the late Qajar period, but primarily at the level of historical-philosophical speculation. The ultimate synthesis of form and content would await the Pahlavi period.

SEEING PARIS: THE BEGINNINGS OF URBAN RECONSTRUCTION

The transformation of Iranian cities began during the reign of Naser al-Din Shah. By the late 1860s and early 1870s, when he began to think seriously about developing Tehran along the lines of a modern capital city, urban reconstruction was already under way in other parts of the Middle East. Cairo and Istanbul, in particular, had set out on projects of urban reconstruction. Egypt's Khedive Ismail had visited Paris and the Exposition Universelle in 1867, at the invitation of Napoleon III, and been inspired to carry out a similar set of ambitious changes for Cairo. Upon arriving in Paris, Ismail was given a personal tour of the city by Baron Haussmann, the French city planner responsible for the recent renovations. The khedive observed with rapt attention as Haussmann presented the broad boulevards of Paris and the labyrinth of sewers running beneath the city. French-trained Egyptian architects then carefully studied Haussmann's Parisian designs and conceived a modern Cairo along similar lines.[9]

In Istanbul a similar process was under way by the 1850s and 1860s. Pera, Galata, and Tophana had already come to be recognized as the European quarters of the city, especially after the influx of European denizens during the Crimean War, and by the 1860s they became areas of urban experimentation with the construction of boulevards, monuments, squares, and public gardens. As in Cairo, French-trained Ottoman engineers who had been impressed by Haussmann's Paris carried out the urban restructuring of Istanbul.[10]

Members of the Iranian diplomatic corps abroad informed Naser al-Din Shah of the changes taking place in Cairo and Istanbul. By the 1860s Iran maintained a full embassy in Istanbul, as well as consular services in Bombay, Baghdad, Basra, Cairo, Erzerum, and Tiflis and diplomatic legations in London, Paris, and St. Petersburg.[11] The private letters and official dispatches Iranian diplomats sent back to Tehran most often described political developments in Europe and postulated their possible effects on Iran.[12] But these diplomats were also well placed to observe the rapid pace of changes taking place in European and some Middle Eastern cities.

Urban transformations were some of the most visible signs of European progress and therefore were among the components of modernization most quickly advocated by overseas diplomats.[13] The order, regulation, and civic character of European cities as experienced by the diplomats stood in sharp contrast to the Iranian urban environments with which they were more familiar. This juxtaposition posed Iran's relative backwardness as a stark and tangible reality. The visible quality of Iran's backwardness to some extent explains the emphasis on the outward, visible character of subsequent Iranian nation-building projects. Invariably, among the first projects of reform were those advocating *physical* transformation, whether by focusing on the modern, urban form of the city or by other visible means such as sartorial regulation. Reform and modernization in the colonial and semicolonial world, it seems, reflected an obsession with appearances. The emphasis on the appropriation of outward forms of modernity, such as urban design, public ceremony, and dress codes, emerged in part out of the primarily visible experience of backwardness.[14]

The dispatches sent back to Tehran by these diplomats describing, among other things, the urban changes they witnessed abroad thus became important sources of transmission for the model of the "modern-national" city into the Iranian project of state-building. The Iranian ambassador in Istanbul, the reformist Mirza Hoseyn Khan, was well placed to observe the Tanzimat reforms as well as the urban redesign projects then under way in the Ottoman capital. His appointment to the Istanbul embassy in 1858 and his stay in that city for the next twelve years coincided with the most intensive period of urban reconstruction yet undertaken by the Ottoman state and afforded him a firsthand account of how the form of a modern city could be implemented in a Middle Eastern context.[15] Mirza Hoseyn Khan reported these developments back to the Tehran foreign ministry and to Naser al-Din Shah himself through detailed official dispatches and personal letters advocating the adoption of similar reforms in Iran.[16]

Members of the Iranian mission in Paris—bureaucrats lower in rank than Mirza Hoseyn Khan but closely allied with him, such as Hasan 'Ali Khan Garusi,[17] Mirza Mohsen Khan Mo'in al-Molk,[18] and Mirza Yosuf Khan[19]—also reported back to Tehran about changes taking place in Paris.[20] Both groups of diplomats urged Naser al-Din Shah to accept Napoleon III's invitation to visit Paris during the 1867 Exposition Universelle.[21] Khedive Ismail of Egypt and Sultan 'Abdolaziz of the Ottoman Empire had also received invitations. The presence of the Iranian shah alongside these other regional leaders and European heads of state would, as Mirza Hoseyn Khan urged the shah in one of his dispatches, "give new life to the state and the nation of Iran, and it will leave the shah's great name standing in the history books."[22]

A related motivation, from the point of view of Mirza Hoseyn Khan and the other reformers, was the anticipated effect the shah's experience of Paris would have on the pace of reform in Iran. By 1867 the reformers had come to believe that their advocacy of change had not produced the desired impression on the shah but had fallen largely on deaf ears. A visit by the shah to

Haussmann's Paris would, they thought, inspire Naser al-Din out of his com-placency and help him recognize the importance of the projects they were proposing. Implicit in their position was the assumption that *seeing* Paris would give the shah the necessary perspective to contrast Iran's position with that of the putatively more advanced West.

"A PERPETUAL EXHIBITION": NASER AL-DIN SHAH IN EUROPE

Naser al-Din Shah did not travel to Europe in 1867. He embarked on his first grand tour some six years later, in 1873, after persistent calls by his diplo-matic corps to see "the wonders of European progress" finally convinced him to travel west.[23] His journey by land, rail, and steamer took him across much of the continent, and he visited Russia, Germany, Belgium, England, France, Switzerland, Austria, and Italy. Historians have been ambivalent about the importance of the shah's three tours of Europe, in 1873, 1878, and 1889. Critics of Qajar Iran generally dismiss them as indulgent "pleasure trips" designed as much around the shah's attraction to the entertainments of Euro-pean spas, which he was apparently fond of frequenting, as for any diplo-matic gains to be derived.[24] The timing of the 1873 trip, during the controversy over the so-called Reuter affair, suggests that the tour might also have been part of a broader policy of attracting investment from overseas sources, or "concession mongering." The Reuter concession was negotiated privately between Baron Julius von Reuter and Iranian representatives, including Malkom Khan and Mirza Hoseyn Khan, without the sponsorship or endorsement of the British government. The political imbroglio it caused might have made Naser al-Din Shah's European tour an opportune occa-sion to alleviate the diplomatic entanglements.[25]

More sympathetic observers of the Qajar period see the trip as having been an occasion for the shah to present himself, and Iran, on an international political stage. The trip was timed to follow Naser al-Din Shah's public decree announcing the administrative reform of the state, a decree based largely on the Ottoman Tanzimat reforms observed by Mirza Hoseyn Khan during his tenure as ambassador to the Sublime Porte. The short-lived 1871 decree sought to rationalize the administration of the state and for the first time create min-istries responsible to an appointed prime minister.[26] It was hoped that the timing of the tour would help leave the European states with a positive impres-sion of Iran as a relatively advanced nation. The cultivation of this impres-sion was seen as urgent, given the unpredictability of the Great Game politics of the time and Iran's precarious buffer-state position between imperial Russia and the British Raj.[27] The presence of Naser al-Din Shah in Europe was thus an assertion of Iranian sovereignty and an attempt to elevate Iran's position in an increasingly international system of nation-states.

These interpretations aside, Naser al-Din Shah's 1873 tour can also be interpreted as a seminal *cultural* moment in the history of modern Iranian nationalism. It was the shah's first direct engagement with the fully formed and articulated style of politics used by the late imperial monarchies of Europe to create bonds of loyalty between themselves and the masses. By 1873 the urban redesign of European cities was largely complete in the areas he visited, and the legitimating ceremonial activity that animated life in the new cities was fully in place.[28] The shah's diary of his trip, the English translation of which made a minor literary splash in Victorian London, detailed his fascination with the new cities he visited and the public rituals and ceremonies he witnessed. His scrupulous attention to popular life and the urban environment went beyond a simple chronicling of his daily itinerary as a tourist; it suggests instead an almost conscientious attempt to absorb the dimensions and order of his surroundings. As Naser al-Din stated in the letter of introduction he gave to Malkom Khan to facilitate his making arrangements for the trip, "we desire to personally see and investigate the advances made by the [European] nations."[29] Far from being a leisurely continental holiday, Naser al-Din Shah's encounter with European urban life seems finally to have produced the impression long sought by the reformists in the diplomatic corps. The shah's experience of European urban life would have important effects on subsequent state-building efforts in Iran.

Among the European curiosities that most attracted his attention in 1873 was the ubiquitous presence of crowds in the cities. Urban crowds, created as a result of the redesigns of European cities, became a hallmark of political culture in the nineteenth century. Commentators from Edgar Allan Poe and Charles Baudelaire to Gustave Le Bon, Walter Benjamin, and Georg Simmel reflected on this new social and cultural phenomenon.[30] Naser al-Din Shah's preoccupation with crowds seems to have been unusually acute and suggests that he was unaccustomed to seeing an urban environment characterized by such mass participation. His comments on the crowds in the cities reflect a sensitivity to his position as an object of curiosity for them. He seems to have stepped into a strange new world characterized by an unusual culture of urban spectatorship in which he was the central item on display. His sensitivity to the presence and gaze of the crowds suggests that large numbers of well-wishers and the curious filled the streets, eager to see the "exotic oriental potentate."

No less an observer than Mark Twain, who was commissioned by the *New York Herald* to write a series of articles on the London leg of the shah's journey, was impressed by the size of the crowds the shah attracted: "The streets for miles are crammed with people waiting whole long hours for a chance glimpse of the shah. I have never seen any man 'draw' like this one."[31] Naser al-Din Shah was himself impressed by the crowds. After arriving at Charing Cross rail station in central London, having crossed the channel from Belgium, he described the crowds and the ceremony that greeted him and his entourage:

> There was an assemblage of spectators, and a crowd, beyond all limits; there were the armour-wearing English household cavalry; there was the Nawab the Heir-Apparent of England, known as the Prince of Wales; and the whole of the Ministry, of the notables, and of the nobles, were present. We alighted. I, the Heir-Apparent, the Grand Vizier, and Lord Morley, — the Lord-in-Waiting upon us, took our seats in an open carriage, and drove off. Both sides of the road, the roofs, and upper stories of the houses, were full of women, men, and children, who exhibited much joy and pleasure by shouting hur-rahs, by waving handkerchiefs, by clapping hands. It was a surprising turmoil. I saluted with head and hands. The crowd of spectators was never-ending.[32]

The reaction of the crowd is difficult to judge. Their shouts of greeting might have stemmed from their perception of the shah as an Asiatic odd-ity, on display much like the other specimens of oriental culture in the muse-ums and exhibition halls of London.[33] Conversely, their reaction might have been conditioned by the form of the encounter, in the style of the public rituals and ceremonies common at the time.[34] Naser al-Din Shah's status in the culture of Victorian England most likely lay somewhere between these two extremes. From the viewpoint of the shah, however, the experience was unprecedented as a moment when the city became a stage for a kind of com-munion between himself and the masses. He was suddenly transported into a new subject position, seeing the city from the vantage of a late imperial European sovereign receiving mass adoration in an officially staged urban choreography.

Similar encounters with the admiring gazes of crowds followed the shah all through his European tour. In England alone, popular receptions were staged for the welcoming ceremony upon his landing at Dover, during mil-itary reviews in and around the city, and at ceremonies greeting him at the port of Liverpool and the textile factories of Manchester.[35] Naser al-Din thus became intimately acquainted with the public ritual life of Victorian England, a ritual life characteristic of much of Europe during the late imperial period.

The shah's marvel at the crowds was matched by the attention he paid to sites of public entertainment in and around London. His visit to the Albert Hall, which he described as "an exceedingly spacious enclosure with a roof in the shape of a dome, very vast and very lofty,"[36] seems to have left an important impression on him, perhaps influencing the design of the Takyeh Dowlat, the royal amphitheater then under construction in Tehran.[37] He also visited Madame Tussaud's Gallery of Waxwork Figures, the Royal Opera, and the Crystal Palace, home to the original "Great Exhibition of the Works of Industry of All Nations" held some twenty-two years earlier. The Crystal Palace has been described as the first great edifice of modernity, as well as, perhaps, the progenitor of *les grands magasins* of the nineteenth-century Parisian bourgeoisie, not to mention the latter-day suburban shopping mall.[38]

The site of the original exhibition had been in Hyde Park, but after its closing in October 1851, popular demand encouraged investors to relocate the exhibition hall to Sydenham, just outside London, and to establish the venue there as a permanent exhibition. The Crystal Palace became a popular site of entertainment for several generations of Britons from all social strata. It consisted of exhibit rooms, performance halls, an aquarium, a zoo, and a large garden and park where fireworks displays were presented and hot-air balloons gave visitors aerial views of the surrounding area. As one contemporary Londoner wrote, the Crystal Palace was "the first great venture in mass provision for the safety and amusement of the masses."[39] The site's reputation soon drew visitors from all over the world; as one commentator for the *Times* wrote: "Foreigners also came, their bearded visages conjuring up all the horrors of Free Trade."[40]

Naser al-Din Shah and his entourage may have been uncouth by the standards of Victorian England, but his talent for observation was acute, and the Crystal Palace proved a source of great fascination to him. Indeed, he was so impressed that he visited the grounds on two occasions during his stay in London, the first time with an official reception and tour in his honor. On his second visit—having extended his stay in London for that purpose— he insisted on exploring the exhibition grounds alone, dressed as inconspicuously as possible in "a simple tunic," trying to experience the amusements much like a common Londoner.[41] As he walked through the galleries, passed the Greek, Byzantine, Renaissance, and Gothic exhibits, marveled at the taxidermy display and the marine aquarium, and admired the replica of the Alhambra, he gained firsthand knowledge about the popular amusements of a modern metropolis. In his diary he described the Crystal Palace as "a perpetual exhibition, with refreshment rooms, . . . places of recreation for the inhabitants of London; and . . . fountains, basins, parks, gardens, and everything that can amuse people. It is now the very best of all places of pastime in London. Every day seven thousand to eight thousand individuals go there for amusement."[42]

Naser al-Din's description of his experience at the Crystal Palace is important on at least two levels. First, it suggests an intuitive awareness of the site's social function. In recounting what he saw, he was quick to point out the quality of amusement and entertainment he had experienced while strolling through the grounds. But amusements were not the only things that concerned him. He also quantified the number of patrons who regularly visited the site, and he displayed the social acumen to judge the exhibition as "the very best of all places of pastime in London." His words also suggest the boundary that separated his perspective from the alien cultural milieu he was observing; the amusements were, as he affirmed, "for the people of London." His description therefore suggests a kind of sophistication in which his observation of these amusements transcends the category of his individual experience and approaches an assessment of the social function of an alien cultural practice. As in his description of the crowds, he seems to have been intrigued and engaged in experiencing, examining, and cataloging these forms of urban life.

Second, the shah's experience at the Crystal Palace was important for the introduction it gave him to another cultural practice, the assigning of politico-cultural meaning to objects and building sites for their public display. As Tim Mitchell argued, this "particularly European concern with rendering things up to be viewed" led to the proliferation of public sites of mass amusement during the second half of the nineteenth century, in the form of panoramas, international exhibitions, museums, theaters, zoos, monuments, cinemas, and public gardens.[43] Such sites of mass entertainment served the social functions observed by the shah, but equally importantly, they were sites for the transmission of values and meanings to an urban populace.

Naser al-Din's itinerary during his European tour was filled with visits to such places, not only the Crystal Palace but also, for example, the "pavilion of nations" at the Vienna Exhibition of 1873 and sites of more strictly national memory such as the tomb of Napoleon I in Paris.[44] As Mitchell argued, the selection of objects at such sites, their arrangement and classification, and the style of their presentation conveyed an order of meaning that, instead of reflecting an external reality, worked to construct that reality.[45] We can observe this in the national displays at the Crystal Palace and the Vienna Exhibition, where pavilions were built according to the authentic architectural styles of the nations they supposedly represented and were furnished with culturally appropriate arts and artifacts. Further, the spatial distribution of the national displays on the exhibition grounds, where individual national pavilions were juxtaposed along a boulevard, courtyard, or exhibit hall, worked to convey a notion of the cultural integration of each display and its location within a chorus of other such national cultures. The style of presentation inscribed national meaning on the displayed objects and conveyed the equal status of cultures arranged in like form.

Naser al-Din Shah's experience at these sites of public display taught him a new way of seeing. But for the shah, as for other nineteenth-century Middle Eastern travelers to the international exhibitions, this new way of seeing initially proved disorienting. The confusion stemmed from the disjuncture separating the apparent realism of the displays from the meaning they were intended to represent. There was indeed nothing "natural" about the production of these artificial environments, complete with imported objects and replicas of authentic objects, all designed to produce the illusion and promise of some external reality. The contrived character of the surroundings, on one hand, and the creators' hypersensitivity to making the displays appear as real as possible, on the other, led to confusion. Mitchell described this experience of disjuncture for Egyptian travelers to European exhibitions: it stemmed from "the peculiar distinction maintained between the simulated and 'the real', between the exhibitions and the world."[46] In the case of the shah, this experience of disjuncture was most vividly recorded during his visit to Madame Tussaud's Gallery of Wax Figures, of which he wrote:

> She originated a place in which are arranged the effigies in wax of monarchs, of men of celebrity, and of great poets, ancient and modern, clothed in the very garments of the persons themselves or of their periods, whether they were men or women, even to artificial jewels, such as crowns, necklaces, finger-rings, and the like. These figures are arranged in rooms and halls, in standing or sitting postures, etc., in such a manner that there is no possibility for one to distinguish whether they are human beings or wax figures.[47]

The shah's description highlights a moment of disorientation when the strangeness of this new way of seeing became apparent to him. The authentic details of the wax figures—their likenesses to real persons, their authentic-looking jewelry, their natural positioning, even the manner of their dress in the "very garments of the persons themselves"—contrasted with the artificiality of the actual objects. The result, as the shah's diary records, was a moment of confusion when there was "no possibility" of distinguishing reality from representation.

In Paris the shah witnessed a similar style of politics. In the first week of July 1873 he concluded his stay in Britain and set out for France, arriving barely two years after the Franco-Prussian war of 1870 and the subsequent struggle for the Paris Commune. His arrival thus took place during a difficult period in French history, after the loss of Alsace-Lorraine and the fall of Napoleon III and the Second Empire.[48] As Naser al-Din himself observed, "they still keep up the state of mourning that followed the German war, and they are all, young or old, sorrowful and melancholy."[49] The defeated French had little cause for celebration just then, and the mass-ceremonial urban culture that had been so central to Napoleon III's Paris was in danger of fading into a discredited past.[50]

For the still struggling Third Republic, the shah's visit to Paris was an opportunity to reinterpret the ceremonial culture of the Second Empire and revive a sense of national pride lost in the immediate aftermath of the military and political defeat.[51] Press accounts of the shah's stay in Paris documented ceremonies and celebrations in his honor, including the official reception at Versailles and visits to the Louvre and the Bibliothèque Nationale.[52] Accounts also exist of the more popular urban ceremonies staged for the shah, such as the gala welcoming ceremony at the Arc de Triomphe, the evening fireworks displays, and the farewell fête at the conclusion of his stay.[53] All these public ceremonies were staged in central Paris and attracted large crowds.

These events further introduced the shah to the forms of urban mass ceremony characteristic of late-nineteenth-century states. In Paris he also experienced the monumental architecture and urban designs of Haussmann. Even more than London, the Haussmanization of Paris presented to the shah the synthesis of symbol, ceremony, and urban form. His description of the welcoming ceremony illustrates this. After crossing the channel and arriving at Caen, he boarded a train to Paris. At the Gare de Passy, on the western edge of the city, a large, elaborately decorated pavilion, extending out from the rail station and encompassing the adjacent avenue, had been erected to receive him. The president of the republic, the newly installed Marshal MacMahon, along with a large crowd of Parisians assembled in the pavilion, was there to welcome him. As the train approached the station, a

FIGURE 2. *Sketch of Naser al-Din Shah's arrival at the Arc de Triomphe, which is decorated with the lion and sun insignia, Paris, July 1873.*

cannon announced the shah's arrival and signaled the military band to begin playing the hastily arranged Persian march.

After a brief welcoming reception, the shah and the president climbed into a waiting carriage and rode through the streets of Paris to the site of the official ceremony, the Arc de Triomphe.[54] Along the way, Naser al-Din saw crowds gathered on either side of the boulevards, as well as street lamps adorned with the Iranian colors and the royal insignia of the lion and sun. In preparation for the welcoming fête, the Arc had been transformed into a ceremonial space. Beneath it had been placed lush red carpeting and two armchairs, one for the shah and one for the president. The boulevards and avenues leading onto and surrounding the Arc were crowded with observers waiting to see the shah's carriage. As the party made its way up the Avenue de Grand Armeé, past these crowds, Naser al-Din could see that the Arc de Triomphe was decorated with the Iranian colors. Atop it his French hosts had placed a large plaster figure of a lion in front of a gold-colored sun with attached banners representing rays of radiating sunlight (fig. 2).[55] The planners of the event had adopted the Iranian royal insignia as part of the ceremonial iconography. The welcoming event thus showed the shah a blending of Iranian iconography into a chorus of symbol, ceremony, and urban form.

When the carriage arrived at the Arc, the welcoming ceremony began. Naser al-Din wrote in his travelogue that

> on both sides of the road were posted infantry of the line, cavalry, and gens-d'armes, all in beautiful uniforms. Behind the rows of the troops, crowds of spectators were standing. We passed through the Bois de Boulogne, which is outside of the fortifications; again entered the enceinte of the city; went along the Avenue de la Grande Armee, and arrived at the Arc de Triomphe, which is of the grand structures of the first Napoleon, is built of stone, and on it are sculptured, within, without, and all round, the battles of that leader. It is a very imposing pile; but in the late wars with Prussia, great damage has been done to it by cannon-balls.
>
> The interior of the Arc de Triomphe was carpeted, chairs were placed there, and much ornamentation had been achieved. Here we alighted and sat a while. The Governor of the city, a fat man and bulky, named M. Duvall, came with the 'Kalantar' (mayor), and made a speech, to which we replied. Several persons charged to represent the Deputies of the city of Paris came also and made a speech, which we answered. We then rose, remounted our carriage, and entered the avenue of the Champs Élysées, which is very spacious and pleasing. On both sides of all these avenues through which we passed they have planted handsome trees and built beautifully grand houses. And so we reached the place de la Concorde, where they have erected a lofty obelisk brought from Egypt. This is a charming public place, having two basins of water with fountains. The fountains do not always play; but whenever they wish, they cause them to flow. Passing by a bridge over the Seine, we entered the edifice which they have assigned to us. At the foot of the steps of this edifice M. Buffet, the actual President of the National Assembly, together with some of the Deputies, made a speech based on congratulations for our arrival; and we replied thereto.[56]

The shah's account of his entrance into Paris can be read on at least two levels. On the surface we can detect a childlike fascination with novel gadgetry—the fountains, he marvels, do not flow continuously but can be made to flow on demand. More importantly, beyond the mundane recording of objects and recounting of events, we can observe the shah absorbing and surveying the order of the city. The buildings, monuments, boulevards, and crowds he described were not disconnected objects scattered across a disorganized urban landscape. Rather, the scope of his observations and the narrative of his experience wove these objects together. He experienced Paris, much as

Haussmann had intended, as a model capital city reflecting a continuity of style and an organic experience of community. The arrangement of objects, such as the boulevards converging on the Arc de Triomphe; the participation of the populace, such as the crowds gathered to watch the passing of the shah's carriage; and the symbolism and choreography of the ceremonies themselves, which brought these elements together, all combined to show Naser al-Din Shah what a city could be—a stage on which to enact public rituals of loyalty between state and society.

Paris and the other European capitals he visited posed for Naser al-Din Shah, as they had for his Ottoman and Egyptian counterparts, a new model of urban experience. Such things as a centralized urban geography, a rich and mass-participatory public life, and the ubiquitous presence of legitimating symbols and iconography characterized this new model. As Hobsbawm and Anderson both noted, in the official nationalisms of late-nineteenth-century Europe, these and other elements were designed to maintain social cohesion between classes and ultimately to promote the loyalty of the masses to the dynastic states.[57] Naser al-Din Shah's account of his experiences in Europe reflects no direct recognition of the function of these urban ceremonies in maintaining loyalty and social control. The still largely vertical, segmented loyalties characterizing Iranian society in the 1870s posed no sustained threat to the authority of the Qajars in the way that popular nationalisms threatened the sovereignty of many European monarchies. The social and economic changes under way in late-nineteenth-century Iran did, however, herald popular movements that would begin to challenge the policies of Naser al-Din Shah. Thus the appropriation of new methods of legitimation was useful as an early attempt to maintain Qajar authority in the face of social and economic changes and the early stirrings of organized political discontent arising from them.

What the shah seems to have been even more aware of was the role of this model of urban life as a powerful international standard of progress. Clearly, the ascendant nations of Europe were characterized by a particular style of urban life that featured legitimating festivals of display and representation. The adoption of this form of urban life became an element in the larger project of modernization, reform, and progress in Iran. Social control and maintenance of loyalty would be important elements in modernization, but from the vantage of Naser al-Din Shah, this urban form of culture and legitimation was more important as a way of associating Iranian forms of statecraft with the putatively more advanced statecraft practiced by the European monarchies.

REBUILDING TEHRAN

Naser al-Din Shah's encounter with European cities and ceremonial activities played an important role in the subsequent transformation of Iranian cities. The attention he paid and the resources he devoted to redesigning Tehran upon his return from Europe in September 1873 bear witness to the influence of the European model. Integrating that model into the Iranian project of modernity became a major preoccupation for much of the rest of his reign.

The modernizing project had already begun in the 1860s upon news of similar projects under way in Istanbul and Cairo. Reports from the Iranian missions in those cities, as well as from Iranian travelers to Paris and other European capitals, had inspired the shah by 1867 to commission a joint group of Iranian and European engineers at the royal college, the Dar al-Fonun to produce a plan for a remodeled Tehran.[58] Now, after the success of his 1873 trip and his firsthand experience of the new cities, the pace of urban transformation in Iran increased.

The new plan, although ambitious, represented an intermediate stage in the reorganization of the city, a stage between the traditional medieval pattern of urban design, dominated by a mosque-bazaar axis, and the new model of a centralized, open city suitable for public rituals. The latter model would be put into place fully only in the Pahlavi period. The Naseri reorganization was crucial, however, in changing the basic scale and structure of the city. The first change called for by the initial plan was the demolition of the old city walls and their reconstruction around a greatly expanded perimeter. The old walls, complete with moat, had enclosed an area of three square miles encompassing the central mosque and bazaar along with the adjoining *mahals*, or neighborhoods.[59] Although the plan retained the concept of a walled city, the new walls were constructed around a much larger perimeter, the number of gates was increased from five to twelve, and the total area of the city grew more than fourfold.[60] This expanded space within a newly symmetrical, octagonal perimeter provided room for the city to grow from the roughly 50,000 inhabitants crowded inside the old city walls in 1860 to the roughly 150,000 inhabitants who lived within the new perimeter by the 1880s.[61]

The expansion of the city's area, however, was meant not only to provide room for a growing population. At least as important was the designers' intention to open up the urban space along the model of the modern cities of Europe. The destruction of the old city walls and expansion of the perimeter were important in fundamentally transforming the spatial organ-ization of Tehran. This is clearest in the new role assigned to the royal com-pound. Previously, the royal compound and citadel (the Arg) had maintained an imposing and detached presence, sequestered in the northern quadrant of Tehran. The compound nestled between the citadel's imposing walls on its southern flank and the moat that formed the city's perimeter to the north.[62] After the redesign, the compound found itself in the geometric cen-ter of the capital, serving as Tehran's central square. It was also developed to be more accessible to the public. The protective walls of the citadel were now supplemented with a series of gates that invited the populace into the compound to enjoy the newly manicured gardens and recently constructed buildings. The citadel, too, was developed; the large open space adjacent to it, the Meydan-e Tupkhaneh, was transformed into an accessible central square or parade ground suitable for public ceremonies.[63]

This spatial reorganization of the capital, centralized on the newly acces-sible royal compound, called for a network of avenues to link the city center with the new outer suburbs created through the expansion of the city walls.[64] The result was a series of meticulously straight avenues, each approximately sixty feet wide, lined on either side by trees, sidewalks, and water channels (fig. 3).[65] These broad new avenues extended from the twelve outer gates of the city through the residential districts and onto the newly configured cen-tral square.

The urban redesign of the Naseri period was by no means transforma-tive, but by 1891, when the conservative British imperial statesman Lord Curzon passed through the streets of Tehran, the change was noticeable. He wrote:

> Shops are seen with glass windows and European titles. Street lamp-posts built for gas, but accommodating dubious oil-lamps, reflect an air of questioning civilization. Avenues, bordered with footpaths and planted with trees, recall faint memories of Europe. . . . We ride along broad straight streets that con-duct into immense squares and are fringed by the porticoes of considerable mansions. In a word, we are in a city which was born and nurtured in the East, but is beginning to clothe itself at a West-End tailor's.[66]

In all these respects—the expanded scale of the city, its newly central-ized spatial organization, and the new network of broad avenues tying the city together—the urban redesign of Tehran in 1867–73 suggests the influence of a newly accessible model of the modern European city. The cumulative

FIGURE 3. *Painting of a new avenue near the Qajar palace as envisioned during the reconstruction of Tehran in the 1870s.*

effect of these reforms was the gradual transformation of the urban experience itself into one that transcended the segmented loyalties of village, tribe, or quarter and helped to produce a unified popular consciousness promoting loyalty to the state.

CEREMONIES OLD AND NEW

The changes made to the city were carried out not only in emulation of a European aesthetic ideal. As Naser al-Din Shah had experienced while abroad, the spatial form of modern cities had important social and political functions as well. Most important was their use as arenas of mass participation in legitimating ceremonial activities. The redesigned Tehran was therefore to maintain a coherence of aesthetic form borrowed from the international model, but at least as important, this aesthetic form was to enact a social function.

Mass-mobilizing ceremonies, however, were primarily a preoccupation of the later Pahlavi period. With important exceptions, public rituals and mass ceremonies like the ones Naser al-Din participated in during his European tour were used sparingly and institutionalized only gradually during his reign. The urban redesign of the late Qajar period was therefore important in setting the stage for later nationalizing activity, but the Naseri period itself remained largely a transitional one in the use of legitimating mass ceremonies.

The gradual adoption of mass rituals reflected the macro-historical transformation that took place in conceptions of political authority in nineteenth- and early-twentieth-century Iran. Despite the appropriation of some legitimation practices from European late imperial states, Naser al-Din and the other late Qajar shahs remained largely conservative in their self-conscious conception of political authority, continuing to see themselves as bearers of the traditional Persianate theory of kingship. Grounded in a notion of pre-Islamic sacral kingship, this conception of legitimacy had been eroded during the Islamic period as the doctrine of salvation stripped the crown of much of its sacral authority. Yet despite the ruler's diminished status, for much of the Islamic period the Persianate theory of kingship managed to negotiate a synthetic sacral status for the shah, especially with Iran's conversion to Shi'ism in the Safavid period (1501–1722), through the title bestowed on him, "Shadow of God on Earth."[67] Naser al-Din and the other late Qajar shahs thus saw themselves as managing a continued, if precarious, balance between monarchy and religion and ultimately laid an approximate claim to a divine right of rule.

During the nineteenth century, with its social and cultural changes, this age-old basis of legitimacy was increasingly challenged by groups ranging from free-thinking constitutionalists and nationalist intellectuals of various stripes to sectarian religious movements and an increasingly assertive Shi'a clerisy experimenting with new and newly revived doctrines of authority and leadership.[68] The contrasting conceptions of political authority in nineteenth-century Iran—a theory of kingship that saw legitimacy grounded outside or *above* society versus new, national-popular doctrines that conceived of legitimacy as emanating *from* society—reflected precisely the dilemma of legitimation that confronted all the conservative monarchies of the nineteenth century, whether they were dynastic states led by the Habsburgs, Hanovers, Hohenzollerns, Romanovs, and Ottomans or the nationalizing dynasties of Japan and Siam.[69]

The dilemma of legitimation, characteristic of this transformative phase in conceptions of political authority, played itself out in the style, symbolism, and choreography of state ceremonies. In the documented cases of Europe and Japan, the dilemma led to robust policies of cultural and political centralization—what Anderson called a "willed merger of nation and dynastic empire."[70] Such policies began in mid-century in response to the national-popular claims of political authority percolating from below, and they took the form of the Russification, Anglicization, Japanification, and Ottomanization programs of the late imperial states.[71] All these political and cultural centralization programs used instruments including the promotion of official languages, military conscription, and increased reliance on urban mass ceremonies to legitimate the rulers in the eyes of the masses.

The implication of this new strategy of legitimation was a conceptual compromise on the part of the dynastic states regarding their notions of political authority. The publicly choreographed pomp and ceremony of the late imperial dynastic states conceded a shift away from a divine right of rule and toward the political premise of the new age, in which even the most remote dynastic families had to cultivate the favor of their respective "publics."

In the Qajar Iranian case, the adoption of new strategies of legitimation came both in emulation of Western models and in response to the same macro-historical crisis of legitimation experienced by other, contemporaneous dynastic states. The Qajar state's response to this common set of circumstances, however, was largely piecemeal and muted. The projection of legitimacy in the late Qajar period ultimately came to reflect an uneasy coexistence between a traditional system of legitimation based on the old model of Persianate kingship and a new system conscious of the need to ground political authority in a popular-urban social base.

Naser al-Din's increased preoccupation with being seen at Friday religious services and his public pilgrimages to popular local shrines suggest an interest in maintaining a visible presence in the urban life of the capital.[72] Public displays of religiosity on the part of the shahs had in fact been part of the traditional conceptual compromise between the Persianate theory of kingship and the demands of popular religion. As early as 1815 the then governor of Bombay, Sir John Malcolm, in his *History of Persia*, keenly observed:

> The kings of Persia have always been very observant of the forms of religion. They say their prayers at the appointed hours: as it is the habit of Mahomedans to do this in public, the neglect of it would excite notice; and nothing

would tend more to weaken their authority than a belief that they were irreligious. They sometimes attend divine worship in the principal mosque of the capital; and, like their subjects, pay their devotions, whenever they have an opportunity, at the sepulchres of those sainted persons who are buried within their dominions.[73]

Much more common, however, were official state ceremonies, which remained in the traditional mode. They were generally restricted to the confines of the royal palace and reserved for audiences of selected court dignitaries, including members of the royal family, members of the ʿulama, officials in the state bureaucracy, tribal heads, and provincial governors. Such court ceremonies, or *salaams*, despite their elaborate and ornate displays of symbolism, were largely private affairs, devoid of mass participation.[74] Salaams might be held on special occasions such as coronations, religious holidays, new year celebrations, receptions for foreign envoys, and the shah's birthday.[75] The last of these, the shah's birthday celebration, was initiated by Naser al-din Shah in the 1860s, likely borrowed from the royal practices of European courts.[76] These court ceremonies represented the persistence of the traditional structure of legitimation well into the Qajar period—a structure that carefully regulated a regime of symbols and choreography but that also remained fundamentally self-referential and confined to the palace grounds. John Malcolm, observing the court of Fath ʿAli Shah at the beginning of the nineteenth century, documented the nature of such ceremonies:

> In no court is more rigid attention paid to ceremony. Looks, words, the motions of the body, are all regulated by the strictest forms. When the king is seated in public, his sons, ministers and courtiers, stand erect with their hands crossed, and in the exact place belonging to their rank. They watch his looks, and a glance is a command. . . . It presents a scene of the greatest magnificence, regulated by the exactest order. To no part of the government is so much attention paid as to the strict maintenance of those forms and ceremonies, which are deemed essential to the power and glory of the monarch.[77]

At the end of the century, Lord Curzon recorded another court ceremony, this time in the court of Naser al-Din:

> I was conducted to a room next to that in which the shah was about to appear, the uplifted sashes of both apartments opening on to the garden, where, on the broad, paved pathway running in front and down the central alleys

between the tanks and flower beds, were disposed in order the various par-
ticipators in the ceremonial. . . . The whole of the assemblage was now
arranged, every man stood shoulder to shoulder with eyes fixed in front, and
absolute silence prevailed. Suddenly a cry was raised. The shah appeared in
the room adjoining that in which I was placed and took his seat upon a gilded
chair in the window. His principal ministers accompanied him and stood in
the background. As the king appeared every head was bowed low, the hands
outspread and resting upon the knees. . . . Then a mullah, standing behind,
recited in a loud voice the khutbah, or prayer for the sovereign. This done
the poet laureate advanced, and, pulling out a sheet of paper, read a com-
plimentary ode. . . . When the ode was at an end, the Shah rose from his chair,
and slowly stalked from the chamber.[78]

The symbolism and choreography of this and other ceremonies taking
place inside the palace—later moving into slightly greater public view when
performed on the veranda of the palace garden—affirmed the basic insularity of ritual life in Qajar Iran. This insularity was grounded in the persistence of the traditional conception of political authority, in which
legitimacy emanated not from a romantic union between state and people
but from the sovereign himself. The self-referential structure of legitimacy
had the desired consequence of balancing the discreet political interests of
those participating in the ceremonies—rival princes, the ʿulama, tribal
heads, provincial governors, and heads of bureaucracies, each positioned
by rank during the proceedings. The reciting of sermons and panegyrics in
the shah's honor during the salaams projected a regime of symbolism within
a carefully demarcated arena that encompassed the participants in the ceremony but did not extend beyond the halls of the palace or the veranda of
the garden.

The rituals Malcolm and Curzon described were typical of ceremonial
life in the Qajar court. During them the princes, governors, ʿulama, tribal
heads, and bureaucrats were assembled in groups, facing one another as they
took their places around the audience hall in descending order of rank.[79]
The shah was positioned at the apex of the ceremonial space, with the assembled dignitaries before him. There was nothing *imagined* in the structure of
this ceremonial form. The ceremony and its symbols were designed to circulate within a narrow arena of elites participating face-to-face in a self-
affirming community of authority.

Ultimately, despite the redesign of the capital, ceremonial activity in late
Qajar Iran remained grounded largely in a premodern conception of polit-

ical authority. The expansion of the walled area of the city, the network of new boulevards that tied it together, and the promotion of the central square of the capital succeeded in transforming the urban geography of Tehran along the lines of a modern national capital. But the persistence of a traditional conception of political authority prevented the Qajar state from utilizing this new national space as a public arena for the articulation and dissemination of legitimating symbols. The partial nature of the change in ceremonial form in late Qajar Iran is best illustrated by an example from the memoir of the court observer ʿAbdollah Mostowfi, who recalled the sudden break with tradition when Naser al-Din Shah dispensed with his traditional regalia and presented himself at a royal salaam dressed in a military frock.[80] Although the shah's choice of costume represented the gradual adoption of a national style of dress, the structure and choreography of the ceremony itself remained unchanged.

THE TAKYEH DOWLAT

The singular and centrally important exception to this pattern of partial transformation in the style of legitimation rituals was the newly constructed Takyeh Dowlat, the royal amphitheater built as part of the 1867–73 plan for the redesign of the capital.[81] The Takyeh Dowlat was built as a public theater for the performance of the taʿziyeh, the passion play performed annually during the month of Moharram to commemorate the martyrdom of Imam Hoseyn. As part of the ceremonial calendar of Shiʿi Islam, the public performance of the taʿziyeh was traditionally central to the series of rituals that encompassed popular Shiʿi religiosity. Scholars of the taʿziyeh have either focused on its strictly religious significance or, just as commonly, cited its importance as a literary form representing an early stage in the development of Iranian dramatic theater.[82] Less attention has been paid to the social function of the taʿziyeh performance.[83]

The social function of the taʿziyeh is important in that traditionally it stood in sharp contrast to the insular ceremonies performed in the royal palaces. The taʿziyeh was performed in public—in the open spaces adjoining mosques and bazaars, in the courtyards of residences and neighborhood buildings, and in makeshift or sometimes permanent theaters provided by devout patrons.[84] Arthur de Gobineau, in residence in Tehran as the official envoy of the French government between 1855 and 1858 (before the building of the Takyeh Dowlat), observed that every quarter in Tehran had its own small theater for performances of the taʿziyeh. The smaller ones housed two hundred to three hundred spectators; the larger ones, built by wealthy patrons, had room for two thousand to three thousand.[85] Until the Takyeh Dowlat was built in the early 1870s, the ta'ziyeh and the building of theaters for its performance were thus supported by private patrons. The theaters were erected with the blessing of the shah but with no official state endorsement or state funds.[86]

Public performance of the ta'ziyeh thus remained largely unregulated prior to the building of the Takyeh Dowlat. It can be described as an autonomous reflection of popular Shi'i religiosity, a form of religiosity that remained external to the domain of state-sponsored ceremony. This autonomy ultimately gave the ta'ziyeh a socially popular and inclusive character. By one estimate in the late Qajar period, during the month of Moharram no fewer than two hundred productions of the ta'ziyeh were mounted in Tehran alone.[87] Peter Chelkowski noted: "Its genius is that it combines immediacy and flexibility with universality. Uniting rural folk art with urban, royal entertainment, it admits no barriers between archetype and the human, the wealthy and the poor, the sophisticated and the simple, the spectator and the actor."[88]

The inclusiveness that Chelkowski described should, however, be placed against the backdrop of state-sponsored ceremony in Qajar Iran. The social function of the ta'ziyeh before the construction of the Takyeh Dowlat is another indicator of the bifurcation of traditional Iranian ceremonial activity. The openness of the ta'ziyeh and associated Moharram processions contrasted sharply with the insularity of traditional court ceremonies. These contrasting ceremonial forms belonged to distinct zones of symbolic articulation, one demarcated within the confines of the palace, the other situated in the segmented popular sphere. This bifurcation is emblematic of a premodern structure of legitimation in which state and society remain fragmented and only loosely tied to one another. Court ceremonies in Tehran reflected a self-referential conception of legitimacy, and rulers saw no need to project this conception outward to society. Conversely, urban mass ceremonies such as the ta'ziyeh and Ashura processions reflected popular religiosity, unlinked to the legitimacy of the state. These bifurcated ceremonial forms suggest that state and society in premodern Iran still ran along parallel trajectories.

The construction of the Takyeh Dowlat in the early 1870s as the official site for the ta'ziyeh marked a turning point in this traditional structure of Iranian ceremonial activity. In many ways anticipating the construction of the sports stadiums of the Pahlavi period and the mass rallies staged in them, the Takyeh Dowlat was the first attempt to build a site for the participation of a sizable segment of the urban populace. The amphitheater's social function thus worked to transcend the traditional bifurcation between court and popular zones of symbolic articulation. This was a site where, for the first time, the two zones could join in a common ceremonial space.

The Takyeh Dowlat performed this new social and cultural function through a number of novel means. Among the most important was the location chosen for it. As part of the overall redesign of the capital, the team of European and Iranian architects and engineers, supported by the shah and other patrons from among the notables, chose to situate the new amphitheater in the royal compound itself.[89] Construction of the Takyeh Dowlat thus became part of the project to reposition the royal compound as the city's central hub and make it a usable, accessible public space.

The new structure had an impressive presence in the compound.[90] It was a large, circular, brick building with a vaulted vestibule three stories high and an iron-frame domed roof with a removable canopy (fig. 4). The interior of the arena was two hundred feet in diameter. In the center stood a circular platform where the drama was staged (fig. 5). The bulk of the audience sat on the ground around this stage, sometimes crowded closely together. The remainder of the audience sat in private boxes on the upper three floors of the arena. These boxes, including the royal box from which the shah watched the ceremony, were reserved for members of the notables and other dignitaries. The total audience capacity of the arena is difficult to judge, but estimates range as high as twenty thousand observers.

Regardless of the exact number, the Takyeh Dowlat became an important place for the convergence of thousands of urban denizens on the royal compound during the annual taʿziyeh performance. The selection of the royal compound as the site for the amphitheater worked to transform the taʿziyeh into an annual state-sponsored event designed to encourage public participation. As the popularity of the site grew, the frequency with which the theater was utilized also increased. Initially, the taʿziyeh was expanded from its traditional ten-day Moharram performance into a two-month event. Beyond the taʿziyeh, the theater became a site for state-sponsored public gatherings of other types, such as at the successful conclusion of a journey by the shah and other occasions of thanksgiving.[91] The somber high point of the theater's public use came during the funeral of Naser al-Din Shah, when his body lay in state there so that visitors could pay their final respects.[92] In all these examples, the convergence of the urban populace on the royal compound inevitably invited association of the site and ceremony with its royal patron.

The physical structure of the amphitheater can also be read as significant.

FIGURE 4. *Exterior view of the Takyeh Dowlat.*

The spatial division of the audience—the urban popular classes assembled on the ground floor, around the stage, and the shah and notables in their private boxes on the upper levels—can be interpreted in two ways.[93] First, it reproduced the Qajar social hierarchy. Each participant was positioned according to rank, much as in the meticulous social choreography of the official court salaams. Such use of ceremony as a legitimator of social hierarchies was common to the cultural practices of the dynastic states of the late imperial period. The structure of the Takyeh Dowlat is thus another indication of the appropriation of that model of legitimation.

FIGURE 5. *Interior view of the Takyeh Dowlat.*

Simultaneously, however, the theater was also a place where people from disparate social strata, both men and women, participated in common ceremony. The Takyeh Dowlat was unique in providing an arena for a set of symbols that circulated across social and physical divisions. Despite their spatial separation, the popular classes and the elites were united in their mutual consumption of a common set of symbols. The location of the stage at the center of the auditorium, with the spectators gathered on all sides, also worked to break down the separation between performers and spectators and heightened the dramatic effect of the performance. The physical space of the theater at once reproduced existing social hierarchies and articulated symbols that suggested the transcendence of those hierarchies.

While the selection of the site for the amphitheater and its physical design are important in understanding the changing use of ceremony in late Qajar Iran, elements in the choreography of the ta'ziyeh itself, as it was performed in the new amphitheater, are also suggestive of a new form of ceremonial activity. Of the few accounts we have of the actual performance of the ta'ziyeh in the Takyeh Dowlat, S. G. W. Benjamin's description in his *Persia and the Persians* is the most detailed.[94] Benjamin spent two years in Iran, between 1883 and 1885, as part of the American delegation charged with establishing the first permanent United States mission in Iran. His stay in Tehran afforded him the opportunity to observe many aspects of late Qajar culture, including the Moharram ceremonies and the ta'ziyeh itself, which he described as "the most remarkable religious phenomenon of the age."[95]

Benjamin's description of the 1884 Moharram ceremonies reveals a great deal about the changing forms of ceremonial activity in late Qajar Iran. Most importantly, it reveals the persistence of the bifurcated zones of symbolic articulation that separated court ceremonies from popular ceremonies, as well as the Qajar state's attempt to use the ta'ziyeh as a legitimating ceremony to crosscut these zones. Benjamin described a variety of ceremonies performed during the month of Moharram in addition to the ta'ziyeh itself. By the late Qajar period, a distinction between the ta'ziyeh and the popular processions seems to have been important, suggesting that although official sponsorship of the ta'ziyeh changed the political nature of the ritual, the more traditional Moharram processions persisted as expressions of popular religiosity. With the construction of the royal amphitheater, the performance of the ta'ziyeh moved gradually out of the popular zones of the city and became in effect monopolized by the state. Other forms of popular ceremony associated with the Moharram festivities continued to take place. Benjamin described one of them:

> One procession which passed my gate on the morning of the tenth day presented a sickening spectacle. Preceded and followed by an admiring crowd of the rabble, a troop of some sixty men hurried by stripped to the middle, and in several cases completely nude. They all with one accord smote their

bare bosoms with their right hands with a certain rhythm of sound. Their bosoms were raw from the oft-repeated blows; all carried naked swords or daggers in their left hand, with which they gashed themselves, generally on the crown of the head; a number were covered with streams of blood. As they rapidly strode in this manner from street to street they continually shouted or groaned, "Ya Hoseyn!" The impression left on my mind for days by this hideous sight was like that of a fearful nightmare.[96]

The disturbing sight to which Benjamin awoke that morning—a band of self-flagellating devotees roaming from street to street—represented a popular and ecstatic form of religiosity that, by the late Qajar period, was coming increasingly into conflict with the more sober and regulated performance of the ta'ziyeh in the royal amphitheater. Not surprisingly, as Benjamin also described, these bands of devotees occasionally clashed with authorities.[97] The sober ta'ziyeh performances at the royal amphitheater and the popular processions can be seen as demonstrations by competing communities vying for space in the nascent public sphere emerging as a result of the urban redesigns of the Naseri period. Although the redesign of the city offered the possibility of transcending the older bifurcation between court and popular ceremonial forms, the conflicts arising from the popular processions indicate the contestation that perhaps inevitably accompanies the consolidation of a unified urban space.

As for the ta'ziyeh performed in the Takyeh Dowlat, what is most apparent from Benjamin's description is the close regulation of the choreography and the attempt to use the ritual as a publicly staged legitimating ceremony. The ceremony began with a series of processions, each filing slowly from the outer arena into the main hall in columns of two, passing the seated audience and singing in slow, melodic chants, accompanied by musicians.[98] The first procession Benjamin described consisted of two hundred men dressed partly in black, bare chested, rhythmically striking themselves in a slow, deliberate march. This "chorus of lamentation" was followed by a smaller group dressed in Arab costume, no doubt characters in the drama meant to represent the army of Yazid, the slayer of Hoseyn and his company. Next Benjamin described another group as it filed slowly into the hall and around the stage and then exited the arena. At the point where each group circled the stage, the procession paused momentarily, its members standing opposite the royal box and saluting the shah. The carefully staged choreography thus culminated with the performers acknowledging the shah's presence.[99] This use of choreography was even more pronounced in the next procession. After the first three groups had exited, the next to enter represented Hoseyn and his party—the martyrs and thus the heroes of the tragedy. Benjamin described the atmosphere as they entered the arena:

> In front, facing the audience, were several children dressed in green; at their side warriors gathered glittering in the chain-armor and gold-inlaid helmets of past ages. Suddenly on the solemn silence, like the thrill of a bird at night, came the voice of one of the children, low and solemn, then rising to a high, clear tone indescribably and thrillingly pathetic—a tragic ode of remarkable power. . . . This song of lamentation was an announcement to the spectators that they were to prepare themselves to behold a soul-moving tragedy,—the martyrdom of Hoseyn and the grandchildren of the Prophet.[100]

As the procession entered the hall, this "song of lamentation" accompanied it. Other children joined the first child in the chorus. Marching past the audience, the actors approached the stage, circled it, and then, unlike in the previous processions, ascended the three steps leading onto the platform. There they sang the tragic ode in unison with the surrounding audience. And precisely at this moment, when the choreography had produced its most dramatic effect, the martyrs turned toward the royal box and saluted the shah. The symbols, choreography, and physical space in which the ceremony was performed worked together to unite the popular classes assembled around the stage with the shah and the notables in their private boxes. The social divisions separating the two groups became momentarily submerged through the combination of symbol, choreography, and space. The spectacle of Hoseyn and the martyrs onstage saluting the shah produced the symbolic equivalent of Hoseyn recognizing the shah's political authority.

The staging of the ta'ziyeh in the royal amphitheater is suggestive of the new character of legitimation practices in late Qajar Iran. The state's sponsorship of the event, the public nature of the spectacle, and the attention devoted to the legitimating use of symbol and choreography all suggest the novelty of the performance as a ceremonial form. At least in the case of the ta'ziyeh performance at the Takyeh Dowlat, the Qajar state had decidedly moved outward from the insularities of traditional ceremony and recognized the political importance of managing the loyalty of its public. This recognition had come largely through the encounter with the legitimating practices of the dynastic states of late imperial Europe. Observation by Iranian diplomats abroad and Naser al-Din Shah's direct experience during his 1873 tour of Europe were the most important mechanisms by which the

European model of urban ceremony entered into the Iranian project of modernity and reform. The subsequent redesign of Tehran into a modern capital and the gradual changes in the form of ceremonial activity, such as the ta῾ziyeh performance at the Takyeh Dowlat, suggest the attempt to put a new model of politics into practice in Iran.

At the same time, the changes enacted in the late nineteenth century remained partial. The modification of the urban form of the city, although an important beginning, did little to fundamentally transform Tehran into a public stage. The construction of the royal amphitheater and the shah's periodic public appearances were exceptions to the more general rule of royal insularity. Just as important was the nature of the symbols selected for public ceremonial display. Invariably they emphasized the person of the shah and the religious basis of his authority. The ta῾ziyeh at the Takyeh Dowlat was emblematic of Naser al-Din Shah's political self-conception; the narrowly Iranian basis of his legitimacy was downplayed in favor of the more resonant Islamic basis. The sermons and panegyrics delivered from the stage pronounced Naser al-Din the shah of *Islam*. In the same way, despite the transformation of Tehran into a "modern-national" city, its official title, *dar al-khalafeh,* retained its religious identification.

Seen in this way, late Qajar Iran can be judged a period of contradictions in which decidedly modern legitimating practices stood alongside more traditional cultural forms. The seeming contradictions suggest that the late Qajar period was a transitional stage in Iranian nationalization. The simultaneous projection of religious, dynastic, and national forms and symbols— which from the vantage point of more than a century later seem an odd assemblage of contradictory elements—was not, from the perspective of the late Qajar state, a recipe for conflict. The late Qajar era was a period of experimentation by the state in contriving a suitable synthesis of state, society, and culture around a common set of legitimating symbols. Seen in this light, Naser al-Din Shah's and the late Qajar state's attempt to form a new basis of popular legitimacy—what might be described as a *Qajar royalist Shi῾ism*—stands alongside the other failed projects after which it was patterned: the legitimating efforts of imperial Russia and Austria and, most notably, the "Ottomanism" of Naser al-Din Shah's neighbor and contemporary, ῾Abdolhamid. In this regional and global context, the flux of religious, political, and national loyalties made the Qajar state's attempt to fashion religious and dynastic loyalty within a modern style of politics ultimately a conservative response to a larger macro-historical process.

The assassination of Naser al-Din Shah on May 1, 1896, largely terminated the late Qajar project of legitimation. Ironically, the preparations made to celebrate the golden jubilee of his reign were now used for his funeral ceremony, a fitting culmination to his attempts to project a new public image of the monarchy. His casket was brought to the Takyeh Dowlat, the most important public stage in the city, where government officials, foreign representatives, and urban denizens all paid their final respects. Amin al-Soltan, who had taken charge in the immediate aftermath of the assassination, staged the funeral ceremony, hastily arranging a performance by the minstrels and bards who had prepared for the jubilee. Before the casket and the public, the theater group performed a drama extolling the virtues of Naser al-Din Shah, whom they declared the "martyred king." Afterward, the casket was carried through the streets of Tehran amid thousands of onlookers and laid to rest at the shrine of 'Abdolazim. In what was perhaps the first in a century of urban ceremonies and demonstrations, the funeral procession of Naser al-Din Shah at last transformed the city he himself had rebuilt into a public stage on which state and society were brought together.

Ironically, the funeral of Naser al-Din Shah was the most elaborate legitimating spectacle of his reign. Its choreography suggests the importance the public image of the monarchy had acquired by the end of the nineteenth century. The state's new, self-conscious awareness of its public role in turn suggests the way that role itself was changing. The state no longer took its legitimacy for granted but now sought to use symbols and ceremonies derived from Iranian culture to cultivate legitimacy and loyalty from society. What lay ahead was the political and ideological battle over exactly what the content of those cultural symbols should be.

2 NATIONALIZING PRE-ISLAMIC IRAN

The Return of the Archaic and the Authentication
of Modernity

WHEN THE IRANIAN DEMOCRATIC AND NATIONALIST LEADER HASAN TAQIZADEH
(1878–1970) arrived in Berlin on January 9, 1915, the world was at war.[1] The
early victories of the Central Powers on both the western and eastern fronts,
and the menacing presence of the German submarine fleet in the sea lanes
of the Atlantic, seemed to promise the Reich's victory over the now weak-
ened empires of Britain and Russia. The cataclysm of the Great War—
described by one European playwright, without too much hyperbole, as "The
Last Days of Humanity"—was, if not humanity's end, then certainly the
terrible crucible through which the late imperial world passed on its way to
becoming something entirely new. Hasan Taqizadeh was aware, as was much
of the politically conscious intelligentsia of the colonial and semicolonial
worlds, that the outcome of the Great War would decisively influence the
political status of the nations he and his comrades understood themselves
to represent.

By 1915 Taqizadeh (fig. 6) was already a veteran of war and revolution.
He had taken an active role in the 1905–11 constitutionalist struggle in Iran,
distinguishing himself as a strong advocate of the constitutionalist cause
against the increasing autocracy of the Qajar state. E. G. Browne, the Cambridge University professor of Near Eastern literatures, sympathizer with
the Persian cause, and correspondent of Taqizadeh's, wrote of his friend that
"he struck me as a man equally remarkable for his high-minded disinter-
estedness, his honesty, his veracity, and his courage."[2] Another observer of

Taqizadeh during his years in the movement wrote that he was "one of those whose genius is capable of inspiring great enthusiasm, great sacrifices, and whose influence leaves a lasting impression on the history of nations."[3]

After his early years of religious education, his subsequent encounter with European history and philosophy via his contact with the American Presbyterian Mission School in Tabriz, and his joining the constitutionalist movement, Taqizadeh was elected in 1906, at the age of twenty-seven, as a representative from Tabriz to the first Majles, or Iranian parliament.[4] His performance there, and his sharp criticisms of both continuing Qajar autocracy and clerical conservatism, made him a target first of Mohammad 'Ali Shah during the failed royalist coup d'etat of 1908 and then of the religious forces in the Majles, who accused him—almost surely erroneously—of taking part in a successful plot to assassinate the conservative cleric Sayyed 'Abdollah Behbehani in July 1910.[5] The reaction to Sayyed 'Abdollah's assassination precipitated a violent showdown between the secular and religious elements in the Majles and encouraged Taqizadeh to leave Iran in October 1910.[6]

From the time of his flight from Iran until his arrival in Berlin in January 1915, Taqizadeh lived the life of a traveling scholar-revolutionary. He made his way first to Istanbul, where he spent two years (October 1910–October 1912) working as a teacher. From that vantage he observed the politics of the late Ottoman state during the critical second constitutional period (1908–13) of the Young Turk Committee for Union and Progress (CUP). It was during the eventful years of 1911 and 1912 that the Ottomans lost Libya to the Italians, Albania declared its independence, and the military alliance of Bulgaria, Serbia, Greece, and Montenegro inflicted further territorial losses during the first Balkan war.[7] Moreover, Russia finally invaded Iran and put a violent end to the Majles in November 1911.[8] From Istanbul Taqizadeh observed not only these events but also the internal struggle between the CUP and the religious, nationalist, and other heterodox ideological opposition groups contending for state power. The fractured nature of Ottoman politics during the last years of the empire no doubt reminded him of the strikingly similar array of forces in play during Iran's constitutional movement. The result of his stay in Istanbul was a series of articles, all signed "X," for the *Revue du Monde Musulman.*[9] They make it clear that for both Taqizadeh and many others on the eve of the First World War, the national question was rapidly crystallizing out of the dynamics of political contestation.

Frustrated by the deteriorating political situation in Iran in the wake of the Russian invasion, Taqizadeh left Istanbul in October 1912 and traveled

FIGURE 6. *Hasan Taqizadeh (1878–1970).*

to Paris, London, New York, and Berlin in order to rally Iranian exiles and expatriates, as well as to advocate for the Iranian cause in the capitals of Europe. In London he worked with E. G. Browne and the Persia Committee to encourage the British House of Commons to check the Russian presence in Iran.[10] In May 1913 he abruptly left England for the United States, staying in New York City for the eighteen months leading up to the war. The time he spent there (May 1913–November 1914) is shrouded in some mystery. Given the detachment of the United States from European affairs on the eve of the war, it is unclear what Taqizadeh believed he could accomplish from the trip. It was during his stay in New York, however, that he was contacted and recruited by German agents to participate in anti-Triple Entente agitation in the Middle East.[11] Seeing the Germans as a potential check against the twin menace of the Russian Bear and the British Raj, Taqizadeh, like many of his Democratic Party colleagues of the now defunct Majles, sought to pursue a Young Turk policy of bringing Iran into the war on the side of the Central Powers.

Against this background, Taqizadeh arrived in Berlin in January 1915 and immediately began to gather a circle of agitators and intellectuals—including such luminaries in the pantheon of Iranian nationalism as Mohammad Qazvini, Mohammad 'Ali Jamalzadeh, Hoseyn Kazemzadeh-Iranshahr, and Ibrahim Purdavud—to cooperate with the Germans in charting a new nationalist course for Iran.[12] The group incorporated itself as the "Iranian Committee for Cooperation with Germany" and undertook a series of initiatives including dispatching emissaries to the south of Iran to help Colonel Wassmuss, the "German Lawrence," in his mission to rally the tribes of southern Iran against British interests in the region.[13]

Most important was the Iranian Committee's publication of *Kaveh,* a semimonthly Persian-language periodical (fig. 7). Under Taqizadeh's editorship, it began publication in January 1916 and continued until March 1922. The journal was named after the legendary blacksmith who revolted against the tyrant Zahak, a story told in the *Shahnameh* (Book of kings), the epic poem written by the tenth-century Persian poet Ferdowsi, recounting pre-Islamic Iranian myths and legends. *Kaveh* combined markedly Germanophile political coverage of the war with cultural, historical, and literary articles referencing Iranian antiquity. It circulated widely among Iranian expatriates in Europe, the Ottoman Empire, and India, as well as within Iran, where it quickly became the leading voice of the generation that came of age during the constitutional revolution and its immediate aftermath.

Taqizadeh's personal, political, and intellectual development from the

FIGURE 7. *Front page of the journal* Kaveh, *edited by Hasan Taqizadeh and published in Berlin from 1916 to 1922.*

years of his participation in the constitutional movement to the years of his editorship of *Kaveh* reflects the broader cultural and political trajectory of the national movement in Iran. It was during this period that the process of reform and modernization underwent a crucial shift away from the late imperial project of the Qajar state and toward the nationalist project that would dominate Iranian politics for much of the twentieth century. The years during which this transition took place, from the Russian invasion in 1911 to the rise of Reza Khan (later Reza Shah) in 1921, have usually been considered a time of political disintegration and have fallen out of conventional narratives of modern Iranian history. It is precisely during these years, however, that we can locate the political origin of modern Iranian nationalism. In an important sense the history of Iranian nationalism began with the publication of *Kaveh*, which combined the political commitment born of the constitutional movement with the promotion of an "organic" cultural conception of Iranian identity. That conception was now slowly being pieced together from a newfound awareness of Iran's pre-Islamic past. The discovery of this past and its politicization as the basis of modern identity became the major preoccupation in the cultural process of modernization, leading directly into the rise of the Pahlavi state.

In several important ways this shift marked an important departure from the late Qajar structure of legitimation, which followed the modernist style of the late imperial projects of Britain, Austria, Russia, the Ottoman Empire, and Japan. These states had discovered their respective publics but, at least in the Austrian, Russian, and Ottoman cases, had remained for the most part unable to retain the loyalty of their newly mobilized masses. In Qajar Iran, especially from the latter half of the reign of Naser al-Din Shah, the monarchy began increasingly to make its presence known in urban life. Nevertheless, the projection of political authority reflected the classic pattern of a monarchy that was patrimonial and self-referential, equating the nation with the person of the shah. Culturally and symbolically as well, the late imperial project of the Qajar state reflected overlapping religious, royalist, and nationalist identifications, which, from Taqizadeh's political vantage point in 1916, must already have seemed a strangely eclectic mix of ideological elements.

In place of the late imperial model, Taqizadeh and his like-minded colleagues posed a new construction of the nation that followed "*volk*-ish" and romantic conceptions of community. This model was premised on an organic understanding of culture, an idealized construction of a "golden age" of authenticity, and a rigidly historicized conception of time in which the nation acts as the subject of history and, in the words of Benedict Anderson, "loom[s] out of an immemorial past . . . and glide[s] into a limitless future."[14] Like its late imperial predecessors, this organic conception of political community became an increasingly ubiquitous model by the beginning of the twentieth century. Whether in Europe or across Asia, the elevated status of antiquity and the scientific study of culture seemed to provide the blueprint for constructing modern national identities; what remained was only the diligence of cadres of patriot-scholars to recover these lost national essences.

Thus several generations of intellectuals from across Europe and Asia were engaged in a common project of recovery premised on a fundamental cultural break with the past. In Germany, Tacitus' *Germania* became, as George Mosse wrote, the "favorite source of reference and the favorite authority on the history of the ancient Germans."[15] In Greece, as Anderson noted, young Greek intellectuals, having imbibed the tonic of philhellenism during their student days at German, French, and British universities, set out on an intellectual project of "recreating a glittering, and firmly pagan Hellenic civilization."[16] Similarly in China, as Prasenjit Duara explained, turn-of-the-century narratives of Chinese history emphasized "an antiquity which saw the birth of the true China—a China of China."[17] And in India, according to Partha Chatterjee, the Bengali intelligentsia's reassessment of the Sanskrit-mediated Vedic culture meant that "ancient India became for the nationalist the classical age."[18]

Iran's construction of its classical past followed this global pattern. Like its counterparts in Europe and Asia, Iran's discovery of antiquity served several purposes. First, the classical period became the foundational epoch of the national myth, the formative period in which the nation-subject existed in its homogeneous, unsullied form. For Iran, national authenticity became associated with the pre-Islamic period of the Persian empires. The nationalization of pre-Islamic history emerged out of a complex interplay between, on the one hand, dormant but now mobilized myths and legends representing pre-Islamic Iranian culture and, on the other, a growing awareness and appropriation of European forms of knowledge involving scientific discoveries about Iran's antiquity. Iranian intellectuals paid attention to philology, the Indo-European hypothesis, race science, the Aryan theory, archaeological findings, and the prolifically published European historiography on the classical period.

Second, beyond the discovery of the classical period and the formation of the nation-subject, the construction of Iranian antiquity allowed for invention and creative anachronism. The classical period became a template on which decidedly modern and scientific characteristics were inscribed. In this way the tension between traditional culture and modern standards of progress could be negotiated by discovering nineteenth-century standards of progress in the national past. This *authentication of modernity* became a central trope in the construction of Iran's antiquity.[19]

Finally, the construction of antiquity fitted the project of reform and modernization in another way. The rearticulation, or "refashioning," in the words of Mohamad Tavakoli-Targhi, of the classical past—now infused with authenticated modern European characteristics—produced a new historical consciousness that invited comparisons with the present condition of decay and backwardness. The invention of the archaic inevitably became juxtaposed against "the present," triggering the trope of degeneration and a political call to arms.

Although the publication of *Kaveh* and its close intellectual cousin, *Iran-*

shahr, marked an important moment in the formation of this nationalist narrative of modern Iran, the two periodicals were in some sense the culmination of a process that had commenced in the mid-nineteenth century. The genealogy of this (re)articulation began with cultural innovators at that time who produced experimental narratives combining long dormant local myth-histories with new forms of knowledge derived from Enlightenment and post-Enlightenment Europe. The rogue Qajar prince Jalal al-Din Mirza, the polemicist and dragoman of the Russian viceroy in the southern Caucasus Mirza Fath ʿAli Akhundzadeh, and the Babi dissident and radical journalist Mirza Agha Khan Kermani were among the most important of the early innovators. Their writings reflect a synthesis of cultural and religious heterodoxy with European orientalism, anthropology, and historiography.

By 1915, however, the political environment had changed dramatically. With the failure of both the late imperial style of legitimation of the Qajar state and the constitutional movement of 1905–11, that environment was ripe for the emergence of a new attempt to synthesize state, society, and culture. As Hasan Taqizadeh's personal and political development reflects, it was out of the failure of the Qajar and constitutional projects that the nationalist narrative emerged from the political contestation of the first two decades of the twentieth century.

THE REVIVAL OF ANTIQUITY: HYBRID NARRATIVES AND THE CONSTRUCTION OF A MODERN IRANIAN NATION-SUBJECT

Much as in the case of India, the politicization of Iranian nationalism in the first two decades of the twentieth century was rooted in cultural and philosophical changes that had taken place in the mid- and late nineteenth century. As Partha Chatterjee noted, the political manifestation of Indian nationalism was preceded by several generations of cultural and intellectual work carried out by an emerging nationalist sector of culturally hybridized middle-class Bengalis.[20] Conventional histories of Indian nationalism—and of non-Western nationalisms more generally—have, as Chatterjee argued, focused almost exclusively on nationalism in its later, political manifestation. The result of this preoccupation has been, as Chatterjee described it, a neglect of the formation of non-Western nationalism as a "cultural complex" or "mode of thought." Describing the conventional historiography of non-Western nationalism, Chatterjee wrote: "It does not let us into that vital zone of belief and practice . . . where the new disciplinary culture of a modernizing elite has to turn itself into an exercise in self-discipline."[21] Thus,

the story of Indian nationalism is conventionally told from the founding
of the Indian National Congress in 1885 without taking into account the work
of the Bengali intelligentsia, which, from the mid-nineteenth century, was
experimenting with ways of "mediating" between traditional forms of
thought and new European systems of knowledge.[22] This process of "medi-
ation" was critical in recasting traditional conceptions of loyalty and
identification into modern national forms, laying the groundwork for
Indian nationalism's later political manifestation.

In Iran as well, the cultural and intellectual rearticulation preceded the political manifestation of Iranian nationalism by at least two generations. As in
India, it was in the earlier period—beginning in the mid-nineteenth century—
that a new conception of the Iranian nation emerged from a complex interplay between traditional Iranian myth narratives and new European styles of
thought. The first producers of this conception were members of a hybridized
Iranian intelligentsia who, like their project, were situated between these
increasingly overlapping and intertwined systems of knowledge.

Among the earliest of the cultural "mediators" who articulated a modernist construction of Iranian national history was Jalal al-Din Mirza Qajar,
the forty-eighth son of Fath 'Ali Shah Qajar. Jalal al-Din Mirza's political
activities with the nascent Iranian Freemasons, his copious correspondence
with Iranian dissident intellectuals in the Caucasus, the Ottoman Empire,
and India, and his parsimonious but ultimately important literary production are indications of the experimental and heterodox ideas that were
beginning to circulate among a small sector of Iranian intellectuals during
the Qajar period. His *Nameh-ye Khosravan,* an imaginative narrative of Iranian history from a creation myth to Qajar times, is suggestive of the
influences converging in the narratives of an emergingly modern Iranian
intelligentsia.[23] Among these influences we can identity knowledge of European scholarship on Iranian antiquity derived from European instructors
at the newly constructed royal college, the Dar al-Fonun, as well as important traces of a resurgent neo-Zoroastrianism that was entering elite consciousness through contact with the long detached but now reconnected
Zoroastrian-Parsi community of Bombay. These and other elements were
important parts of the early attempt to construct Iran as a modern nation
capable of serving as a political subject of history.

Jalal al-Din Mirza was born to Fath 'Ali Shah Qajar (r. 1797–1834), second monarch of the Qajar dynasty, in 1827. By that time Fath 'Ali Shah, in
the closing years of his reign, had resigned himself to a quiet life of leisure
and the prolific production of offspring. As one of Fath 'Ali Shah's last chil-

dren, Jalal al-Din was born a low-ranking Qajar prince. His low social status in the Qajar family positioned him ultimately as a marginal figure in the politics of the Qajar elites while retaining for him access to some of the privileges of royalty—notably, education. He is in this sense analogous to Anderson's "creole pioneers" of the nationalisms that emerged out of the Spanish Empire in the Americas and to the "hybrid Indochine" of Dutch Indonesia.[24] Like marginalized and hybridized social actors elsewhere, Jalal al-Din Mirza—and all the other Iranian figures discussed in this chapter—was a marginal member of a social elite who had access to the most advanced forms of knowledge but was ultimately excluded from holding the reins of power.

The most formative period of Jalal al-Din's intellectual development came during his years of education at the Dar al-Fonun.[25] The college was established in 1851 by the reforming Qajar minister Mohammad Taqi Khan Amir Kabir as an institution of modern learning in Iran. It employed French, Austrian, Italian, and Prussian instructors—all from politically neutral states—to train members of the Qajar elite for careers in government service.[26] Beyond the practical purpose of training efficient administrators, the Dar al-Fonun quickly became a major site of cross-cultural contact between Europeans and members of the Qajar elite. It was out of this encounter that Jalal al-Din Mirza and others of his generation began grafting Enlightenment and post-Enlightenment forms of knowledge onto a reconstructed Persianate historical and literary tradition. The discovery of Iranian antiquity and the casting of this history into the form of a modern nation-subject thus emerged from the interplay between these systems of thought at the Dar al-Fonun.

The curriculum and the texts used for instruction at the college are telling indications of the components that went into this cultural synthesis. Aside from European languages—French, the nineteenth-century lingua franca, being the most important—students at the Dar al-Fonun received instruction in the natural, physical, and military sciences and in medicine, mathematics, and philosophy.[27] Most of the texts were used as practical manuals of instruction and were compiled, summarized, and translated into Persian from their original languages by the visiting instructors, in collaboration with local scholars. The translation of these scientific texts at the Dar al-Fonun was an important episode in the encounter between modern European scientific knowledge—such as advances in astronomy, chemistry, and biology—and the tradition of Islamicate science.[28]

Of particular interest in locating influences on the writings of Jalal al-Din Mirza are the literary, philosophical, and historical texts used at the college.

Joseph Arthur de Gobineau, dilettante anthropologist and the French second empire's special envoy to Iran between 1855 and 1858, while visiting the Dar al-Fonun, observed that students were reading Descartes' *Discours de la méthode*.[29] E. G. Browne, in his *Press and Poetry in Modern Persia,* included a list of more than 160 texts in use at the Dar al-Fonun. Although by his own admission the list was not a complete catalogue of the Dar al-Fonun library, he did name approximately fifty works in circulation at the college that can be considered important historical, philosophical, and literary texts. Among them were Sir John Malcolm's *History of Persia,* George Rawlinson's *History of the Sassanian Kings of Persia,* the *History of Nadir Shah,* and several translations from Voltaire including *History of Peter the Great, History of Alexander,* and *History of Charles XII of Sweden.* Also listed were translations of Fénelon's *Les Aventures de Télémaque,* Verne's *Around the World in Eighty Days,* Defoe's *Robinson Crusoe,* and Moliere's *Le Misanthrope*.[30]

These texts, in circulation at the Dar al-Fonun during the second half of the nineteenth century, might have been among the sources of information from which Jalal al-Din Mirza compiled his *Nameh-ye Khosravan.* Jalal al-Din mentioned his encounter with "European writers" in connection with the writing of the text, but he mentioned few of them by name.[31] Among the texts he did mention was a translation of Herodotus' *History of the Persians.* His encounter with European thought and scholarship is most clearly detailed in his inclusion in the text of portraits of the Sassanian shahs as traced from coins.[32]

One of the reasons the *Nameh-ye Khosravan* was so seminal a text was its inclusion of images and visual motifs from Iranian antiquity. The circulation of images from pre-Islamic history would become ubiquitous in Iranian public life in the generations to follow, as part of the larger practice of reproducing nationalist imagery on flags, maps, architecture, currency, and stamps.[33] In an important sense Jalal al-Din Mirza began this process with his reproduction of portraits of the Sassanian shahs as derived from numismatic sources. By the mid-nineteenth century the science of numismatics had developed to the point that Jalal al-Din could make use of its scholarship in reconstructing his narrative of Iranian history. Adrien de Longpérier's *Essai sur les médailles des rois perses de la dynastie Sassanide* and Edward Thomas's *Early Sassanian Inscriptions: Seals and Coins* were important works that included reproductions of Sassanian coinage.[34] Jalal al-Din Mirza neither cited these texts nor otherwise mentioned them by name, but he did state that in reproducing the portraits of the Sassanian shahs, "I have taken images from European sources and traced them."[35]

Jalal al-Din Mirza's tracing of Sassanian portraits from European sources is an apt metaphor for the process of interpellation by which pre-Islamic images were filtered into modern Iranian consciousness through contact with European scholarship. It was out of the interplay between local material culture and European forms of knowledge that Sassanian antiquity was recast as part of Iranian national history. Jalal al-Din's use of visual motifs of antiquity from numismatic evidence forged a direct link between the viewer and the pristine past. For him and his readers, the use of coins and other archaeological relics as evidence of a national past worked to enframe that evidence around an aesthetic ordered by nationalism. Once the archaeological object was understood as a national relic, the visual experience of it reinforced the powerful metaphor of a cultural renaissance emerging organically from the soil of the nation.[36]

Also indicative of the interplay between European forms of knowledge and the rediscovery of a lost authenticity is the renewed interest in Persianate narratives of pre-Islamic culture and history that arose in nineteenth-century Iran. The *Shahnameh* revival is an important example. Although wealthy patrons had long sponsored the production of illuminated manuscripts of the epic poem, the advent of the new print culture allowed for more widely available editions.[37] By the mid-nineteenth century, J. G. Herder's notion of *nationalliteratur* had also set a global standard by which every nation possessed an epic.[38] Consequently, the promotion of the *Shahnameh* and its growing circulation were in part a function of exterior standards shaping the selection of a national literary canon.

Other myth narratives that began to find a growing readership as a result of global standards of selection and new technologies of print were the *Dasatir,* the *Dabestan,* and the *Sharestan.*[39] The *Sharestan* was originally written by members of a small, heterodox community of neo-Zoroastrians in Akbar's India during the early seventeenth century. Akbar's project of creating an ecumenical, if not syncretic, religio-cultural milieu in North India promoted the production of texts such as the *Sharestan,* which combined Islamic Sufism, Hindu philosophy, and Zoroastrian cosmology.[40] When intellectuals such as Jalal al-Din Mirza, who were aware of the importance of antiquity for nineteenth-century European scholarship, expressed an interest in antiquity, texts such as the *Sharestan* became newly empowered and began to recirculate. Long marginal and often suppressed as heretical, these texts gained status under the influence of new global standards that assigned value to them as national artifacts. The technological miracle of the new print culture now enabled them to circulate on an unprecedented scale. Between 1846 and 1904 the *Dabestan,* for example, went through seven editions.[41] Along with Rawlinson, Malcolm, Herodutus, and numismatic scholarship, these new editions of old myth narratives were likely also to have been part of the cultural and literary world in which Jalal al-Din Mirza lived.

Of central importance in tracing the cultural and intellectual environment in which Jalal al-Din Mirza and others began producing pre-Islamic revivalist narratives was the figure of Manekji Limji Hataria (fig. 8).[42] Manekji was the son of Limji Hushang Hataria, a leading member of a prominent Parsi family in Bombay. In the early 1850s Manekji was sent to Iran as an emissary from the Bombay Zoroastrian community to strengthen ties between Zoroastrians in India and Iran. The Parsi community of Bombay had undergone a reform movement since the late eighteenth century that had altered much of its theological and ritual life;[43] Manekji's mission to Iran was to asses Zoroastrianism as practiced there and to promote the position of the Zoroastrian community in Iranian society.

For more than three decades he lived in and traveled around Iran, making contact with Zoroastrian communities in Yazd, Kerman, and Tehran. With the help of the Bombay Parsi-sponsored "Persian Zoroastrian Amelioration Fund," under Manekji's direction, the Iranian Zoroastrian community repaired fire temples and gained schools, orphanages, and hospitals. With Manekji's persistent lobbying of government officials, in 1882 Naser al-Din Shah granted the community an exemption from the *jizya* poll tax levied on non-Muslim communities within his domain. Manekji also became a fixture in Tehran's cultural and literary life during the second half of the nineteenth century.[44] In Tehran he became acquainted with Jalal al-Din Mirza and others who showed an interest in Iran's Zoroastrian past. Jalal al-Din Mirza mentioned Manekji's presence and cultural influence in his correspondence with the prominent nationalist and literary figure Mirza Fath 'Ali Akhundzadeh, and Manekji, also a correspondent of Akhundzadeh's, mentioned his acquaintance with the young Qajar prince.[45]

As part of his mission to revive Zoroastrianism among Iranians, Manekji's other major activity was publishing on and promoting neo-Zoroastrian and Iran-centered myth-histories in Tehran. He contributed an important preface to the 1854 edition of the *Sharestan,*[46] the myth narrative written in seventeenth-century India recalling the legends of the ancient kings of Persia. In 1857 he assisted Reza Qoli Khan, the Qajar court scholar and director of the Dar al-Fonun, in writing *Nezhad Nameh-ye Padeshahan-e Iran Nezhad,* an Iran-centered history that traced mythic genealogies of Iranian and

FIGURE 8. *Manekji Limji Hataria (1813–90), a Parsi emissary who lived in Iran for many years and was instrumental in promoting Zoroastrianism and the pre-Islamic revival.*

non-Iranian dynasties to pre-Islamic Iranian kings.[47] He edited and wrote an introduction, appendix, and notes for A'in-e Hushang, a collection of ancient Zoroastrian texts translated into modern Persian from the original Pahlavi.[48] In 1877 he edited Javidan Kherad, a collection of moral precepts attributed to the ancient sages of Iran, India, and Greece.[49] He was instrumental in encouraging and assisting Ismail Khan Zand Tusarkhani in compiling and editing the myths and legends that became the Farazestan.[50] Manekji also frequented Babi circles in Iran, and it was on his suggestion that Mirza Hoseyn Hamadani compiled the Tarikh-e Jadid, the first account of the Babi movement. E. G. Browne eventually translated this text into English in 1893.[51] Most important for his relationship with Jalal al-Din Mirza was Manekji's Tarikh-e Parsian,[52] a brief narrative of the history of Zoroastrianism in ancient Iran. Jalal al-Din Mirza felt the work to be so important that he included it as an appendix to the first volume of his Nameh-ye Khosravan.

The Nameh-ye Khosravan was thus the product of several intersecting sources of influence. Jalal al-Din Mirza's encounter with European scholarship on Iranian antiquity at the Dar al-Fonun provided him with the most advanced nineteenth-century scientific findings. At the same time, the revival of traditional myth narratives and the renewed encounter with Iran's Zoroastrian past via contact with the Bombay Parsi community gave the appearance to Jalal al-Din and others that an authentic national essence existed and could be retrieved by reconstructing a lost antiquity. It was at the intersection of these influences that Jalal al-Din produced his Nameh-ye Khosravan, a work best described as a transitional narrative or hybrid text in which he grafted elements of myth-history derived from recently recirculated myths and legends onto knowledge derived from European scientific scholarship. It was out of the interplay between these cultural forms that the Nameh-ye Khosravan articulated the first quasi-modern narrative placing Iran as the nation-subject of history.

The work's most striking modern-national characteristic was its narrative structure. The Nameh-ye Khosravan was the first text to include both pre-Islamic and Islamic history in a single narrative. Traditional Islamicate narratives conventionally marked a sharp break between the pre-Islamic and Islamic periods, the former being the "age of ignorance" (jahaliya).[53] Traditional Persianate myth narratives such as the Shahnameh were bound entirely in the pre-Islamic period, from the Persianate creation myth of Kyumars, the first man, to the fall of the Sassanian dynasty and the Muslim invasion.[54] The three-volume Nameh-ye Khosravan was unique in encompassing both periods in a single narrative and subsuming both in the subjectivity of Iran. The first volume, appearing in 1869, followed the conventional myth-histories in reproducing the pre-Islamic narrative. The second volume, published the following year, continued the story from the Arab invasion to the twelfth century, and the third volume, another year later, spanned the time from the Mongol invasion to the aftermath of the Safavid dynasty. Although a fourth volume was planned, Jalal al-Din Mirza died before it could be completed, a victim of the syphilis epidemic of the late Qajar period.[55]

Despite the work's being cut short by its author's premature demise, the narrative structure of the *Nameh-ye Khosravan* should be familiar to students acquainted with the later tradition of Iranian historiography. That tradition describes an elevated, classical civilization that came to an end with the Arab-Muslim conquest of the seventh century, only to have a recurring Iranian identity assert itself despite the "yoke of Islam" and the indignity of further alien invasions. This narrative projects Iran as a conceptual and territorial unit existing in history alongside—and in competition with—other conceptual-territorial units similarly bound in time and space. The Arab-Muslim invasion of the seventh century and the Mongol invasions of the twelfth century are explained as assaults that only momentarily disrupted the underlying continuity of Iran's indivisible existence. This assertion of indivisibility, built into the structure of the narratives, was uncommon in Qajar historiography before the *Nameh-ye Khosravan* and in this sense was the novel ingredient that projected Iran as a modern nation-subject. As possessor of an autonomous and continuous history, Iran could now lay claim to a core identity, a national essence, born in a barely perceptible mythic past and remaining pure down to the present, despite the vicissitudes of history.

Although the structure of the *Nameh-ye Khosravan* posed the possibility of a national essence, the nature of that essence remained to be identified. Its contents had yet to be retrieved, reconstructed, and given voice. In this context, Jalal al-Din's use of language becomes the other issue of importance in assessing the *Nameh-ye Khosravan*. He was the first modernist writer to write history in "pure Persian," a somewhat stilted literary style that consciously avoids the use of Arabic and Turkish loan words.[56] In this sense he associated his narrative with Ferdowsi's *Shahnameh,* which the poet likewise composed largely in pure Persian. Jalal al-Din Mirza's style was part of the broader *Shahnameh* revival of the nineteenth century, which produced a burgeoning genre of poetic works written in imitation of Ferdowsi's epic—hence Jalal al-Din's consistent use of the Persian *nameh* instead of the Arabic *ketab, dastan* instead of *tarikh,* and *payqambar* instead of *rosul.*[57] The "pure Persian" of the *Nameh-ye Khosravan* might also have been in emulation of the *Dasatir,* the *Dabestan,* and the *Sharestan,* which were composed in a curious, stilted Persian dialect devoid of Arabic and Turkish vocabulary. Not only did these newly recirculating myth narratives pose the revival of lost and putatively authentic legends from a pristine past, but also the language in which they were written was felt to reflect an unsullied and archaic Iranian essence.

The empowering of language as a marker of identity was ultimately derived from the broader global discourse of nationalism in the nineteenth century. Jalal al-Din Mirza, a cosmopolitan intellectual, was situated between dominant nineteenth-century standards of culture, politics, and identity, on one hand, and local cultural forms, on the other. His reading of dominant global standards of identity—such as the equation of language and nationality—into indigenous cultural forms shaped his association of a purified and pristine Persian language with Iranian national identity. Thus, as with much else in the revival of Iranian antiquity, global standards of culture and politics were used to reconstruct the past and in the process transform Iran into a modern nation-subject.

The effects of global standards of culture and politics in regard to language are also seen in the literary style of the *Nameh-ye Khosravan.* Jalal al-Din Mirza wrote in a simple, austere style, in contrast to the flowery and ornate Persian panegyrics that were still the norm in the late Qajar period. He may have been following the examples of Malkom Khan and Mirza Fath 'Ali Akhundzadeh, with both of whom he was associated and intermittently corresponded. Malkom and Akhundzadeh had worked together on ideas for a reform of the language and had experimented with prototypes including a Persian written not in Arabic script but in either the Latin or a modified Cyrillic alphabet.[58] As part of their proposed reform, the two had also advocated a general simplification of the literary style to make the language more amenable to modern, scientific concepts and modes of thought, as well as more direct and accessible to readers of the gradually increasing print culture. Thus the problem of language, like much else, was situated between the recovery of an archaic subjectivity and the transformation of traditional cultural forms to cohere with new, modern standards of progress. Jalal al-Din Mirza's purified vocabulary and simplified style were in keeping with these Janus-like goals. His purified Persian was intended to embody an archaic and pristine cultural authenticity, while his simplified literary style was intended as a modern reform to make that authenticity accessible to the public.

MIRZA FATH 'ALI AKHUNDZADEH: ANCIENT
IRAN BETWEEN ORIENTALISM AND RACE SCIENCE

At least as important for the project of constructing a classical past as the basis of modern Iranian national identity was the work of Mirza Fath 'Ali Akhundzadeh (1812–78), perhaps the most intriguing and important personality to participate in the nineteenth-century Iranian national revival. A poet, playwright, and polemicist, he pioneered the grafting of Enlightenment and post-Enlightenment modes of thought onto a Persianate cultural idiom and in the process recast Iran into modern national form. His seminal treatise, *Alefba-ye Jadid* (1863)—in which he decried the deficiencies of the Arabic alphabet and proposed a modification of the script or its complete substitution by either the Latin or Cyrillic alphabet in the writing of Ottoman and Persian—was one of the earliest tracts to acknowledge the importance of language in the project of reforming culture and society in the Middle East.[59] In this way he anticipated the language reform projects of Kemalism in Turkey and the language policy of the Soviet state in the Caucasus and Central Asia.

Akhundzadeh's important literary works include his plays—such as *Molla Ibrahim Jalil Kimiagar* (Mullah Ibrahim, the alchemist), *Mard-e Khasis* (The stingy man), and *Musyu Jordan* (Monsieur Jordan)—which were among the earliest adaptations of the modern dramatic form in Middle Eastern literature. They were also early works of social criticism, satirizing what Akhundzadeh perceived to be traditional impediments to progress, such as popular superstitions among the masses and the corruption and incompetence of clerics and civil authorities.[60] His most important work, however, is arguably his polemical-literary work *Maktubat-e Kamal al-Dowleh*,[61] a fictional correspondence between an Indian prince, Kamal al-Dowleh, and an Iranian prince, Jalal al-Dowleh, no doubt patterned after Montesquieu's *Persian Letters*. The two characters engage in a correspondence after Kamal al-Dowleh has traveled through Iran and writes to his counterpart lamenting the sorry state of Iran's once elevated civilization. Like Jalal al-Din Mirza's *Nameh-ye Khosravan*, Akhundzadeh's *Maktubat-e Kamal al-Dowleh* (The correspondence of Kamal al-Dowleh) was one of the earliest narratives that challenged dominant Islamicate narratives of Iranian history with an alternative born out of a synthesis of Enlightenment and post-Enlightenment thought and reconstructed Persianate cultural forms.

Also like his contemporary and correspondent Jalal al-Din Mirza, Mirza Fath 'Ali Akhundzadeh was a quintessentially nineteenth-century hybrid intellectual, bringing his synthesis of a recast Iranian identity out of an assortment of disparate influences. It is one of the strange—but ultimately understandable—ironies of Iranian nationalism, and of nationalism more generally, that hybridized and thoroughly cosmopolitan persons such as Akhundzadeh became the progenitors of a nationalism that would in turn lay claim to an exclusivist and unsullied conception of authenticity.

Akhundzadeh was born in 1812 in the town of Nuka, an Azeri Turkic-speaking region along the unstable frontier separating the Russian, Ottoman, and Qajar empires in the southern Caucasus.[62] Nuka was then nominally part of the Qajar dominion, but with the Russo-Persian war of 1828 and the Treaty of Turkomanchay, Nuka, along with the remaining territories in the Caucasus once ruled by the Qajars, was annexed by imperial Russia. The world in which Akhundzadeh spent his early years was thus one of shifting boundaries. It saw the shifting of Russian and Qajar political boundaries and of Muslim and Christian religious ones, the overlapping of Turkic, Persian, Russian, Armenian, Georgian, and Kurdish linguistic boundaries, and the erosion of boundaries between what was perceived as a decaying and impotent world of tradition and a new world of progress made unmistakable by the incendiary effects of Russian arms. Added to the mix was Akhundzadeh's partial African ancestry; his mother was descended from an African slave in the service of Nadir Shah.[63] Like the partial African descent of Alexander Pushkin, Akhundzadeh's great intellectual role model and literary forebear, to whom he wrote an elegy in Persian upon the former's death, Akhundzadeh's ancestry further complicated the cultural, religious, linguistic, and ethnic sources from which, in an increasingly national age, he felt compelled to construct a synthetic identity.

He negotiated these boundaries and constructed his synthetic conception of Iranian identity from Tiblisi, the seat of the Russian viceroy in the Caucasus and the largest and most cosmopolitan city in the region. He arrived there while still in the care of his maternal uncle, who had become his presumptive guardian after the dissolution of his parents' marriage.[64] After his early religious education, which included Arabic and Persian grammar and the rote memorization of the Qur'an, Akhundzadeh was enrolled in one of the new Russian schools that now dotted the southern Caucasus, spreading Russian enlightenment among the newly conquered peoples. By his own account he quickly excelled in the study of Russian, and because of his equal proficiency in Azeri Turkish, Persian, and Arabic, he was eventually enlisted as a dragoman in the service of the viceroy.[65]

It was in Tiblisi that Akhundzadeh absorbed Enlightenment and post-

Enlightenment thought as filtered through the Russian language and Russian imperial culture. As the seat of the Russian viceroy, Tiblisi was the most important cultural center in the region, with a cosmopolitan population that included Decembrist exiles, Armenian intellectuals, and Georgian nationalists. Coupled with this cosmopolitanism was a multilingual political and literary print culture as well as Russian-sponsored universities, theaters, and other cultural institutions that provided forums for contact and the circulation of ideas among the diverse communities of the region.[66]

Among the immediate and traceable influences that can be associated with Akundzadeh are the ideas of Khachatur Abovian (1805–48), the Armenian reformer and celebrated novelist, who was director of a Tiblisi gymnasium where Akhundzadeh was a sometime teacher of Azeri Turkish.[67] Abovian was a noted advocate for simplifying and standardizing the Armenian literary language, an idea foreshadowing similar ones that Akhundzadeh would advocate for Ottoman and Persian in the 1860s and 1870s. Also chief among Abovian's achievements was his work as a novelist and social critic. His anticlericalism, in novels such as *Verk Hayastani* (Wounds of Armenia), in which he satirized the Armenian clerisy's fatalism, would find later echoes in Akhundzadeh's literary and polemical writings about the Muslim ʿulama.[68] Akhundzadeh's Tiblisi interlocutors also included progenitors of a Georgian national literary renaissance such as Ilia Chavchavadze and Grigori Orbeliani. Among his Russian associates was the exiled Decembrist revolutionary A. A. Marlinsky, who introduced Akhundzadeh to the works of Pushkin and Gogol and of radical Russian Enlightenment critics such as Chernyshevsky, Derzhavin, Ostrovsky, and Griboyedov.[69]

That the Russian language offered Akhundzadeh's sole window onto Enlightenment and post-Enlightenment European thought necessarily narrowed the influences to which he had access. Among the non-Russian influences he mentioned in his letters and other writings were Voltaire, Shakespeare, and John Stuart Mill, to whose works he had access through Russian translations.[70] His encounter with nineteenth-century European anthropology was also important in shaping his reconstruction of Iranian identity, but that encounter, too, was mediated by Russian as his exclusive European literary and scientific language.

The most important non-Russian influence in this regard was the work of Ernest Renan, a central cultural figure in the French second empire and Third Republic and among the transcendent intellectuals of the nineteenth century. Renan's most widely accessible work was his *Vie de Jesus*, which became a focus of international attention and controversy when it was published in 1863 and immediately translated into several other European languages, including Russian.[71] Akhundzadeh mentioned Renan sporadically throughout his writings but did not mention which of Renan's writings he was familiar with. Besides *Vie de Jesus,* few others of Renan's works appeared in Russian translation during Akhundzadeh's lifetime. Among those that did were an 1866 translation of the 1858 work *De l'origine du langage,* an 1864 translation of the 1853 article "Des religions de l'antiquité et de leurs derniers historiens," and an 1865 translation of the short piece "Les antiquités égyptiennes et les fouilles de M. Mariette."[72] Akhundzadeh might also have come into contact with Renan's thinking indirectly via Russian scholarship that was influenced by, if not derivative of, his work.[73]

Akhundzadeh was clearly attracted to several strains of Renan's thought, including his critique of religion and his anthropological notions. Renan's strikingly secular and historicist reading of Jesus, which attracted the ire of the Catholic church,[74] would find a later parallel in the iconoclastic tone in which Akhundzadeh would treat Islam and the Prophet Mohammad. And like Renan, who from the safety of his chair in Semitic philology at the Col-lege de France could issue his pronouncements on the historical Jesus, Akhundzadeh, under the protection of the Russian viceroy in Tiblisi and far removed from the long arm of the Shi'ite clerisy, could give free rein to his call for an "Islamic Protestantism" and forge his reconstructed notion of Iranian identity—a notion formed from the intersection of influences he had encountered in Tiblisi.[75]

In the *Maktubat-e Kamal al-Dowleh,* Akhundzadeh brought together the strains of thought he had synthesized during his intellectually forma-tive years. Most important were Enlightenment ideas of secularism, anti-clericalism, and religious reform, all of which he repeatedly traced to an abstract notion of *civilization.* At least as important were post-Enlighten-ment ideas, which are also readily discernable in the *Maktubat.* Among them can be highlighted a romantic notion of a classical past and a racialized understanding of culture. Writing in the latter half of the nineteenth cen-tury, Akhundzadeh had access to both the Enlightenment thought of the late eighteenth century and post-Enlightenment, nineteenth-century ideas such as romanticism and the then vogue of racial anthropology.

His incorporation of eighteenth-century Enlightenment ideas in the *Mak-tubat* is clearest in his pronouncements on Islam. He wrote the *Maktubat* as a series of three letters between a fictitious Indian prince, Kamal al-Dowleh, and a fictitious Iranian prince, Jalal al-Dowleh. The second letter is devoted almost entirely to a wide-ranging criticism of Islamic legal institutions and cultural practices. The tone of its pronouncements and the nature of its criticisms clearly derive from Enlightenment forms of thought. The transposition of Enlightenment categories and vocabulary is most evident in Akhundzadeh's adoption of terms such as *progress, civilization, fanaticism, charlatan, revolution,* and *despot*.[76] He used these categories in his intellectual arsenal to challenge the existing social, cultural, and political state of affairs in Islamic Iran and to pose an alternative construction of a redeemed classical past and a newly popularized national culture.

In considering Islamic legal institutions, Akhundzadeh claimed that they were flawed both in their basic Qur'anic foundation and in their system of practical adjudication.[77] He argued that the perception of the Qur'an as both a divinely revealed sacred text and a source of positive law made it unsuitable as the basis of a modern judicial system. In an exaggerated polemical tone, he argued that the perceived sacred status of the Qur'an infused a transhistorical value into the text's prescriptive legal pronouncements, rendering the law immutable and resistant to change. "How is it" he asked, "that the laws of Islam have not changed in twelve hundred years?"[78] The answer, echoing radical eighteenth-century Enlightenment thought, was that the system of law was based on a false premise of divine revelation.

At least as important was the corruption of the Muslim ʿulama, to whom Akhundzadeh habitually referred, using a directly transposed term, as "charlatans."[79] Their corruption, he believed, was among the chief causes of Iranian backwardness. Their obsession with the ritual profession of faith and their role in maintaining illiteracy and ignorance were among the major indictments he levied against them: "Only one in a thousand of the people of Iran can read, because of the corruption and 'despotism' of the ʿulama, and because of the existing alphabet."[80] Here he combined his anticlericalism with his advocacy of a reformed Arabic script; the existing script, he argued, was too difficult to learn and was thus a major obstacle to mass literacy. In addition, it was in the interest of the ʿulama to maintain Arabic as the exclusive language of law, thus keeping their monopoly over the adjudication of justice.

In ritual life, Akhundzadeh was critical of both the taʿziyeh and the hajj, describing them as outward professions of faith that reinforced uncritical obedience and fatalism. "The taʿziyeh has no use," he wrote. "Spend your time on lofty deeds, consider how the people of the world are advancing and likewise move in the direction of progress and achieve civilization."[81] The hajj, he said, was a mindless ritual that reinforced the insularity of the

Muslim world; the exclusion of non-Muslims from Mecca segregated Muslims from the mainstream of civilization. Similarly, the convergence of national groups in participation in the hajj neither promoted the unity that the ritual was supposed to foster nor served the national interests of the participating groups.[82]

Akhundzadeh next focused on the status of women in Islamic societies. He criticized the legal strictures that limited the rights of women in cases of divorce as well as the legally sanctioned practice of polygamy.[83] He was bold enough to single out for criticism Mohammad's relations with his wives. The Prophet's wives could not have married him willingly, Akhundzadeh claimed, pointing out the youthful ages of some of them and the practical considerations of tribal politics that no doubt also factored into the marriage alliances.[84] "A young woman," he wrote, "would not have wanted to marry an old man who had some twenty-two wives and concubines."[85] As in many of his other criticisms of Islam, Akhundzadeh argued that these practices derived from traditional "Arab customs" that became institutionalized in the faith during its formative years.

Akhundzadeh's association of Arab cultural and ethnic characteristics with what he decried as undesirable and antimodern practices in Islam reflected the synthesis of Enlightenment and post-Enlightenment thought in his construction of Iranian political-historical consciousness. From Enlightenment thought came an abstract notion of civilization and progress, while from post-Enlightenment thought he seems to have borrowed a racialized understanding of modernity in which traits he designated "Arab-Islamic" were labeled antimodern. The lack of progress and civilization that he argued were endemic to Iranian society were said to be caused by Iran's long association with Arab-Islamic culture. The logic of this argument is congruent with much of post-Enlightenment European thought, especially important currents of orientalism and romantic nationalism. Among Akhundzadeh's many correspondents were Russian and French orientalists and anthropologists to whom he sent manuscript copies of the *Maktubat* in his unsuccessful attempt to have the work published. His relationship to their scholarship is complex and suggestive; many of his criticisms of Islamic legal institutions and cultural practices were grounded in familiar nineteenth-century orientalist tropes of Islamic backwardness.

For Akhundzadeh, however, orientalism did not represent a scientific-imperial discourse of domination in the familiar Saidian sense. In his mind, orientalism and the Persianate philosophical-historical tradition were associated with each other, and he fused them into a common discourse that had as its ultimate goal the inclusion of a reconstructed Iran into the philosophical orbit of a universal modernity. The price to be paid for entering this orbit was the dissociation of Iran from its Arab-Islamic heritage and the marking of that heritage as an external and antimodern element within Iranian tradition. Orientalism was thus central in Akhundzadeh's discovery of a pure Iranianness, in that it posed for him a fault line separating the authentic from the inauthentic, which in turn corresponded to the division separating the modern and the antimodern. Iranian authenticity, for Akhundzadeh, could thus be represented as congruent with modernity, whereas the Arab-Islamic elements in Iranian culture came to represent the inauthentic and antimodern.

We see this most dramatically in his invocation of a mythic Iranian classical past as a golden age of progress. He described its authentic Iranian institutions as congruent with Enlightenment and post-Enlightenment values. Geographically, his idealized Iran encompassed all of the Middle East and the Caucasus, as well as parts of Central Asia and North India: "In the ancient period the kingdom of Fars was at the center of the world: [in] the north was the river Jeyhun and the Urals, in the south was the Persian Gulf, to the east was the river Suteg between Send and India [north of Gujarat], and [to] the west [it extended] all the way to the Bosphorus, that is, the strait of Istanbul and the White Sea."[86] This greater Iranian landmass was "all under the supervision of the Iranian state and was administered with great justice."[87]

This mythic kingdom of perfect justice was ruled by a king who provided jobs for all, created a system of regular stipends for the elderly, and established hospitals for care of the sick.[88] No one was poor or homeless in this mythic Iranian state. The authorities did not abuse the citizens or inflict severe punishments, but rather administered an equitable and enlightened system of justice.[89] "People resided under your [Iran's] civilization with comfort. They did not beg, they did not want; inside the country they were free, and outside of Iran they were proud."[90] Surrounding the king were wise counselors and *mobed*s (Zoroastrian priests), who supported the king and encouraged the achievement of great deeds. "There was a time," Akhundzadeh wrote, "when your culture was dynamic, and for several thousand years you were important in the pages of history. . . . Oh, Iran, where is that dignity which existed under Kyumars, Jamshid, Anushiravan, Khosrow, and Parviz?"[91] He answered this question by laying responsibility for the decline of the mythic past on the Arab-Muslim invasions of the seventh century CE: "The barefoot and hungry Arabs twelve hundred years ago produced your misery."[92] It was their "violent assault" that "caused your backwardness."[93]

Like Akhundzadeh's criticisms of Islamic legal institutions, Islamic cultural practices, and the Arabic script, his polemic against the Arab-Muslim invasions was flavored with racial undertones. He seems to have followed the logic of nineteenth-century racial thought, which classified national groups according to a hierarchy of racial attributes. Central to this classificatory scheme were the racial and linguistic divisions separating the Semitic family of languages from the Indo-European, or Aryan, family. Akhundzadeh made no direct reference to the Aryan theory but did periodically refer to the work of Ernest Renan, who, along with Max Müller and others, was among the most important popularizers of the Aryan theory in nineteenth-century Europe.

Although the Aryan theory is most often remembered as part of the history of European anti-Semitism, its importance also extended to the formation of Iranian and Indian national consciousness.[94] The discovery of the Indo-European family of languages by Sir William Jones in 1786 suggested that languages such as Greek, Latin, Sanskrit, Persian, German, and Celtic were all descended from a common linguistic ancestor.[95] Although somewhat displaced by the controversies surrounding the publication of Darwin's *The Origin of Species* (1850), the Indo-European hypothesis became widely accepted in the mid-nineteenth century, popularized as the most advanced form of scientific knowledge accounting for the ethno-linguistic genealogy of humankind. The work of Schlegal, Bobb, and Grimm, among others, extended and confirmed some of the provocative ideas first put forward by Jones.

By the mid-nineteenth century, however, the implications of the Indo-European hypothesis were very different from those Jones had conceived of two generations earlier. For Jones, the Indo-European theory was grounded in a monogenetic conception of humankind that sought to reconcile the new ethno-linguistic classificatory scheme with biblical and Mosaic conceptions of history. Two generations later, it was no longer a theory of the common history of humankind but the basis for constructing new hierarchies of racial-linguistic value. The most powerful of these was the linguistic division separating the Semitic from the Indo-European language group.

Two developments account for this shift in the emphasis placed on Jones's discoveries. First, the wide-ranging public controversies surrounding Darwin's theory of evolution changed the nature of anthropological thought more broadly. Darwin's emphasis and that of many of his followers on evolutionary change and on a hierarchy of species with humans as the most "advanced" form shaped the terms in which the Indo-European hypothesis was discussed. The classificatory schemes separating the Indo-European, Semitic, Turkic, Mongol, African, and Aboriginal language families became, under the influence of Darwinian notions of evolutionary progress, increasingly ordered according to new hierarchies of cultural and civilizational worth. Second, the popularization of the Indo-European hypothesis led to mythic and romantic conceptions of linguistic categories as markers of broader cultural-social characteristics. Proponents of the politics of romantic nationalism seized upon the hypothesis as scientific confirmation of national distinctiveness and repackaged the scientific findings for a mass audience.

Among those who contributed to this popular mythologizing of the Indo-European theory was Friedrich Max Müller, the great German-born British philologist who edited the definitive edition of the *Rig Veda* and was professor of Sanskrit at Oxford University in the latter half of the nineteenth century. Müller was one of those rare figures in nineteenth-century science who managed to gain a wide audience for his writings.[96] His well-attended public lectures in London and elsewhere, along with his readable and hugely successful *Lectures on the Science of Language*,[97] were among the most important channels through which the Indo-European theory became popularized.

It was Müller who first sought to historicize the Indo-Europeans as more than a linguistic category by using the Sanskrit term *Aryan* to name them. He also looked beyond linguistic evidence to interpret social and cultural practices as distinguishing markers of Aryan culture. It was Müller, too, who popularized the Aryan invasion theory of India, in which he sketched the historical process by which the early Aryans swept across the Iranian plateau from their mythic, primordial origins and into the Indus Valley. In Müller's popular writings—as in the writings of others who worked to draw a more vivid and romantic portrait of the early Indo-Europeans—the connections between language, culture, and race became increasingly solidified.[98] Indeed, as the Indo-European theory circulated beyond the narrow circles of scientists and pedants and made its way into the print culture of the reading public, the Aryans increasingly became the stuff of myth and legend. By the end of the nineteenth century, the increasingly popular scientific findings successfully conjured up in the imaginations of those familiar with the most advanced knowledge a romantic, idealized image of a primordial Aryan community bound by language, culture, and race.

Among those readers was Mirza Fath 'Ali Akhundzadeh. The racialized undertones of his polemics against the Arabs and his romantic descriptions of Iranian antiquity can best be understood as extensions of this broader, popularized Aryan mythology. His participation in the discourse of Aryanism worked simultaneously on at least two levels. On the first, his anti-Arab and anti-Islamic pronouncements and his glorification of Iranian antiquity were direct echoes of the scientific judgments made by orientalists and anthropologists of the time. On the second, his use of this discourse as part of a nationalist polemic worked to authenticate those judgments within an Iranian discourse of national identity. As used by Akhundzadeh, race science was no abstract scientific pronouncement but a way of asserting Iran as an equal and authentic member of a trans-European modernity.

The nature of race science itself allowed for this type of assertion. Iran and India were the only two extra-European cultural zones positioned at the peak of the nineteenth-century racial hierarchies, alongside the advanced European states and in contradistinction to the Semitic, Turkic, Mongol, and Aboriginal ethno-linguistic families. Nineteenth-century cultural science implied that Iran and India, unlike the other groups, possessed a proto-Aryan national essence that could be reformed and redeemed by modernity. Following this logic, race science implied that antimodern elements had caused Iran and India's decline, and these elements were external—they had entered into and corrupted those regions' national essences.[99] Akhundzadeh and others seized upon this implication in their construction of an Iranian national-cultural imagination. The Semitic-derived Arab and Muslim heritage, woven into the fabric of Iranian culture for over a thousand years, now became distinguished as external to a newly discovered, pristine national essence that could be linked to a new Aryan subjectivity associated with a trans-European modernity.

Ultimately, Akhundzadeh situated his construction of Iranian identity between orientalism and race science. From orientalism he borrowed an Enlightenment universalism that was critical of traditional religious institutions. In his hands orientalism became a discourse to use in criticizing what he perceived as an ossified and medieval Islam. At the same time, his appropriation of race science and his romantic description of Iranian antiquity allowed him to find a cultural space in which to associate a reconstructed Iran with dominant nineteenth-century standards of progress. Thus, a dual process of disengagement and reconstruction distinguished Akhundzadeh's scenario of Iranian identity—disengagement from a derided Arab-Muslim culture and a simultaneous recasting of Iran as an Indo-European nation worthy of participation in the new universalism.

TAQIZADEH AND THE POLITICIZATION OF THE NATION-SUBJECT

Although Jalal al-Din Mirza and Mirza Fath 'Ali Akhundzadeh were instrumental in constructing Iran as a modern subject of history, the cultural and philosophical process of reconstruction that they and others pioneered underwent a decisive shift with the work of Hasan Taqizadeh and publication of the journals *Kaveh* and *Iranshahr*. The Berlin journals were bridges connecting the foundational work of the earlier generation of nationalists with the statist project that was to emerge with the ascendancy of Reza Khan (Reza Shah after 1925). The progenitors had done the job of constructing Iran as a cultural complex capable of serving as a modern subject of history. Jalal al-Din Mirza's was perhaps the first nationalist narrative to project a singular Iran as an organic nation-subject bound in time by a unified history. Akhundzadeh infused this nascent Iranian nation-subject with values derived from Enlightenment and post-Enlightenment universalism, projecting modern standards of progress onto a mythic antiquity.

Kaveh and *Iranshahr* took this project a step further by politicizing Iran as the basis of a mass movement. The nationalists who came of age before the constitutional revolution had crafted the conceptual framework of Iranian nationalism, but it circulated within only a narrow stratum of society. The politicizing and popularizing of Iranian nationalism began with the constitutional revolution of 1905–11 and the burgeoning of a journalistic print culture that circulated nationalism beyond the culturally heterodox elites. The political invocation of Iran, as mediated through the popular press, was targeted against the late Qajar structure of legitimation.

But although the generation of 1905–11 owed a great debt to its nationalist predecessors, its members were ambivalent about the myth of pre-Islamic antiquity that was so central to their work. The constitutionalists' political and instrumental interest in forging a broad coalition of political parties—including, importantly, the religious modernist groups—led them to deemphasize the radically secularist, pre-Islamic-based nationalism of Akhundzadeh and his colleagues in favor of a style of nationalism that, although conceptually grounded in the same modernist-nationalist framework, was politically ambivalent and ideologically ecumenical.[100]

The constitutionalist movement, however, was short lived. With its collapse following the Russian invasion of 1911, the fragments of its coalition began to be pieced back together around a new nationalist model. The decade from 1911 to 1921 was a critical one of political contestation and ideological experimentation. Instead of the constitutionalists' broadly conceived political coalition, the new nationalist movement drifted increasingly toward a version of Iranian nationalism that was statist, secularist, and grounded in a mythic antiquity. In this sense the national project that began to take shape after 1911, succeeding and responding to the politically ecumenical interlude of the constitutional era, was directly descended from the version of Iranian nationalism first conceived by Akhundzadeh's generation.

The Berlin journals with which Taqizadeh was associated, *Kaveh* and *Iranshahr*, best represent this post-1911 political drift. They brought together the cultural-philosophical nationalism of the earlier generation and the populist political commitment of the generation of 1905–11. While grounding their invocation of Iran in a romantic construction of a mythic antiquity, they used a populist language aimed at a broad audience. They also made use of the widely circulating newspaper format that, during the constitutional era, had become the new staple of Iranian politics.

The new tone is evident throughout the pages of *Kaveh*. Taqizadeh's introduction in the inaugural issue captures the sense of urgency and anticipation common to political journalism during the First World War. He wrote that "the fate of the nations of the world is being determined in the arenas of war. . . . those who are aware in the nations of the world are in a state of anxious frenzy and excitement. . . . they become agitated by the news of the day and are concerned for their own nation and its success and happiness."[101] His language also highlights a new set of global assumptions being brought graphically into focus by the war. The new world that Taqizadeh saw around him was a world of nation-states engaged in a global competition of national self-assertion and political independence. He believed that people must claim identification with a particular nation-state on this global stage and show concern "for their own nation." It was the tangible reality of the war that brought this set of assumptions sharply into focus for Taqizadeh.

Against this backdrop he wrote that he and his colleagues had taken up the task of producing a newspaper in order to represent the national interests of Iran:

> In the midst of this day of resurrection for the nation, several individuals from a poor and unfortunate nation—that is Iran—have gathered in Berlin—the seat of war—to consider the fate of their nation. . . . our intention is to not sit idle but to awaken our compatriots. . . . this is the intention of this small newspaper, to project its weak voice from Berlin to reach the ear of Iranians. . . . our destiny is tied to the outcome of this war and our duty is to fight

our enemies with all of our strength to secure our independence. . . . our hope is that Iranians will show that the spirit of the nation has not died and that a wise movement will emerge which will again raise the flag of Kaveh.[102]

The combination of a popularizing tone and a new nationalist sentiment is best represented in the selection of *Kaveh* as the name of the newspaper. In its inaugural issue, Taqizadeh devoted a long article to explaining why the name was selected and detailing the historical basis of the myth of Kaveh and his legendary banner. Kaveh was, "according to the ancient legends, a blacksmith from Isfahan who launched a national uprising against the evil foreign tyrant Zahak, expelled the foreigners and restored the pure race of the Iranian Fereydun to the throne, and achieved independence for Iran."[103] Examining the written sources discussing the legend of Kaveh, beginning with Ferdowsi's *Shahnameh* and the medieval historians Tabari and Beyhaqi, Taqizadeh tried to establish the legend's historicity. Of particular interest was the banner that Kaveh was said to have hoisted as a rallying point during the national uprising. After the uprising, the sources suggested, the banner became a revered symbol of the pre-Islamic Iranian nation. Taqizadeh included in his article a traced image from a Sassanian coin showing a Zoroastrian fire temple and a banner that he described as the banner of Kaveh. He also mustered evidence in the form of archaeological finds from Pompeii. In 1831, he wrote, excavations there uncovered material evidence of contact between Pompeii and ancient Iran. Among the finds were coins and stone inscriptions that included representations of Kaveh's banner.

On the basis of these sources, Taqizadeh attempted to render a physical description of the banner. He said it was made of leather and had an X-shaped pattern across it, with a circle at the center. Its colors were red, yellow, and purple. He concluded by suggesting that the banner of Kaveh was the true flag of the nation. The famous lion and sun symbol of the Iranian flag, he argued, dated back only to the Seljuq period of the twelfth century, whereas the banner of Kaveh dated to the pre-Islamic "heroic age." The invocation of the banner was thus designed to bring together a populist political project and a new set of nationalist symbols. "This," he said, "is why we have named this newspaper *Kaveh*."

At least as important was the process of cultural recovery in which Taqizadeh seems to have been engaged as he looked back in history to find precedents and precursors for the project he saw himself launching. The banner of Kaveh was important as a populist political symbol, but it was also representative of the cultural, intellectual, and ideological maneuvers that came together to invent and recast Iranian history in the form of modern nationalism. The legend of Kaveh had always maintained a place in the broader domain of Persianate myth-culture, but its reinvention by Taqizadeh as the precursor of a modern nationalist movement was a novel procedure that infused the legend with new political meaning.

As experienced from inside the discourse of nationalism, the double maneuver of recasting and inventing was elided in favor of a procedure expressed in terms of a scientific process of *excavation,* of *uncovering* a lost authenticity. The difference between these two procedures was subtle but crucial. Whereas Taqizadeh's cultural maneuvering actually worked to invent, construct, and assign new meaning to old myths, legends, and symbols, the assumptions underlying the presentation of these procedures were put in terms of a "return of the repressed." The elision in the self-presentation of the discourse was not born of a lack of philosophical sophistication but rather was grounded in an awareness of the politically and culturally empowering effects of the newly recast myths. Reading modern nationalism into the banner of Kaveh unleashed the creative possibilities of inventing and reinventing Iranian identity from within the broadly conceived parameters of a Persianate cultural universe.[104] Taqizadeh's engagement with this universe and his dialogue with a broadly defined Persianate culture allowed him to invent "the new" while simultaneously *authenticating* his inventions by laying claim to an archaic self.

Throughout the pages of *Kaveh* Taqizadeh employed the maneuver of engaging the deep reservoirs of Persianate myths, legends, and symbols and reformulating those elements in modern national form. Of central importance to this maneuver was his encounter with European oriental scholarship. More than any of his intellectual predecessors, Taqizadeh was steeped in the European historical and philological scholarship of his day. He devoted no fewer than five major articles in *Kaveh* to summarizing the historical and philological findings by German, French, and British scholars of Iran.[105] He devoted one full article to the contents of the two-volume *Grundriss der Iranischen Philologie* (1896–1904), edited by Wilhelm Geiger and Ernst Kuhn, which was perhaps the most comprehensive work summarizing orientalist discoveries concerning Iran.[106] Its first volume was devoted entirely to Iranian languages and included the writings of the noted Sanskritist and Aryanist Christian Bartholomae (1855–1925). His pioneering work in the phonology and morphology of the Old Iranian languages was crucial in detailing the historical transformations and underlying continuities in the development of the Iranian branch of the Indo-European language family.

Not only did Geiger and Kuhn's book summarize findings about the linguistic continuity between Avestan, Pahlavi, and Persian—all within the
Indo-European family—but it also paid attention to the dialects of Persian
and the broader Iranian branch of the Indo-European family, including
Afghani, Kurdish, Pamir, Kashi, Gabri, Naini, Behbehani, Shirazi, and
Tajiki. Taqizadeh summarized these findings for his Iranian audience. He
also summarized Geiger and Kuhn's second volume, which he described as
focusing on Iranian history and civilization. In this case he emphasized the
history of the Sassanian period and Zoroastrianism.

In another article on European scholarship on Iran, he described the contents of Rawlinson's volumes on the great oriental monarchies, including
volumes 6 and 7, which focused on the Parthian and Sassanian empires,
respectively.[107] He wrote that these works were "important without measure"
and encouraged his readers to read translated excerpts from them in the works
of Zoka' al-Molk and E'temad al-Saltanah.[108] Yet another article summarized
the work of Friedrich von Spiegel (1820–1905), the great German orientalist whose three-volume *Iranische Alterthumskunde* (1871–78) is one of the
most important works concerning Iranian history, ethnography, culture, and
religion in the ancient period. Taqizadeh described how the first of the three
volumes dealt with the geography of Iran and delineated its historical territorial boundaries. The second volume considered the racial characteristics of the Iranian nation and examined the ethnic composition of the
population, and the third covered the history of the ancient period, from
the Aryan migrations, and subsequent relations with the Semites.

Taqizadeh's encounter with European orientalism is of central importance for understanding his construction of Iranian nationalism. The
assumptions underlying his construction ran directly parallel to the assumptions underlying European orientalist scholarship on Iran. In some respects,
Taqizadeh's construction of Iran's national past was entirely derivative of
European scholarship.[109] Significantly, however, he seems to have been aware
of the sociology of knowledge that mediated his relationship to orientalism, and he exhibited a sophisticated analytical position on the issue. In the
first of five articles discussing European scholarship on Iran, he wrote:

> Some have argued that those who study the nations of Asia and Africa do so
> with the political motives of the European powers and work to prevent the
> freedom and independence of the societies. . . . But others in my opinion do
> so for the greater good of knowledge. . . . Some of them have been heroes of
> the weak nations and done great service to them against the interest of their

own nations. They have rescued objects by archaeology. . . . Manuscripts have been edited and published. . . . all of this has helped the nations of the East to regain their identity. . . . they [Europeans] know more about our history and culture than we do. . . . not one Iranian knows Pahlavi. . . . it is only because of Europeans who deciphered the old scripts of Avestan, Sanskrit, and Pahlavi that today we know about our kings and ancestors. . . . Iranians must become aware of their ancient culture and their thinkers, artists, and kings so that they will be aware of their great nation in the past before Islam and of what race they derived from, how they have reached their current condition, and how to regain their original greatness as a nation. . . . For this reason we are suggesting the following books by European Iran scholars.[110]

Taqizadeh's position on orientalism is revealing in a number of ways. Most important is his awareness of the politics of knowledge that orientalism represented. He seems to have had an intuitive understanding of the power relationship that mediated his position, as a consumer of orientalism, relative to that of European knowledge, the producer of orientalism. He was aware of the unequal balance of power that this relationship represented and yet was able to transcend it.

For Taqizadeh, orientalism represented a universalist scientific project designed to excavate and recover lost authenticities. Archaeology, anthropology, philology, and history thus gave back to Iranians their forgotten national identity. In making this point he conceded to orientalism—and to European knowledge—the position of final arbiter of universal standards of culture and identity. But in the process he managed to find a philosophical passageway through which Iran could come to participate in that universalism. The elevated status enjoyed by ancient Iran, according to orientalist-arbitrated knowledge, made this concession an easy philosophical bargain to make. Once the dominant standards of knowledge and identity were acknowledged, Taqizadeh was free to find and reconstruct Iranian national identity as associated with and conforming to those standards. Orientalism, therefore, was the cultural and philosophical apparatus that Taqizadeh appropriated and used to forge a reconstructed Iran capable of participating in modernity.

Through orientalism Taqizadeh gained a new understanding of Iranian history, which led to his advocacy of a national transvaluation—the reestablishment of a mythic and ancient past in the modern era. His invocation of a revived antiquity was similar to the broader discourse of romantic nationalism of his time, but for Taqizadeh, as for many Asian nationalists, the revival of antiquity brought with it a modernizing agenda. The discovery of the archaic past allowed for a process of creative anachronism and invention through which Taqizadeh infused modern values and standards into the past as part of a newly recovered authenticity.

This process implied a form of historical consciousness that had profound political implications. When juxtaposed against an orientalist-derived mythic antiquity infused with modernist values and standards, the present became recognizable as a moment of decay. Taqizadeh's encounter with orientalism thus led him to a new form of historical consciousness in which the present was juxtaposed against a mythic past. From this consciousness Taqizadeh took the next step and launched his movement of national reform. His call for a transcendence of the present condition of decay became a call for a return to a once elevated authenticity. He did not passively engage the parameters of orientalist discourse; in his hands the parameters of orientalism moved beyond abstract scientific pronouncements and became politicized as part of a national movement.

We see this in his concrete calls for cultural and political reforms. In a series of articles, some of them entitled "A New Path," he outlined his proposals for national reconstruction.[111] Among the most important themes were mass education, the emancipation of women, the centralization of government, the settlement of tribes, the prohibition of opium, and a call for religious tolerance. His proposed policies were in keeping with the examples of the modernizing states of Europe, particularly the late-developing German state, with which he was most familiar. In advocating these policies, however, he not only referred to the examples of European states but also looked to orientalism and myth-history to find precedents and precursors for modernist reforms in the ancient past. Especially on the questions of mass education and the emancipation of women, his proposals followed this logic.

In the first issue of the new edition of *Kaveh* he began by excerpting and translating a key article summarizing the history of higher education in Germany.[112] The article described the pioneering work of the Swiss-born social reformer and educator Johann Heinrich Pestalozzi (1746–1827), who helped to establish a modern educational system in Prussia based on Rousseau's principles. Taqizadeh outlined the process by which German education became compulsory and universal for all German children from the age of six in the period following the Napoleonic wars. The leadership of Fredrick Wilhelm I, the article continued, was important in making education a priority in Germany's national project.

Taqizadeh's inclusion of this article was designed to make his Iranian readers aware of the policies in place in the states of Europe. It was also intended to invite readers to compare Iran's educational situation with Germany's. The lack of mass education, and of education for women in particular, was, according to Taqizadeh, the greatest social ill facing Iranian society. He argued that Tehran was the only city in Iran in which even limited access to education was available for females. He estimated that no more than five thousand girls were enrolled in school in all of Iran. According to Taqizadeh, the obstacles to women's education were religious prejudices that made physical differences sufficient grounds for denying education to women. In contrast, he argued, the emancipation and education of women were central to Iran's renewal: "Much has been stated about the position of women, and it is true that if ignorance did not exist, and if the people of Iran were aware of civilization, they would realize that the education of women and their emancipation and guarantee of basic rights is a prerequisite for a Muslim nation to reach the position of the states of the West."[113]

His discussion of women's education, like much else in his program for reform, was thus set against the backdrop of European standards of civilization. At the same time, educational reform and the emancipation of women were also situated within *Iranian tradition*. For Taqizadeh and his Berlin associates, the intellectual challenge of reform was to find correlates and precursors from within an authentic tradition that would help to bridge the divide between a pristine past and the project of a modern future. In the journal *Iranshahr*—the successor to *Kaveh*, published by Hoseyn Kazemzadeh-Iranshahr from 1922 to 1927—the intellectual labors of authenticating modernity were most clearly expressed on the issues of women's emancipation and education. No fewer that seven articles were devoted to those topics, including some describing the position of women in ancient Iran and others discussing issues relating to the selection of spouses and women's roles within the family.[114]

Of particular interest is a series of articles in *Iranshahr* describing women from the Zoroastrian-Parsi community of Bombay and the levels of education they had achieved. By the 1920s the relationship between Iranian nationalists and the Parsi community of Bombay was solidifying into one of shared memory. The Parsi community imagined Iran as a lost homeland from which it had been separated after the coming of Islam to Iran. Iranian nationalists perceived the Parsi community as representing the core of Iranian authenticity, which had been preserved in India, removed from the Islamization and Arabization that had followed the Arab-Muslim conquests of the seventh century. The Iranian nationalists in Berlin used the example of the Bombay Parsis in advocating a nationalist revival. The status of Parsi women in particular was made an example for an authentic Iranian woman who was educated and emancipated.

Several issues of *Iranshahr* contained articles describing the achievements of Parsi women. One issue reproduced a letter from Zarbanu Dinshah Molla, a woman from a prominent Bombay Parsi family. According to the article's introduction, she was a practicing lawyer and active in Bombay politics. Her letter, written originally in Gujarati and translated into Persian by Ibrahim Purdavud, was addressed to "our Iranian sisters":

> I send greetings to all my Iranian sisters of pure spirit. The purpose of this letter is to send greeting to Iranian women and also to remind them of our mission. Although we Indian Parsis have been separated from our original home for more than one thousand years, the blood which runs in our veins is still from that land, and the passion for our sacred homeland is in our hearts and is the source of great emotion. In these days when Iran is looking for new progress I find it necessary to remind Iranian women of two points: one relates to ancient Iran and the other relates to the future of Iran. In ancient Iran women were possessors of a position of esteem, and according to the laws of the sacred Avesta and the days of old, women were strong and had stature, and in contrast to today, their honor was preserved and they participated in social life with men.[115]

Zarbanu Dinshah went on to discuss points from the Avesta, the Zoroastrian scripture, and from the Gathas, Zoroastrian hymns, in which she saw references to the elevated status of women. After the Muslim conquest of Iran, she wrote, the old ways of the past had been gradually forgotten. However, "we Parsis sought refuge in India and preserved the ancient beliefs."[116] In the modern period, she continued, Parsi women were the most educated women in India. The first female doctor in all of India was a Parsi, and other Parsi women were lawyers and leaders in education. The purpose of listing these achievements was not to boast of them, she said, but rather to remind Iranian women that "we Parsi women in our blood, race, hearts, and minds are with you Iranian women. The worthiness which you see today in Parsi women is from the veins and blood which they have brought with them from Iran."[117]

Zarbanu Dinsha's letter is emblematic of the intersection of Iranian nationalism with the discourse of race and gender. Its publication allowed the Berlin nationalists to include their advocacy for reform of the position of women within their broader project of using antiquity and race as the basis of modern nationalism. The idea of the modern woman as educated, emancipated, and active in the public domain was projected back onto a mythic and racialized antiquity. Like the broader discourse of nationalism, the discovery of these modern values in a mythic past was used to authenticate modernity and to participate in the new universalism while preserving a national distinctiveness. The example of the Parsi women was therefore a living reminder of the Iranian past, as well as a promise of a modern future.

The nationalism that emerged in newspapers and journals such as *Kaveh* and *Iranshahr* after 1911 did not spring fully formed from a cultural and political vacuum. From the mid-nineteenth century the cultural process of rearticulation had been carried out by marginal members of an intellectual elite who had access to the myth-narratives of the Persianate literary tradition as well as the most advanced sciences of orientalism and racial anthropology. The heterodox and experimental narratives produced by the progenitors reflected a cultural synthesis of these disparate sources. In the process, pre-Islamic Iranian history became a template for a national history on which were drawn nineteenth-century standards of progress and modernity. This *authentication of modernity* ultimately produced the cultural synthesis capable of projecting Iran as a modern nation within a global system of national communities.

The gradual success of this construction of Iranian nationalism after 1911 was not without rival possibilities. Indeed, the construction of a mythic national past was situated within an array of rival constructions also laying claim to political authority. The most important alternative was the Qajar state's projection of a legitimacy grounded in a royalist Shiʻism, in the style of the late imperial dynasties of Europe, the Ottoman Empire, and Japan. In addition, after 1905, the constitutional movement posed the alternative of ideological ecumenism, inclusive of Islamic modernism and democratic liberalism. This rival construction successfully challenged the Qajar state between 1905 and 1911 but was ultimately incapable of consolidating its version of a cultural-political community.

With the collapse of the late Qajar and the constitutionalist projects, political dynamics within Iran shifted dramatically. The new arena of contestation was favorable to a model of political community that could impose political order and offer a new cultural synthesis to mediate the relationship between state and society. It was out of these political dynamics that Reza Khan would emerge in 1921 and make use of the pre-Islamic-based nationalism that had developed since the late nineteenth century as the basis of a new relationship between state, society, and culture.

3 THE PEDAGOGIC STATE

Education and Nationalism under Reza Shah

AS REZA SHAH STEPPED ONTO THE NEWLY BUILT QUADRANGLE OF THE UNIVER-
sity of Tehran on February 5, 1935, to lay the dedication plaque inaugurating Iran's first university, he saw only an empty space devoid of the usual
hum of a college campus.[1] 'Ali Asghar Hekmat, Reza Shah's minister of education and one of the chief planners of the project, recalled in his memoir
that the weather that day was cold and ominous. The impending thunder
in the gathering clouds contrasted with the calm of the well-ordered network of newly paved sidewalks linking the buildings of the campus.[2] The
shah's comments, as he stood on the platform and looked out across the
quad, captured the mood of the day and his understated determination:
"[T]he establishment of a university by the Iranian nation is something that
should have been achieved much sooner, but now that it has been initiated
it must be completed quickly."[3]

The shah's impatience for the virtues of education was not entirely
justified. Although the building of a university was indeed a new initiative
sponsored by a new government, education had remained an element of
continuity in Iran's project of modernity since the nineteenth century. As
far back as the early part of that century, Qajar attempts at modernization
had emphasized the role of education in reforming and strengthening the
Qajar domains.[4] The Qajar prince 'Abbas Mirza had enlisted British and
French military advisors to train standing regiments of local military forces
in the use of artillery along the Russian-threatened frontier in the north-

west province of Azerbaijan. French Lazarists and American Presbyterian missionaries had educated Iranian Christians and others since the nineteenth century, and the Alliance Israélite Universelle had educated Iran's long-standing Jewish community.[5] The establishment of the Dar al-Fonun in 1851, under the initiative of the reforming vizier Mirza Taqi Khan Amir Kabir, to educate a cadre of modernizing elites in the most advanced European knowledge was perhaps the most important nineteenth-century initiative in the field of education and the most direct precursor of the establishment of a university.[6]

During the constitutional period and the interim prior to the ascendancy of the Pahlavi state, educational reforms had been central to the agenda of parliamentary reforms. A small number of so-called *rushdiye* schools— among the first of the state-initiated primary schools based on the French model—were established on the eve of the constitutional revolution.[7] In 1900 the Qajar government established the Anjoman-e Ma'aref (Council of Education) to begin assessing Iran's educational needs. Among the first initiatives of this precursor body to the Ministry of Education was the building of the Madreseh-ye 'Olum-e Siyasi (School of Political Science) to train the sons of the elites in the burgeoning work of the foreign service.[8]

During the constitutional period, educational reform became a major policy concern for the newly formed Majles. Laws passed in 1907, 1910, and 1911 established national priorities pertaining to education. The first of these, the 1907 Education Law, formally established the Ministry of Education (Vezarat-e Ma'aref) as the state institution directly responsible for implementing education policy. Subsequent laws further determined the role and operations of the ministry, including the establishment of the Supreme Council of Education as the deliberative body responsible for establishing educational goals. By the end of 1911 the council had set as a goal the universal primary education of children aged seven to twelve.[9]

Yet despite these precedents, in several important ways the Reza Shah period did mark a new beginning for Iranian education. Nineteenth- and early-twentieth-century policy makers had conceived and established a new system of education, but many of their goals were left unrealized. A lack of resources, a scarcity of qualified teachers, political instability, and the clerisy's opposition to a new system that threatened its traditional educational prerogatives were among the reasons enrollment in modern primary and secondary schools numbered fewer than 30,000 students by 1921. Although the Reza Shah years were hampered by many of the same obstacles, the relative stability of that period and a continued focus on the virtues of education led to an expansion of the primary and secondary school population to more than 400,000 students by 1941.[10]

Statistics, however, tell only part of the story. Conventional discussions of education in Iran and other parts of the non-Western world have traditionally focused on questions of scale and access in determining the social consequences of education. Numbers of schools built, numbers of teachers trained, and numbers of students taught-these types of data have often been invoked, usually uncritically, as indices of modernization and progress.[11] Discussions of education as part of the cultural history of nation-building have been less common, especially in Iranian historiography. In this context, education policy in the Reza Shah years can be seen to have marked the beginning of a radical new relationship between state, society, and culture. Most fundamentally, the advent of a national system of education represented the final dissolution of the boundary between state and society.

That boundary had begun to erode in the late Qajar period, during the reign of Naser al-Din Shah. With the advent of the Pahlavi state and the establishment of an educational system, the state began to construct an official nationalism. In carrying out this project, the Pahlavi state presented itself as the embodiment of national culture, the bearer of a common authenticity shared by state and society. Its mission became to nationalize the Iranian polity through a system of institutions and practices seen as remedial, designed to correct an existing cultural deficiency. As 'Ali Asghar Hekmat, one of the major architects of this policy, described in his memoir, his mission was to make Iran "of a single cloth."[12]

The state thus became the vanguard of national authenticity, and society in turn was seen to need the moralizing leadership of a pedagogic state. This new pedagogic mission could most efficiently be carried out through an educational system administered through schools to what Eric Hobsbawm called "the captive public of school children."[13] In this way the nationalizing practices of Reza Shah's state had much in common not only with those of its immediate neighbor, the Republic of Turkey, but also with those of nationalizing states such as Germany, Italy, and the newly formed polities of eastern Europe that emerged from the Hapsburg, Ottoman, and Romanov empires. Like the educational policies of all these new states, the policy of the Pahlavi state intended to make manifest that which was felt to be latent, to help bring about a new polity in which state and society were unified and mediated by a singular national culture. What remained was to define the nature and parameters of this national culture.

Doing so became the chief concern for state educators and cultural

bureaucrats of the Reza Shah years. Their deliberations and resulting policies to a large extent followed the reasoning of the nationalist intellectuals
discussed in chapter 2. State educators such as 'Isa Sadiq, 'Ali Asghar Hekmat, and Hasan Pirniya were given the task of implementing, through an
educational policy and bureaucratic apparatus, the ideas on education and
national culture first put forth in the radical treatises of Jalal al-din Mirza,
Akhundzadeh, and Kermani and in the pages of the journals *Kaveh* and *Iranshahr*. Like their philosophical predecessors, these educators and bureaucrats
sought to construct a national culture that appropriated the instrumental-
ities of modernity while rediscovering a putatively lost authenticity. National
education under Reza Shah framed its modernizing project in terms of a
return to a pristine modernity that was felt to exist within the deep reservoirs of Iranian tradition. Once this authentic national culture was rediscovered, the policy of Reza Shah's state was to institutionalize it and
administer it to the public through the bureaucratic apparatus of an educational system. Education under Reza Shah thus brought together for the
first time in Iran the cultural and philosophical efforts of a nationalist ideology and the administrative and technical apparatus of a nationalizing
bureaucratic state.

BACK TO THE FUTURE: NATIONAL EDUCATION
AND THE DISCOURSE OF AUTHENTICITY

The formation of a nationalist discourse of education policy was greatly
intensified in the early years of Reza Shah's rule. Newspaper, magazine, and
journal articles from this period reveal an increasing public awareness of
the important relationship between national culture and the administration of an education system. In 1924 the Ministry of Education itself began
to publish a monthly journal called *Ta'lim va Tarbiyat* in order to discuss
issues of education.[14] In cultural, political, and literary periodicals such as
the important journal *Ayandeh*, questions of education were also regularly
discussed by political and cultural figures of the day.[15] Such discussions generally addressed the basic questions of establishing a system of national education and the priorities of such a system. How should it be organized?
Should it emphasize primary and secondary education, or should higher
education be the immediate priority? What should be included in the content of education? These were among the substantive questions and prob-
lems faced by the early builders of a national system of education. Invariably,
the point of departure for the debates was an invocation of the classical past.

Education, like the national project itself, looked to an idealized ancient past in charting a course for Iran's future.

Among the best examples of this type of educational thinking are found in the pages of *Iranshahr,* the Berlin-based journal edited by Hoseyn Kazemzadeh-Iranshahr from 1922 to 1927.[16] *Iranshahr* provided an important arena for the discussion and circulation of ideas related to many aspects of national reform. Its influence on cultural and political policy-making was crucial in establishing the tone of debates taking place inside Iran, and it played a critical role as a bridge between the philosophical and polemical tracts of the nineteenth century and the more practical, administrative thinking of policy-makers during the Reza Shah years.

Kazemzadeh wrote a series of articles for *Iranshahr* detailing the history of education in ancient Iranian civilization. One such article published in an early issue of the journal was titled "Education among the Ancient Iranians."[17] Kazemzadeh began by comparing ancient Iranian education with education elsewhere in the ancient world: "In the science of education, the ancient Iranians were very advanced in terms of progress and civilization in comparison with neighboring nations. For example, whereas in the civilization of ancient India education was confined to the domain of religion, the ancient Iranians had taken it out of this restricted state and placed it in a more social and practical setting."

He continued the article by invoking the roots of education deep in the history of Iranian civilization. He also compared the role of education, as he perceived it to have existed in ancient Iran, with its role in ancient India. Despite the common Iranian nationalist practice of finding shared characteristics between ancient Iran and India, Kazemzadeh noted an important distinction. Iranian education, he argued, was "very advanced" and tied to values of "progress and civilization." These values were clearly identified with the separation of education from the domain of religion. Because of this separation, ancient Iranian education was more advanced than ancient Indian education. Clearly, Kazemzadeh was using the modern standard of secular education as a measure by which to judge ancient Iran. By infusing ancient Iran with these modern values, he blurred the distinction between modernity and Iranian authenticity. He managed to authenticate modern values by tying them to the national past.

Next he attempted to illustrate how the ancient Iranians had used education as a socializing institution through which to pass on national characteristics: "In the opinion of ancient Iranians, the essential purpose of education was to train children in such a way that they would interact with the people in society and express a lofty morality that is characteristic of the Iranian race: that is, good thoughts, good words, and good deeds." The last phrase was a reference to one of the basic ethical precepts of Zoroastrianism. For Kazemzadeh, the first task of an educational system was to pass on these sorts of national values, an ideal for which he found precedent in the ancient period. Once again his conjuring up of an ancient and authentic national past was an invocation of the way he envisioned a modern future. By finding a blueprint for a national education system in the ancient past, when children were socialized into a national culture, he authenticated a modern innovation.

He went on to describe more of the values and characteristics the ancient Iranians inculcated through education. He paid particular attention to the role of education in preserving national culture. Families from all social strata—here he acknowledged the existence of social stratification in ancient Iran but argued that national culture worked to transcend such divisions—considered it important to preserve the "beliefs and customs" they valued. It was through education that these beliefs and customs were passed from one generation to another. He highlighted "diligence and perseverance" as one set of values central to education in ancient Iran: "The ancient Iranians would train their children from a very young age to be accustomed to work diligently and to overcome trials and tribulations." For this reason, he concluded, "in ancient Iran there were no beggars and thieves."

In contrast to this golden age of antiquity, in which education was the basis of an advanced public morality, Kazemzadeh drew a bleak picture of contemporary Iranian decline and decay. The breakdown of the ancient system of education has caused a decline in public morality, he explained. His remark about the absence of begging and thievery in ancient Iran was a thinly veiled reference to the conditions of social corruption and decline that in his time had led precisely to such social ills. Here the connection between an idealized ancient past, the current conditions of decline, and a prescription for reform in order to regain the virtues of the past is made most explicit.

In another important article, "The War on Moral Decay," published in the October 25, 1922, issue of *Iranshahr*, Kazemzadeh devoted more attention to the social causes of decline and called for a comprehensive effort of moral reform in Iran through education. "We must recognize that the greatest enemy facing the Iranian nation, which causes great distress, is moral decay. We must therefore declare war against this enemy. . . . We must uproot this corpulent tree of corruption and decay with the ax of knowledge and social education."[18] Articles extolling the virtues of ancient Iran and articles decrying contemporary conditions of decline repeatedly complemented each other in the pages of *Iranshahr*. The ancient past was idealized as a golden age characterized by authenticated modern values. The present was a period of "moral decay." To move forward into modernity, therefore, Kazemzadeh prescribed a return to the pristine past. The instrument for this return was education. Kazemzadeh saw education as the ultimate cultural and political panacea—an "ax of knowledge." Under conditions of decline, decay, and cultural dissipation, a properly administered system of national education was the ideal solution. He understood education as a remedial exercise to bring to the fore a latent potentiality.

Social change and modernization were thus linked closely to the discourse of education in Kazemzadeh's writings—but that was not what made him unique. The connection between social change, modernization, and education had been well established in the discourse of Iranian education since the nineteenth century. What made Kazemzadeh unique, and what makes him important for the subsequent history of Iranian education, was his unparalleled ability to tie these themes into the nationalist project. Modernity and educational reform now became tied to the rediscovery of a lost authenticity. Kazemzadeh's critique of Iranian culture and his call for educational reform went along with a rhetorical maneuver that discovered modern education in the ancient past. In the critique of education, the ancient period became a template on which modern values could be inscribed and in the process authenticated. Modern education was naturalized into the national past. Henceforth the call for educational reform would be tied to the national project; the establishment of a modern educational system would be part of the larger project of promoting a national culture. This convergence of educational reform and the ideology of nationalism would have profound implications for the development of educational policy and the cultural form of education administered to a generation of Iranians reared during the Reza Shah years.

PRIESTS AND PEDANTS: MISSIONARIES
AND EDUCATION UNDER REZA SHAH

The educational policies initiated during the Reza Shah years, reflecting the state's desire to reconcile the dual interests of modernity and nationalism, involved adopting forms of modern education while tying them to national tradition. The most direct example of the nationalizing of education was the state's policy regarding foreign mission schools, which had existed in

Iran since the early nineteenth century. By the mid-1920s, their status had become precarious as new emphasis was placed on national education.

The debate over the status of the mission schools was, on one level, tied to the state's desire to terminate the capitulations that, since the nineteenth century, had sanctioned the ceding of legal and political sovereignty and the granting of privileges to citizens of European states living in Iran. Many of the schools had come into existence as part of capitulation agreements in the nineteenth century, and they were now seen as relics from the age of imperialism.[19] Although proselytizing was legally prohibited in Iran, Bible study had always been compulsory for students at the mission schools. Their immediate objective might have been to provide students with modern knowledge and practical skills, but their broader goals could hardly be concealed. As the American missionary Henry Schuler put it, echoing much of the standard racial thinking of the day: "The Persians did not accept Islam of their own choice; it was forced on them at the point of a sword. And they have been trying ever since to get rid of some of its teachings, against which the Aryan mind rebels."[20] Another zealot put it even more bluntly: "We are put here to fight Mohammadanism."[21] Thus, by 1927, as the capitulations were being reviewed and renounced by a state eager to exert its newly discovered national interests, the question of the mission schools also emerged. Although they offered the best form of modern education in Iran, their parochial status and proselytizing mission made them inappropriate from the perspective of the new national project.

The architects of Iran's education policy therefore sought to appropriate the practical advantages of the mission schools, with their modern style of education, while situating them within the new national project. We see this policy initially in Reza Shah's education decree of 1927, issued scarcely a year after his coronation.[22] The decree required all schools with foreign names to adopt Persian names. The American College of Tehran, for example, which had been the private institution of Presbyterian education in Iran since 1871, became Alborz College of Tehran. It is important that the content of the curriculum was not the shah's main concern in issuing the decree. Instead, he and his educational planners and policy-makers were concerned that the modern education taught at the school be perceived as Iranian.

In subsequent years, further decrees and laws increasingly nationalized education in the foreign and mission schools. First, the Ministry of Education began to impose a gradual standardization of the language of instruction.[23] English, French, Armenian, and Turkish were common languages of instruction at the mission schools, but a decree issued in 1928 required Per-

FIGURE 9. *Alborz College of Tehran (formerly the American College of Tehran) in the 1920s.*

sian to be used as well. Soon other laws and decrees began to regulate the contents of the curriculum. The ministry became concerned that Muslim students, who were attending mission schools in large numbers, were being proselytized through the schools' curricula, which included extensive Bible study. Besides imposing the standardization of language, the 1928 decree regulated religious instruction in the mission schools.[24] Bible study was now prohibited for Muslim students, and the schools were required to teach Islamic law in its place. Arthur Boyce, the vice-president of the college, wrote: "The demands that our Christian schools should teach Mohammadan Law to our students and give up the teaching of the Bible were particularly hard to accept. Such a course seemed a total reversal of our whole purpose."[25] In subsequent negotiations, the mission schools and the ministry agreed to restrict religious education to the teaching of general religious principles, including the lives of the "great prophets," in a new ecumenical tone as part of general course on ethics.[26]

Another part of the 1928 decree was the requirement that all graduates of the mission schools take compulsory examinations administered by the Ministry of Education upon graduation. The exams were tied to military conscription, now a requirement for all male citizens.[27] Students who passed the exams were commissioned as officers in training; those who failed were sent to boot camp in the regular army.[28] Not only were the exams conducted exclusively in Persian, but their contents were tailored toward the newly standardized curriculum of the national educational system. Students graduating from the mission schools were at a disadvantage in passing the exams and thus qualifying for the officer corps, because the curricula of the mission schools were seldom standardized in accord with the examinations.

The prospect of boot camp made the mostly elite student population eager for a curriculum that would help them pass the exams. Boyce recalled: "In the years that followed, 'passing the examinations' was the only object of education in the minds of most students. Students became increasingly unwilling to give time to anything which did not prepare them for the examinations."[29] The compulsory exams thus put additional pressure on the mission schools to standardize their curricula in line with the new national standards.

The 1928 educational decree marked the beginning of the end for the mission schools in Iran. Further decrees in 1932 and 1939 guaranteed their demise. The 1930s saw rapid expansion of the national project in all sectors of Iranian society, not least in education policy. In 1932 a new decree prohibited the enrollment of Iranian children in missionary primary schools. As Arthur Boyce recalled, the closing of the primary schools was a "tragic loss," for it meant that henceforth students educated at the mission schools would start only after age twelve: "Instead of beginning school with us at the age of six, boys entered the Middle School at twelve and often older, with habits of study and character already formed and therefore less responsive to the ideals of work and conduct we aimed to inculcate."[30] Iranian nationals, whether of Muslim, Christian, Jewish, Baha'i, or Zoroastrian background, made up 75 percent of the student population at the schools, according to Boyce.[31]

Clearly, the decree was intended to drastically curtail missionary education in Iran. Part of the rationale for maintaining the missionary schools had been to fill the gap in the government's ability to provide universal education. By 1932 the Ministry of Education believed that in the areas where missionary education was administered, the state could now provide universal primary education. 'Ali Asghar Hekmat recalled in his memoir that 1932 was the year in which public school construction dramatically increased throughout Iran. At least ten schools were built in Tehran alone, and Tabriz, Kerman, Reza'iyeh, Ahvaz, and Khorabad were also sites of new schools with modern facilities.[32]

Boyce argued in his memoir that the government's position that the mission schools were no longer needed "was only partly true, for even up to the present time, twenty-two years later, there are far from enough schools to supply the need of the country."[33] As he suspected, the ministry's intentions were as much political as practical. The missionary schools, while providing the modern forms of knowledge desired by the new state, did not situate this education within a nationalist framework. The ministry's work was to provide just such an education, which would be presented to students as both modern and national.

The 1932 decree did not require the closure of the missionary primary schools, but the effect was the same, for they were now limited to taking only the children of resident foreign nationals. In 1939, a new decree continued where the 1932 effort had left off. It demanded that all foreign schools be closed and their property turned over to the ministry. The tersely worded notice informing the mission schools of the government's decision was delivered directly by the Ministry of Education to the president of Alborz College, Samuel Jordan: "The government desires all properties turned over to it within the next two weeks, that is, before the opening of the fall term. It promises compensation for the properties and may retain some of the American personnel."[34]

The reaction of the mission educators was one of shock and amazement, as an official cable sent by the Board of Foreign Missions to the Iranian government makes clear:

> For over one hundred years American missionaries have been giving their services in educational work in Iran. Thousands of young men and women have gone out of the Mission schools to make rich contribution to many phases of the life of Iran. . . . [The mission] has rejoiced in the recent rapid advance of the nation and has ungrudgingly given of its best in support of the progressive features of the government program. . . . The Board hoped that it would have received more consideration than the present action of the Government would indicate.[35]

The disappointment felt by the mission educators was in part justified. Both the mission schools and the new national schools had similar goals, the provision of education to children in their preparation for the work of a modern society. The missionaries felt the decision to nationalize their schools was a betrayal of this common cause. From the perspective of the government, however, the importance of the decrees of 1928, 1932, and 1939 lay in their attempt to standardize and nationalize a modern system of education throughout Iran. The mission schools had provided the bulk of modern schooling during much of the nineteenth and early twentieth centuries, but their work was neither standardized throughout the country nor sufficiently national in its form. The educational policy of the Reza Shah years sought to provide a system of education that was modern and yet formed within a standardized, universal, and national framework. In this effort the goals of the mission schools and the Ministry of Education diverged. Having curtailed the missionaries' educational efforts, the new state now took upon itself the task of providing the form and content of its educational objectives.

THE SWORD AND THE PEN: THE MINISTRY OF EDUCATION AND TEXTBOOKS

The state's control over and eventual elimination of missionary education ran in parallel with the growing role of the Ministry of Education in Iran's educational and cultural life under Reza Shah. The most important educational policy-makers who oversaw this period of tremendous expansion were 'Isa Sadiq and 'Ali Asghar Hekmat. Both served in administrative positions in education and culture throughout their careers, including positions as ministers of education and of culture, and both had tenures as chancellors of Iran's flagship university, the University of Tehran. Both became members of the Iranian Senate. Hekmat, in the memoir he wrote in the 1970s, recalled the rapid pace of change during his years as minister of education under Reza Shah. In one year during that time, the ministry's budget was increased by 400 percent.[36]

Along with building new schools and training new teachers, the expanded resources of the ministry during Hekmat's tenure went toward developing a universal curriculum, including textbooks for the new schools. In their memoirs, Hekmat and Sadiq both discussed the difficulty of producing textbooks and the important role they felt such books played in the work of the ministry. Sadiq, for example, wrote that prior to the educational reforms of the Reza Shah years, textbooks were "incorrect, unpedagogical . . . and badly printed."[37] His own education had given him an understanding of what a good textbook should be. He had received a PhD in education in 1931 from the International Institute of Columbia University's Teacher's College, during the years of John Dewey's work there. Paul Monroe, director of the International Institute, had been his PhD advisor.

Sadiq recalled later that the Ministry of Education had commissioned him to produce two books to be used as the main texts for the newly established Teacher's Training College in Tehran.[38] The books, which he remembered producing at a feverish pitch in the sixteen months before the new school opened, were his *The New Method in Education* and *A Brief History of Education.* They were among the first books produced at the newly acquired press of the university. Along with his *History of Iranian Education from the Beginning to the Present Age,* they would become required reading for all graduates of the Iranian Teacher's College well into the 1960s.

The greater resources provided by the government thus allowed the ministry to invest in a press to satisfy the growing publication needs of the new national schools.[39] The production of textbooks was important for a number of reasons. On a practical level, it enabled the state to standardize the education of its citizens. Previously, locally produced teaching materials such as textbooks had been nonexistent, outdated, or untranslated from their original European languages. Students often had to learn a European language before they could make use of existing textbooks of high quality. The textbooks that were available were often poor translations or reproductions of European textbooks left over from the Dar al-Fonun.[40] The expansion of textbook production during Hekmat's tenure at the Ministry of Education thus made a standardized form of education available on a large scale to Iranian students.

Textbooks were important symbolically as well. By reproducing the most advanced and modern knowledge in the standardized format of a national textbook, the ministry could convey to Iranian students that their culture and language were suitable vehicles for transmitting such knowledge. Textbooks were markers of modernity but also of nationalism. Written in the national language and distributed through the institutions of the state, they clearly were objects of national culture. Conspicuously adorned with national symbols, sometimes pictures of the shah on the book's frontplate, they were unmistakable as products bestowed on children by the state. The ministry's textbook policy followed the broader logic of Iran's nationalization project: textbooks became conspicuous markers of modernity just as they were conspicuous markers of nationalism. In keeping with the broader logic of educational policy under Reza Shah, the nationalization of education was a strategy meant to negotiate between the parochialism of national identity and the universalism of modern knowledge. Textbooks allowed Iranians to participate in a universal modernity but also placed that participation within the framework of a distinctive national culture.

Nowhere was this strategy more clearly expressed than in the production of history textbooks during the Reza Shah period. The writing of history had been an important part of the national project since the mid-nineteenth century, but early nationalist historiography was characterized by a style different from that now produced by the Ministry of Education. The historiography of nineteenth-century nationalists such as Jalal al-Din Mirza Qajar, Mirza Fath 'Ali Akhundzadeh, and Mirza Agha Khan Kermani was written in a polemical style, challenging the legitimation practices of the Qajar state and dominant Islamicate narratives. During the Reza Shah years, the interests of the state lay in producing an official history of Iran suitable for mass dissemination through the expanding educational system.

This narrative was produced deliberately, under the supervision of 'Ali Asghar Hekmat and the Ministry of Education. Beginning as early as 1923, Hekmat and the ministry began making plans for history textbooks for what was intended to become a universal system of education.[41] The task of producing the books was assigned to a special committee, the Commission on Education (Anjoman-e Ma'aref), whose eight members were prominent in political and cultural life.[42] Among them were Hasan Taqizadeh, veteran of the constitutional revolution and editor of the Berlin journal *Kaveh*, 'Abbas Eqbal, an important intellectual and publisher, and Mohammad Mossadeq, the Majles deputy who would later become prime minister during the oil nationalization of the early 1950s.

Also on the commission was Hasan Pirniya (Moshir al-Dowleh), son of an important Qajar notable, another veteran of the constitutional revolution, a former Majles deputy, and several times prime minister. Pirniya's massive three-volume *Iran-e Bastan* (Ancient Iran) would arguably become the most important work of historiography produced during the Reza Shah years. An unfinished, three-thousand-page manuscript, it was the definitive Persian-language account of Iran's pre-Islamic history.[43] It became the basis of many shorter, more accessible, mass-produced books published during the Reza Shah years. These works were instrumental in popularizing the pre-Islamic period as the basis of modern Iranian national identity. Among the more widely circulating texts was a two-hundred-page abridged version of *Iran-e Bastan*, titled *Iran-e Qadim*,[44] the earliest history textbook produced during the Reza Shah years. The work became one of the standard textbooks for middle school students.

The publication of *Iran-e Qadim* in 1928 was the culmination of the first stage of the Commission on Education's work. The commission had met regularly under the auspices of the Ministry of Education since 1923 and had worked to plan and produce the history curriculum for the new national schools.[45] Among the first decisions the commission made was to divide the history curriculum into three parts: ancient, medieval, and modern.[46] The selection of this common periodization is suggestive of the commission's attempt to present an official version of Iranian history within a modernist framework of historiography. As 'Abbas Eqbal later recalled, the commission's task was collectively to "present a public history of Iran in the style of the collaborative histories produced by scholars in Europe."[47] Presenting the narrative in this familiar nineteenth-century European framework clearly marked the modernist style in which the commission conceived of its work.

The commission's decision to produce a grand narrative spanning all of Iranian history from the beginning to the present was a decision to create an unprecedented coherence or unity to Iran as an object of historical knowledge. Further, the ancient-medieval-modern periodization was designed to present Iranian history in familiar nineteenth-century nationalist terms. The ancient period became the "golden age," in which the nation had its greatest political victories and expressed its cultural essence most authentically. The medieval period was the "dark ages," in which foreign conquest extinguished the greatness that was ancient Iran. The modern period represented the renaissance of that lost authenticity and an attempt to recapture Iran's lost stature.

After deciding to present Iranian history in this way, the members of the commission asked three of their own to write different portions of the narrative.[48] Hasan Pirniya was selected to write about the ancient period. Hasan Taqizadeh was assigned the middle period, from the Arab-Muslim invasion to the Mongol invasion, and 'Abbas Eqbal was selected to cover the modern period, from the establishment of the Safavid state to the Pahlavi period. Between 1923 and 1928 the three worked to produce the new narrative. When in 1928 the Ministry of Education established a new set of official curriculum guidelines, the work of the Commission on Education became the formal basis for history instruction in all Iranian schools.

In the end, Hasan Pirniya's portion of the narrative was the only one completed as scheduled. 'Abbas Eqbal's part was never finished, and Hasan Taqizadeh composed seventy-eight pages before abandoning the project.[49] He seems to have become disillusioned with the work of the commission. In 1932 he published an article in the education journal *Ta'lim va Tarbiyat* entitled "Jonbesh-e Melli Adabi," in which he criticized the work of the Ministry of Culture and one of its main institutions, the Farhangestan.[50] The work of the ministry had become too politicized, he argued, and its role in determining Iranian culture was detrimental to the natural development of Iranian cultural and intellectual life. The state, he said, should not have the role of determining Iranian culture; "tradition tells us that 'the sword' should not interfere with the work of 'the pen.' "[51]

The article touched off a heated debate in Iran and was eventually reprinted in the major Tehran daily *Ettela'at,* where it was read by Reza Shah. According to Taqizadeh, Reza Shah did not usually read the education journals, but when the article was reprinted in the newspaper he was "enraged" by its contents.[52] Taqizadeh had intended the article to be published anonymously and, according to his memoir, had explicitly asked Hekmat, the minister of education and editor of the education journal, to withhold his name.[53] Anonymous publication was something Taqizadeh had practiced before; just before and during the war he had signed a series of articles for *Le Revue du Monde Musulman* as "X," presumably to avoid drawing attention to himself during that volatile period. The attachment of his name to an article criticizing the cultural and educational policies of Reza Shah was the beginning of the end for his public career during Reza Shah's reign.[54] He was already in Paris when the controversy emerged, and from there he accepted a teaching position in London.[55]

Criticism of Reza Shah's cultural policy was unacceptable, as Taqizadeh was well aware. Others who had run afoul of the state had paid dearly for their indiscretions, with punishments that included prison sentences, forced exile, and mysterious hunting accidents. The controversy surrounding the article, however, was indicative of the broader tensions that existed in Iran over the nationalizing project itself. Although Taqizadeh and others were determined to reform and modernize Iran, his experience with the Commission on Education's textbook program and his comments from this period indicate that he was increasingly distressed that the reform and modernization of culture and society should come at the price of a powerful and undemocratic state.

Ultimately it was Pirniya's portion of the narrative that left the most lasting mark on education in the Reza Shah years. The contents of his 1928 *Iran-e Qadim,* the first history textbook published under the auspices of the Ministry of Education, require some consideration.[56] The text is significant in that it reflects not only the perspective of Pirniya and the Commission on Education but also the broader cultural logic of the nationalization project of the time. Pirniya wove together and negotiated between different styles of historical writing, such as traditional Persianate myth-history and modern rationalist historiography, European scholarship of the nineteenth century and the new sentiment of nationalism emerging under Reza Shah. The result was a unique text that combined these elements in a new framework acknowledging the dominance of a universal modernity while situating that modernity within an Iranian context.

We see this in the opening pages, where Pirniya discussed his approach to history and the writing of the book. Significantly, he began by discussing Ferdowsi's *Shahnameh,* the medieval poem often considered to be the Iranian national epic. Pirniya acknowledged the importance of the *Shahnameh* as a source of myth, legend, and national memory, but he was careful to point out that Ferdowsi's version of Iran's pre-Islamic past did not rise to the level of rational historiography. He delineated two types of historical evidence. The first he described as "inscriptions which remain from the Achaemenid and Sassanian shahs and texts of a religious or nonreligious nature of the Aryan Iranians, as well as conclusions that can be drawn directly or indirectly from documentary evidence from other parts of Asia which can shed light on issues [pertaining to Iranian history]."[57]

In contrast to this type of historical evidence was what he described as "stories which were passed down from generation to generation and in the time of the Sassanians were compiled and then in the Muslim centuries transformed into literature, the most famous of which is the masterpiece of Hakim Abu-Qasem Ferdowsi of Tus."[58] By contrasting these two types of evidence, Pirniya situated his history as the project of a modern, rationalist historian applying high standards of accuracy in determining historical fact. Of the two types of historical evidence, he wrote, "it is obvious that the first type is more valuable for historical research," because "after many centuries of oral transmission from one generation to another there will be a gradual embellishment and a diminution of historical certainty. . . . therefore it is clear that the determination of Iran's past must be placed on the first type of evidence in order to respect its accuracy."[59]

Pirniya's invocation of Ferdowsi and his discussion of the nature of historical knowledge were revolutionary in the way they negotiated between the tradition of myth-history and modern rationalist methods of historiography. In the past, the *Shahnameh* and the Persianate literary tradition had been the main sources of historical knowledge for Iranians. Pirniya's engagement with the *Shahnameh* clearly established the way he saw his role as a *modern* historian of Iran's past. His task was to try to present to Iranian students a new type of historical knowledge that paid respect to the memories and myths of the past but also infused that past with the techniques and forms of knowledge necessary for the modern world. Ferdowsi's *Shahnameh* was an artifact for Pirniya rather than a source of knowledge. He respected it as a "masterpiece" of art, but in acknowledging it as such he changed its status as a source of knowledge. In making this shift, Pirniya's text was emblematic of the role of education in the national project more generally. His text worked to reorder, rearrange, and restructure the reservoirs of tradition and transform that tradition into a new framework of identity simultaneously modern and authentic, universal and national.

We see this even more specifically in Pirniya's rendering of the foundational myth of Iranian history. In the *Shahnameh* that myth was the legend of Kyumars, the first man, roughly analogous to the story of Adam in the biblical book of Genesis. Kyumars was the primordial androgyne who populated the world and established the Iranian nation.[60] For Pirniya this legend was insufficient as the foundational myth of Iranian history. He began his narrative instead with geography, describing the rivers, mountains, lakes, and vegetation of the Iranian plateau, much in the style of nineteenth-century European natural history. "This territory," he wrote, "is possessed of a vast and broad plateau which is surrounded on all sides by tall mountains."[61]

He then described the Aryan migrations that had populated the land, digressing into a discussion of the racial characteristics of the early Iranians. He used a common European fivefold racial system consisting of the categories white, yellow, red, black, and "mixed," and he explicitly used the Indo-European theory to situate the early Iranians. The "white-skinned race," which he made clear included the Iranians, was the Indo-European peoples.[62] He brought in anthropological theories about Indo-European migration onto the plateau: "On the subject of the migrations of the Aryans to Iran, many scholars believe that they arrived on the plateau two thousand years B.C., but more recent scholars argue that it was fourteen hundred years B.C."[63]

We observe Pirniya, therefore, directly appropriating the vocabulary and categories of nineteenth-century anthropological theories of race and geography as a new beginning for his narrative of Iranian history, replacing the myth of Kyumars from the *Shahnameh*. In doing so, he took Iranian myth-history and resituated it within a modernist historiography of nationalism. For him, as perhaps for us, this new narrative point of departure did not seem to be an act of replacing one set of myths with another. His intention was instead to infuse Iranian history with the most advanced forms of knowledge in order to restructure Iranian historical consciousness.

In the process, he had to tread a delicate path between his criticism of

Ferdowsi and the tradition of myth-history, on the one hand, and the scientific discourse of nationalism common during his time, on the other. From Ferdowsi's myth-history he preserved the national or community-centered perspective while abandoning the prerational style. From orientalist scholarship and nineteenth-century historiography he preserved the use of modern, rational categories such as race and geography while abandoning the scientific, Olympian detachment. The result was a remarkable balancing act that produced the first genuinely modern Iranian national history textbook, a book that purported to teach Iranian children national history within a modernist framework.

"TO STRENGTHEN AND UNIFY THE NATION": THE MINISTRY OF PUBLIC ENLIGHTENMENT

The work of the Commission on Education and the publication of the first history textbook were also important in terms of the mass reproduction of knowledge. The circulation of texts under the auspices of the Ministry of Education represented a new mechanization and industrialization of national knowledge, which could now be mass-reproduced through the technologies at the disposal of the state. Created by a small number of cultural bureaucrats, the new national knowledge, such as that found in Pirniya's text, could be disseminated widely throughout society via a highly centralized and bureaucratized educational system.

There is perhaps no better example of this centralized structure of cultural and educational life during the Reza Shah years than that of the Sazman-e Parvaresh-e Afkar, or Ministry of Public Enlightenment. The ministry was a parallel organization to the Ministry of Education, operating as part of the Ministry of Culture. Founded in 1938, toward the end of Reza Shah's reign, it represented the culmination of the state's pedagogic ambitions.[64] Similar in form and function to the ministries of propaganda common in interwar Europe, the Sazman-e Parvaresh-e Afkar was to organize and present lectures, festivals, ceremonies, and other public events for the education of the masses. The first head of the ministry was Ahmad Matin-Daftari, a professor of law at the University of Tehran, as well as prime minister, and later senator during the reign of Mohammad Reza Shah. Writing in his memoirs, Matin-Daftari recalled that the ministry was originally part of a plan to establish a national political party "similar to the People's Party [Hezb-e Khalq] in Turkey."[65] Although a political party closely tied to the state never materialized during the Reza Shah years, the work of the

Ministry of Public Enlightenment made a lasting impression on Iranian national culture.

Matin-Daftari was evangelical in his assessment of the ministry's work. The role of the state in national culture was to "invigorate the spirit of the nation," he said in a speech inaugurating the headquarters of the new ministry in 1938.[66] He continued:

> From the point of view of the state it is not the duty of the state to merely initiate reforms. This is not enough, because a new education and a new way of thinking must also be bestowed on the people so that the meaning of reforms will be understood, and they will be familiar with the reforms and understand their value, and so that they will become interested in the reforms. . . . The duty of the state in public culture is such that it must strive to strengthen the spiritual forces of a nation. It is for this purpose that the Ministry of Public Enlightenment has come into existence.[67]

Matin-Daftari assigned the state a privileged position as the vanguard of enlightenment and modernity. His moralizing tone, however, obscured the ministry's underlying political motives, which were central to its mission. Its mandate was to secure the loyalty of the masses to the state through a highly centralized and bureaucratic system of mass indoctrination. This mandate was made abundantly clear in the ministry's founding document, issued by the prime minister's office in 1938. Through a variety of offices and activities, the Ministry of Public Enlightenment was "to instill and strengthen the love of homeland and monarchism in the people."[68]

In carrying out this mandate, the ministry subdivided its work among a series of specialized offices. The office of publications, for example, was given the task of promoting national values in magazines, newspapers, and books. Headed by Mohammad Hejazi, a writer and later a novelist of some note, the office sponsored the publication of new periodicals deemed to promote the appropriate values and to reflect the interests of the state. It offset their cost of publication and assisted in their acquisition of presses. The publications office was also directed to foster the growth of a cadre of writers who would produce books and articles containing suitable material.[69] In this way magazines such as *Iran-e Emruz, Iran-e Novin,* and *Arya* were published and found distribution in all cities and towns throughout Iran.[70]

The ministry also sent directives to its local offices in the provinces to ensure that the publications were being read by the populace. One letter sent from the Bushire office to the ministry's headquarters in Tehran read:

"[I]n reference to your earlier request that we encourage the sale of the magazine *Iran-e Emruz* to the local population, the task in relation to the aforementioned magazine was quickly achieved and all issues have been sold."[71] This communiqué is representative of dozens of others from other parts of the country collected by the ministry's main office in Tehran.

Other offices of the ministry included the office of public lectures, which commissioned and presented lectures and other events for the moral edification of the populace. Government officials, intellectuals approved by the ministry, and local residents deemed to represent values being promoted by the state gave the lectures in public buildings and spaces throughout Iran. The subject matter usually consisted of social, cultural, and moral topics designed to "enlighten public morality."[72] Some talks dealt with public health; others were more overtly political. The ministry sent lists of potential lecture topics to its satellite offices in provincial cities and towns and kept careful records of all lectures sponsored by its offices throughout the country. The texts of the lectures are not extant, but a sample of proposed topics compiled from ministry documents includes the following:

Nationalism and the Love of Homeland among Iranians
The Effects of Reforms on the Progress of the Nation
The Education of Children
The Homeland's Need for Wise Mothers
The Duties of Women to the Nation
Monarchism and the Love of Homeland
The Love of Work
Our Duty to the Future
The Education of the Next Generation
The Coming of Cinema and Its Usefulness
The Progress of Culture
The Necessity of Kindergarten for the Education of Toddlers
The Comparison of Iran's Culture Today with Its Previous Culture
The Civilization of Ancient Iran
The Love of Homeland among the Ancient Iranians
Work and Discipline
The Usefulness of Exercise for Health and Social Progress
Pleasantness and Truthfulness in Social Interaction
Family Entertainments
Effort and Striving
Respect for Law

The Protection of Ancient Monuments
3,000 Years of Monarchy in Iran
Physical Education and Scouting
Ferdowsi and the *Shahnameh*
Cooperation between Men and Women in Life[73]

Directives to the office of public lectures made it clear that its job was to gather as large an audience as possible for its events. One directive, titled "The duties of provincial officers in the work of public enlightenment," detailed five responsibilities of local officials of the ministry.[74] Number 5 on the list required them to "encourage the people to participate in activities . . . such as public lectures, performances, [and] music, and in the use of radio (which will be operational in six months) and in participation in the arts."[75] Also on the list was the duty to "carry out the orders of the central office as well as the decisions of the council of pubic enlightenment." In addition to the extensive advertising of ministry-sponsored events, which the directive also emphasized, public participation was encouraged through contests and the granting of prizes. In keeping with the ministry's focus on promoting national culture, contests were held for the best essay on a designated topic, the best composition of a patriotic musical anthem, the best composition of a stage performance, and the best public oration on a theme designated by the ministry.[76] A directive said, "the winners of the contests will be selected and prizes will be given at special ceremonies."[77]

The ministry required the office of public lectures to keep careful records of attendance at its events. A great deal of correspondence exists between the main office in Tehran and local offices detailing the number of events, their topics, and the number of attendees. Documents from the ministry indicate that during one month in 1938, for example, nineteen events were sponsored in Tehran alone. Their total audience was recorded as 7,750 persons.[78] A document summarizing the activities of the provincial offices during the first three months of 1940 indicates that they sponsored 920 events, and "240,250 individuals attended and received benefit from these lectures."[79]

Specialized offices were also established for the promotion of national values through theater, cinema, radio, and music. The radio office was given the task of developing programs that could "be distributed to the public through radio in order to foster public enlightenment."[80] In 1938, national radio had not yet been established in Iran, but the ministry's directive to the radio office made it clear that the office had six months to develop enough programming to go on air. By 1941 the technical infrastructure required for national radio transmission had been established, and Radio Iran went on air on April 24 with a message from the prime minister stating that radio was "the voice of a nation . . . and [could] be used as a means to strengthen and unify the nation."[81] Another specialized office, the office of music, was tied closely to the radio office. Its directive instructed it to "produce stirring songs, patriotic anthems, and other recordings which produce excitement."[82]

The work of the Ministry of Public Enlightenment thus spread across the entire spectrum of Iranian cultural life during the Reza Shah years. The saturation of Iran with these new nationalizing cultural practices was facilitated to a great extent by the ministry's use of new technologies of communication. In a society just beginning to develop a public sphere mediated by modern media, the Ministry of Public Enlightenment was the Iranian state's first attempt to present itself to its public through the use of the new technologies. The unparalleled growth of print media and the advent of radio and cinema were immediately seized upon by the state in the conduct of its self-assigned pedagogic mission.

In this way the work of the Ministry of Public Enlightenment was an important extension of the work of the Ministry of Education. Both ministries saw themselves as promoting a homogenized, standardized, and universalized form of Iranian national culture that would help mediate the relationship between state and society. Both carried out their missions through highly centralized and bureaucratic administrative structures. At the Ministry of Education, centralized decision-making resulted in a standardized curriculum and the production of national textbooks. At the Ministry of Public Enlightenment, centralization was manifested in the coordination of activities between the ministry's headquarters in Tehran and local offices throughout Iran to disseminate ministry-sponsored programming in print, radio, and cinema.

The development of these media technologies greatly facilitated the Ministry of Public Enlightenment's nationalizing mission, enabling the distribution of a standardized national culture to all corners of Iran. Central to the ministry's mission was precisely this goal of mass distribution. The ministry's founding document and subsequent directives made it clear that the ministry "must have a branch in every town."[83] Although some cities and towns provided more extensive programming than others—the Isfahan office seems to have been particularly active—ministry-sponsored events had spread to more than thirty-three cities and towns by 1941.[84]

The efforts of the Ministry of Public Enlightenment, together with those of the Ministry of Education, were central to Iran's program of cultural production during the Reza Shah period. The secular national culture, first conceived of during the intellectual and philosophical rearticulation of the late nineteenth century, had now become institutionalized as the official culture and ideology of the state. But however important the work of these two ministries was in cultural production during the 1920s and 1930s, the role of the state in initiating programs of cultural production extended beyond their efforts. Another important way in which this culture became popularized was through the organization of public ceremonies and official commemorations.

4 NATION AND MEMORY

Commemorations and the Construction of National Memory under Reza Shah

ON A FALL MORNING IN NOVEMBER 1934, SEVERAL DOZEN EUROPEAN ORIEN-talists made a pilgrimage to a gravesite in the far corner of Heyreh cemetery, two kilometers outside the city of Nishapur in northeastern Iran.[1] The pilgrims, including such luminaries in the study of Iranian art, literature, and culture as Henri Massé, Jan Rypka, Arthur Christensen, and Vladimir Minorsky, had come to pay their respects at the mausoleum of Omar Khayyam, the thirteenth-century Persian poet whose famous *Rubaiyat* had long been canonized as a masterpiece of Persian literature. After the motorcade bringing the pilgrims to the site made its way down the new road linking the mausoleum to the main highway, the pilgrims exited their cars and gathered around an obelisk erected to mark the resting place of one of the *grand poètes* of Iranian literature.[2] There the visitors and their Iranian hosts read excerpts from Khayyam's poetry and made a toast of wine in the poet's memory.[3] The moment of the libation was captured by a press photographer and found its way into the newspapers in the following days with the headline, "In memory of Khayyam, the orientalists held their cups in hand at the Khayyam mausoleum."[4]

The gathering at Omar Khayyam's grave was more than a casual homage to a long-dead poet. It was what the French historian Pierre Nora described as a *lieu de mémoire*, a symbolic event, site, or object designed to "inhibit forgetting, to fix a state of things, to immortalize death, and to materialize the immaterial . . . all in order to capture the maximum possible meaning with the fewest possible signs."[5] What Nora described in the abstract was indeed a phenomenon universal to the experience of nationalism, whether in France, Iran, or elsewhere—the conscious effort by state elites to organize, construct, and produce a collective historical consciousness for their national polity. Whether in built institutions such as museums and mausoleums or in commemorative festivities such as parades and anniversaries, the preoccupation with assigning a fixed public memory to a given community seems to have been a central characteristic of the modern nation.

The gathering at Omar Khayyam's grave was just one example of this phenomenon. It worked to create a new set of associations with the memory of Khayyam. The construction of the mausoleum and the respects paid to the poet by national political leaders and international arbiters of cultural prestige drew attention to his memory and reinforced his place in the national pantheon. At least as important was the way in which the gathering was represented, portrayed, and made to circulate in the public's mind. The most important detail of the ceremony was neither the toast nor the lines of poetry inscribed at the base of the obelisk but rather the headline, story, and photograph depicting the ceremony in the national press. In understanding the nature of commemorative activity, two basic procedures can be identified: the construction of national memory in its general form and the popularization of that memory as a form of normative consciousness.

The nature and function of symbolic and commemorative activity have been the subjects of numerous works in the comparative nationalism literature. As observers have detailed, among the most common uses of this form of nationalizing practice is that of political legitimation. Monuments and statuary depicting historical personages are among the most ubiquitous expressions of commemorative symbolism. The French Third Republic, as Eric Hobsbawm illustrated, proliferated statuary, placing Robespierre, Mirabeau, and Danton in the "revolutionary pantheon."[6] Similarly, in the Americas, nineteenth-century promoters of commemorative symbolism quickly learned the usefulness of establishing what Hobsbawm called "the cult of the Founding Fathers."[7] This type of symbolism linked the meaning of the image to the authority of the institution or state perceived to be sponsoring the image. Thus, Hobsbawm suggested, commemorative statuary worked—perhaps in the first instance—to build bonds of social cohesion and structures of loyalty.[8]

Just as some forms of commemorative symbolism achieve this legitimating effect by forging symbolic continuities with the past, others emphasize what John Gillis called "the cult of new beginnings."[9] Symbolism tied to the French Bastille Day and the American Fourth of July, for example, emerged out of "an ideologically driven desire to break with the past, to construct as great a distance as possible between the new age and the old."[10] The attempt to memorialize moments of historical rupture suggests that commemorative symbolism is as much an exclusionary cultural practice as it is an attempt to establish connections between past and present. "Collective amnesia," as Benedict Anderson called it, is one of the most commonly recognized features of commemorative symbolism tied to the culture of nationalism. Ernest Renan was perhaps the first to identify it, and recently Pierre Nora analyzed it when he described the "dialectic of remembering and forgetting" as one of the defining features of *lieux de mémoire*.[11]

Another of the most commonly observed features of commemorative activities is their perceived similarity to religious liturgy. All the critics and analysts of the role of memory in the construction of national identity—Mosse, Hobsbawm, Nora, and Anderson, among others—have observed this connection. In tracing the origins of Nazi ritual in interwar Germany, for example, Mosse looked back to eighteenth-century innovations in German Pietism, which "managed to forge a unity between religion and patriotism."[12] Central to this unity was the connection between "liturgical form and the national cult."[13]

Most often the connection between commemorative symbolism and religious liturgy has been explained in terms of the larger process of secularization and the retreat of formal religious practices from public life. Hobsbawm observed that these forms of cultural practice "occur more frequently when a rapid transformation of society weakens or destroys social patterns for which 'old' traditions had been designed."[14] Nora likewise located the emergence of commemorative practices in moments characterized by what he called "the acceleration of history."[15] Anderson's famous invocation of the tombs of unknown soldiers illustrates how nationalism, emerging as a cultural force during "the dusk of religious modes of thought," managed nevertheless to ingeniously explain the mystery of death by transforming "fatality into continuity, contingency into meaning."

Nationalism thus filled the void left by religion's historic decline, according to most theories of nationalism. As religious forms of belief and practice receded, a new "secular religion," as Mosse called it, emerged to take the place of traditional spirituality.[16] Older forms of spirituality were redirected into new categories of belief and practice, such as national history, race, territory, and romanticized depictions of "the people." As Anderson, Mosse, and others have observed, it was therefore no accident that nationalism emerged after the great cultural transformations of the Reformation and Enlightenment. These transformations did not produce nationalism as an ideology, but, as Anderson explained, "nationalism has to be understood by aligning it . . . with the large cultural systems that preceded it, out of which . . . it came into being."[17]

The Iranian state's use of commemorative activity both confirms and complicates these broader generalizations from the comparative literature. There is little doubt that the Pahlavi state made abundant use of commemorative symbolism as a legitimation practice. Not only Omar Khayyam's mausoleum but also those of the poets Hafez, Saʿdi, and Ferdowsi were built under state and public sponsorship and inaugurated with great fanfare and publicity. Other commemorative activities, such as celebrations of the shah's birthday and the annual *nowruz* celebration, were common parts of cultural life during the Reza Shah years. The use of commemorative activities to select and emphasize certain elements of tradition and therefore to exclude others was also a part of Iran's practice, conforming to the broader pattern described in the nationalism literature. The selection of certain poets—whose poetry reflected decidedly earthly, if not bacchic, sensibilities—to be apotheosized marked a clear choice on the part of the cultural bureaucrats of the Pahlavi state to select heroes suitable for a secular and national culture at the expense of Iran's religious heritage.

These secular heroes and icons were selected for ideological reasons, not practical ones. In this sense, Iran's use of commemorative symbolism complicates the generalizations of the nationalism literature. Whereas in the examples highlighted by Hobsbawm, Mosse, and Anderson, national memorials invoked a religious spirituality in an age of growing secularism, Iranian culture in the early twentieth century was not in the twilight of its religiosity, seeking a new spirituality to fill a void left by one fast receding. Iranian culture remained largely unreformed and profoundly religious. The backroads of the countryside were dotted with the tombs of saints and *imamzadeh*s, to which the faithful continued to make dutiful pilgrimages. Building new sites of memory to "national poets" was a dangerous, provocative, and vulgar act in a culture still steeped in formal religiosity. The provocation, however, was necessary from the point of view of a state whose intention was to construct a counterdiscourse to prevailing forms of the sacred. Sites and practices of memory during the Reza Shah years were intended not to fill a void but to create an alternative and parallel spirituality tied to national tradition and capable of taking the place of a still dominant spirituality now deemed lacking in authenticity.

The construction of a new Iranian national memory during the 1920s and 1930s thus served several purposes. First, it was intended to promote a new popular culture designed to mediate the relationship between state and society. The state's interest in promoting a uniform, secular national culture was part of its effort to attain political-cultural legitimacy. Second, the construction of a new national memory was part of the state's project of creating a new culture and a new form of identification born from a negotiation between the demands of a universal modernity and the constraints of local authenticity. Most fundamentally, the construction of a national memory in Iran was a novel and creative exercise designed to uncover, select, and emphasize the elements of tradition that were deemed most compatible with the culture of modernity. The presence of European orientalists at the tomb of Omar Khayyam, for example, was far from incidental. It was a tacit, public sanctioning of the suitability of Iran's culture—or some part of that culture—for membership in the new universalism. The visitors' status as *European* scholars of Iranian culture underscored their implied authority to make such judgments.

In contrast to its more conventional uses, therefore, commemorative activity in Reza Shah's Iran was put to novel use. Not only was its function that of a legitimation practice or an exercise in selective memory, but more importantly, its function was characterized by the unique position of its extra-European context. Commemorative activities like the ceremony at the tomb of Omar Khayyam were designed to highlight the compatibility of Iranian culture with modernity. They were attempts to associate Iranian tradition with modern values while promoting a new culture to mediate the relationship between state and society. In this novel use, commemorative activity in Iran suggests the underlying flexibility and malleability of nationalist practice as it enters specific cultural idioms and is put to use for the achievement of specific political projects.

RABINDRANATH TAGORE IN IRAN: "A POET, NOT OF THIS OR THAT KIND, BUT IN THE ABSTRACT"

Among the most important of the commemorative events during the reign of Reza Shah were the public ceremonies and festivals associated with the visit of Rabindranath Tagore to Iran in April and May of 1932. Tagore (1861–1941) was a major literary, cultural, and political figure in his native India and in the world during the first decades of the twentieth century.[18] He was most famous for his works of poetry. The English-language edition of his collection of Bengali verse, *Gitanjali,* originally published in 1910, received wide acclaim and was singled out by the Nobel committee when it awarded him the Nobel Prize for literature in 1913.[19] He was the first non-European to receive that prize. Tagore's other literary and creative efforts included short stories, novels, essays, musical compositions, and paintings.

Tagore also saw himself as a social reformer and activist working for India's independence. After being knighted by the Raj in 1915, he renounced the honor to protest the Jallianwalla Bagh massacres of April 1919.[20] His most enduring contribution to social reform in India was arguably his work in education. He conceived of and founded the Santiniketan Academy, near Balpur, India, a school self-consciously established on the principle of fusing revived Indian traditions with elements of thought and culture derived from Europe.[21] The academy taught classical Indian literature with the use of modern pedagogic and hermeneutical methods. It also had extensive course offerings in European literature and philosophy as well as the literary and philosophical traditions of China, Japan, and Iran. Significantly, unlike at other educational institutions in India, the language of instruction at Santiniketan was not English but Bengali. The academy's curriculum, combining a cosmopolitan, global outlook with a decidedly Indian and Asian perspective, was characteristic of Tagore's philosophical stance and his ideal of an Indian national culture at home in the modern world.[22] As his admirer Isaiah Berlin wrote, the novelty of Tagore's position was in "choosing the difficult middle path, drifting neither to the Scylla of radical modernism nor to the Charybdis of proud and gloomy traditionalism."[23]

When Tagore arrived in Iran on April 11, 1932, having made the journey from Bombay to Bushire by plane, his reputation as a Nobel laureate and an advocate for Asian cultural revival and political independence preceded him. Members of the Ministry of Culture, including Mohammad Taqi Malek al-Sho'ara' Bahar, chairman of the Iranian Literary Society (Anjoman-e Adabi), had encouraged Reza Shah to issue Tagore a formal invitation. It had been presented by Jalal al-Din Kayhan, the Iranian consul general in Bombay.[24]

By 1932 Tagore had already traveled the world to promote his ideas, including visits to Germany, Russia, England, the United States, and France. His trips to Europe were made in the context of the profound cultural and philosophical crisis of confidence experienced by European society in the aftermath of the Great War. Tagore's visits were presented as those of an oriental sage coming to chastise the West for the devastation its civilization had wrought. The philosophical doubt of the interwar period was reflected in a culture that produced Heisenberg's uncertainty principle, Einstein's theory of relativity, and Picasso's abstract forms. In this climate, Tagore's message of deep spirituality and global peace came as a welcome tonic. As he wrote, "they are waiting for the day-break after the orgies of darkness, and they have their expectations of light from the East."[25]

His presence in Iran in 1932 was viewed very differently. He arrived at the height of the Pahlavi state's promotion of a new, pre-Islamic-based national identity, and his visit gave the state an opportunity to present him to the public as a living personification of the ancient Iranian heritage. That heritage was understood to have been preserved in India and kept away from the Arabizing effects of Islam, which was seen to have long dominated Iranian culture. Since the formulation of the Indo-European hypothesis in the nineteenth century, Indian and Iranian nationalists, as well as European anthropologists and philologists, had noted the cultural continuity between the two nations in the pre-Islamic period. Not only a common linguistic bond but also a common religious history was perceived to tie India and Iran together. The Avestan-language literature of the pre-Islamic period was the basis of both Zoroastrianism and forms of Hinduism. In addition, after the Muslim invasion of Iran in the seventh century, the exodus of many Iranian Zoroastrians to India, where they became known as the Parsi community of Bombay, was an important element of religious and social continuity between India and Iran. Persian poetry, too, had a dynamic presence in the subcontinent, going back at least to the Moghul period, when it spawned a uniquely Persianate literary tradition that transcended formal political boundaries. The symbolism surrounding Tagore's visit to Iran was therefore enormous. The Indian poet, philosopher, and sage served as a personification of, and a living monument of memory to, Iran's ancient heritage.

Both his Iranian hosts and Tagore himself saw the visit in this way. In the weeks preceding his arrival, Iranian newspapers prepared the way for the manner in which Tagore was to be perceived. The April 20, 1932, issue of *Ettela'at* began introducing Tagore to the Iranian public and explaining why his presence was so important. "Our dear readers," the article began, "may wish to acquaint themselves more fully with the ideas and thought of the poet and philosopher from India who is our new guest." He was not just another poet but a poet and sage "whose writings have been translated from Bengali, which is his mother tongue, to many foreign languages and have been published all over the world, placing his poetry and thought in the lofty garden of world literature." Articles lauding Tagore's poetry and his stature as a cultural icon continued to appear during the whole of his month-long stay in Iran.

The April 28, 1932, issue of *Ettelaʿat* contained an article that was particularly important in conveying the cultural symbolism of national revival associated with the visit. The article placed Tagore—"the famous Bengali sage and poet who is one of the most famous luminaries of the present age"— and his visit in the broader context of the cultural history tying Iran and India together. "The people of any nation have a specific destiny," it read, "and the destiny of the Iranian nation is to have a very close relationship with the destiny of the nation of India." The connection between Iranian national authenticity and the classical heritage of India was a common and consistent theme of Iranian nationalism during this period, and Tagore's visit was yet another opportunity to popularize the theme. The article went on to say that

> six thousand years ago our fathers were brothers with the Indians and lived together as one nation. Afterwards these two brothers were separated from one another, and our ancestors came to the Iran of today by way of Transoxiana and the River Oxus. However, during this voyage they brought with them the essence of Indian culture. Even today names such as Jamsheed, Fereydun, Kyumars, and others that are repeated in our language and are part of our mythology have not been separated from the mythology of India, and these names are the same words that our forefathers brought with them.

The article described in great detail the elements of cultural continuity that continued to link Iran and India. Just as elements of Iranian culture could be found in Central Asian cities such as Samarqand, Balkh, Bukhara, Kabul, and Herat, so they could be found in South Asian cities and regions such as the Punjab, Lahore, and Send. "In no way is there any distinction between these people in terms of race, culture, literature, opinion, ways of thinking, or material life," it said. Persian poetry was still recited by India's poets, and the Persian language was known by anyone who claimed to have literacy. "Even down to the present day the non-Muslim population of India uses the divan [poetry collection] of Hafez in religious ceremonies and on Fridays gathers to pay homage to the spirit of Hafez."

Iran and India were thus presented as part of a single national culture. The article suggested that circumstances of history had separated the two, but at their core they continued to share a common authenticity. The implication was that the separation had been effected during the Islamic period, and with the renaissance of national culture then under way, this "unnatural" condition of segregation could be remedied. The author's references to the traces of cultural continuity linking Iran and India were attempts to find and highlight those remnants of "authenticity" and to rekindle them. The promotion of this sentiment in the public's mind established the framework in which Tagore's arrival could be perceived. The article of April 28 concluded, next to a front-page portrait of a wizened and saintly Tagore: "The arrival of Rabindranath Tagore in our country is like the arrival of an elder in the land of his forefathers. With total happiness we Iranians will show hospitality to this brother."

Tagore's presence thus invoked a powerful metaphor of "return" from a long exile. He was portrayed as returning to an original homeland and bringing with him a lost authenticity that had long since been eroded in Iran. The centuries of exile in India had preserved the core and essence of Iranian national culture; the intervening period, the centuries of foreign conquest and Islamic hegemony, had only diminished that essential authenticity within Iran. These were the powerful sentiments that circulated in the press on the eve of Tagore's visit. When he arrived, the symbolism of the event invoked the memory of the lost national authenticity and the even more powerful message of that authenticity now triumphantly reborn.

The ceremonies and activities in which Tagore participated and the speeches he gave during his visit reinforced the metaphor of national revival. He arrived in Iran at the port of Bushire on April 20, 1932, and was met by Abolhasan Foroughi, a former head of the Teacher's College and ambassador to Switzerland. Also at Bushire was Malek al-Sho'ara' Bahar, an Iranian poet and member of the Iranian Literary Society.[26] Tagore, for his part, brought with him Amiya Chakravarty, his literary secretary, and Pratima Devi, his daughter-in-law, who looked after the now aged poet.[27] Also accompanying him was Dinshah Irani, a Parsi scholar and president of the Iran Society of Bombay, an organization devoted to promoting Zoroastrianism and cultural ties between Iran and India.[28] Irani had been instrumental in assisting Ibrahim Purdavud in producing the first translation of the Zoroastrian Gathas, or hymns, into modern Persian in 1928. As his introductory note to that volume suggests, Irani saw the promotion of Zoroastrianism as an important element in the "revival" of Iranian authenticity: "The cultured Persians of today, and educated Persians of whatever denomination, are as interested as the Zoroastrians in the study of their own ancient literature, from a sense of patriotism and cultural habits than as anything else."[29]

In Bushire, Tagore was also greeted by large crowds who welcomed him to Iran.[30] He and his entourage next spent fifteen days traveling through

southern and central Iran, making their way to Tehran. He visited archaeological sites under excavation and made a trip to Kerman, the traditional
home of the remaining Iranian Zoroastrians.[31] In Isfahan the editor of the
local newspaper interviewed him and asked him his impressions of Iran.
He replied that he was pleased to visit the land that had produced poets such
as Saʿdi and Hafez. "The experience [has] gone deep into my heart," he said.
"I had my first introduction to Hafez through my father, who used to recite
his verses to me. They seemed to me like a greeting from a faraway poet
who was yet near to me."[32]

A visit to the shrines of Hafez and Saʿdi in Shiraz culminated the first
part of Tagore's trip (figs. 10 and 11). Like the mausoleum of Omar Khayyam,
the tombs of Hafez and Saʿdi were being rebuilt and embellished into suitable monuments of national culture (fig. 12). At Saʿdi's tomb, with some
fanfare, Tagore was presented with a scroll purported to be in Saʿdi's own
hand. The visit to the mausoleum of Hafez conveyed the continuity between
the Iranian poet and Tagore as his latter-day heir.[33] The event was covered
in the Iranian press, where elements of the ceremony such as Tagore's presentation of flowers and the curator's presentation to Tagore of a copy of
Hafez's poems were described for the public. Tagore was said to have sat
inside the tomb for some time in deep contemplation, eyes closed, and then
to have read and recited some of Hafez's poems in solitude.[34] He was represented as the present embodiment of the ancient tradition of poetry, spirituality, and national authenticity of which Hafez was the paradigmatic
embodiment. His presence at Hafez's grave was a meaningful gesture suggesting that the ancient tradition was not extinct but was in fact being rein-
vigorated with the promotion of the state.

The available excerpts from Tagore's diary suggest that he was aware of
the symbolism surrounding his visit to the mausoleum of Hafez and other
sites:

> Who or what am I to these crowds? . . . These people believe me to be a poet,
> but solely by force of imagination. To them I am a poet, not of this or that
> kind, but in the abstract; so that nothing stands in the way of their clothing
> me with their own idea of what a poet should be. Persians have a passion for
> poetry, a genuine affection for their poets; and I have obtained a share of this
> affection without having to show anything for it in return. . . . In me they saw
> a poet, and that too an Eastern poet, an Indo-Aryan poet like themselves.
> Mohammedans though they are by religion, they have learned to be proud
> of their Aryanhood.[35]

FIGURE 10. *Rabindranath Tagore (right) at the mausoleum of the poet Hafez during Tagore's visit to Iran in 1932.*

FIGURE 11. *Rabindranath Tagore (center) outside the mausoleum of Hafez, 1932.*

FIGURE 12. *The Hafez memorial after its reconstruction.*

His interpretation of the way his hosts viewed him was remarkably vivid and accurate. Tagore was seen as a living monument of national authenticity. The crowds who watched him in the cities, at the archaeological sites, and at the tombs saw him as a spiritual role model akin to the other great Persian poets. His visit coincided with the increasing status of poetry and poets in national culture. The great poets who had long been canonized as part of the literary tradition were now being incorporated into the official nationalism promoted by the state. Poets such as Hafez, Saʿdi, Khayyam, and Ferdowsi were seen to offer an alternative spirituality that was uniquely Iranian and not tied to Islam. Tagore and the Iranian poets of the present age became the living heirs to this tradition and were made to function as a secularized counterclerisy, keepers of the national tradition.

In Tehran, symbols and metaphors of national revival and authenticity continued to abound. ʿIsa Sadiq, chancellor of the Teacher's College and an important player in the cultural life of Iran during the Reza Shah years, spent considerable time with Tagore during the Tehran portion of his trip. Sadiq's memoir, too, invokes an image of Tagore as heir to the national tradition of spirituality. His description of Tagore is detailed and evocative:

> Tagore had a tall, lanky stature and wore a long, simple cloak that only increased his lankiness. With his tousled white and silvery hair and long forehead, an open and elongated countenance, penetrating and engrossing eyes, long and delicate beard, a voice which was mild and pleasing, speech that was measured and deliberate, and movements that were supple and graceful, Tagore exuded a very noticeable and effective presence.[36]

He went on to say that this impressive visage "reminded one of the great sages and mystics and ancient prophets."[37] Tagore's statements and activities while in Tehran reinforced Sadiq's impression of him as an ancient sage, or *hakim*, embodying a faint but rekindled Iranian authenticity.

On May 2, 1932, *Ettelaʿat* described the official reception in which Tagore was formally introduced to Reza Shah. The event was held at the outdoor garden and courtyard of the Ministry of Culture and was attended by over one thousand people, according to press reports and contemporary accounts. At the reception Tagore presented Reza Shah with a painting he had made. Press accounts carefully detailed the central motif of the abstract painting, a figure intended to represent Reza Shah kindling a small flame representing the "light of Iran." A figure representing Tagore was approaching to help the central figure. The imagery captured the intended symbolism of Tagore's trip to Iran.

In his speech following the formal presentation of the painting to Reza Shah, Tagore made this intended meaning clear. Given in English but translated into Persian by Mohsen Asadi, a professor of English and former member of the Iranian Foreign Service, the speech, too, was closely covered in the press. Tagore elaborated on the painting and his trip to Iran by saying, "I am an Iranian and my ancestors emigrated from this land and went to

India. I am therefore pleased to be returning to my homeland. I realize that the kindness shown to me here is because of this unity of race and culture. And the reason for my trip, despite the difficulty of the journey, is precisely to show the sense of unity and affection that I have for Iran."[38]

After referring to the cultural, historical, and racial ties between Iran and India—ties central to the way Tagore had been presented to the Iranian public—he alluded to the painting more directly. "War and disease," he said, had ravaged the "civilization" of Asia, and Iran, like India and China, had fallen "into the shadows."

> [I]n Iran, however, the light entered into Reza Shah's hand. I was in a far cor-
> ner of India when I saw this new light on the distant horizon. And so I came
> here on behalf of India and all of Asia to salute him and to witness his great
> deeds, which are a source of pride and strength for all of Asia. So I have made
> this pilgrimage to gain strength and to take back to my own nation a souvenir.[39]

The metaphors of return and the revival of a lost authenticity were central to the symbolism surrounding Tagore's visit. His presence and the cere-monies and activities in which he participated underscored these metaphors of national renewal. In addition to his formal reception with Reza Shah at the Ministry of Culture, Tagore made speeches at the Iranian Literary Soci-ety and visited Alborz College, the Majles, and the newly established Col-lege of Music. As a social reformer and educator, he was interested in visiting the Zoroastrian Society of Iran and the Zoroastrian School in Tehran. 'Isa Sadiq reported that he and Tagore discussed the Santiniketan Academy and that Tagore suggested that the Iranian government endow a chair of Ira-nian studies at an Indian university.[40]

Tagore's departure from Iran coincided with his seventy-second birth-day, which was celebrated in the streets of Iran with a large, state-sponsored public ceremony.[41] It concluded with Tagore reading to the assembled crowd a poem he had composed for the occasion. It was translated into Persian and published prominently in the newspapers on the following day, along with details of the public event.[42]

Tagore's visit to Iran in 1932 was just one example of the commemora-tive activities sponsored by the Pahlavi state during the Reza Shah years. But unlike museums and mausoleums, parades and anniversaries, Tagore's visit conveyed the commemorative symbolism through the presence of a living figure. He became a living monument placed on display to show mod-ern Iranians quite literally what their lost authenticity looked like. Standing alongside the figures of Khayyam, Sa'di, and Hafez, Tagore reminded Iranians of those premodern poets, who had now been elevated to the status of national icons. He was represented as the living heir of that tradition, a tradition almost extinct but preserved in its purity in India and now being reborn under the leadership of Reza Shah.

THE MILLENNIAL CELEBRATION OF FERDOWSI

The other major commemorative event during the Reza Shah years was the millennial celebration marking the birth of the poet Ferdowsi, held in October and November of 1934. Ferdowsi's place in Iranian national culture, like that of other major Persian poets, became increasingly visible during the 1920s and 1930s. His epic poem the *Shahnameh*, comprising more than fifty thousand couplets chronicling the myth-history of Iran from its primordial beginnings to the Arab-Muslim conquests of the seventh century, had long been an important part of the Persianate literary tradition. By the mid-nineteenth century, as the national model encouraged would-be and emerging nations to tie literary traditions to their political histories, the *Shahnameh* had become canonized as Iran's national epic.[43] The work of the German scholar Theodor Nöldeke was seminal in making this link.[44] Hasan Taqizadeh's and Mohammad Qazvini's articles in the Berlin journal *Kaveh* drew heavily from the work of Nöldeke and were instrumental in bringing Ferdowsi, as a national poet, and the *Shahnameh*, as a national epic, into the discourse of Iranian nationalism.[45]

By the 1930s, poets as national icons were becoming increasingly important in public life in Iran. The rebuilding of the mausoleums of Hafez, Sa'di, Khayyam, and others and their promotion as sites of national pilgrimage were part of this pattern. The symbolism surrounding Tagore's visit to Iran was another example. But perhaps the most important commemorative event elevating the status of poets and poetry as constituents of national identity was the celebration held in 1934 in honor of the millennium of Ferdowsi's birth. The month-long celebration included an international conference attended by scholars from seventeen countries, a major ceremony with a speech given by Reza Shah at the poet's newly restored mausoleum in Tus, and other activities encouraging public participation, such as the showing of a new biographical film based on the life of Ferdowsi by the pioneering Iranian filmmaker Abolhoseyn Sepanta.

The idea of commemorating the millennium of Ferdowsi's birth was conceived by the semi-official Society for National Monuments (Anjoman-e

Asar-e Melli). The society had been founded in 1922 by a group of Iranian statesmen and cultural figures including Mohammad 'Ali Forughi, the historian Hasan Pirniya, the prominent court official Abolhoseyn Teymurtash, and the Majles deputy and prominent member of Iran's Zoroastrian community Keykhosrow Shahrokh.[46] 'Isa Sadiq recalled that it was in 1926, the year of Reza Shah's coronation, that the society first thought of restoring and embellishing the site of Ferdowsi's mausoleum. Sadiq, then a member of the Ministry of Education, was asked to attend an informal meeting with the group in Tehran. "The Society for National Monuments," he wrote in his memoir, "asked me to help raise private funds for the building of a mausoleum for Ferdowsi."[47]

The society wanted to fund the effort privately, and it publicized its fund-raising efforts in order to mobilize popular participation and sentiment for the project. Sadiq remembered: "The opinion of the Anjoman-e Asar-e Melli and the lovers of the homeland was that the national public should participate in this national duty so that the feeling of national devotedness will be more awakened and the value and worthiness of their culture and the high status of Iran's heroes will be appreciated. And this hope was to a great measure achieved."[48] Among the group's initiatives was enlisting school-children in fund-raising. Sadiq recalled gathering the students of one school into its main quadrangle and instructing them in how to go into neighborhoods and solicit donations.[49]

The society also sponsored a national lottery to raise funds for the project, advertised with broadsides posted throughout Iranian cities in 1932. The image on the broadsides was an artist's rendering of the proposed mausoleum and the mythical bird the *simorgh* with a copy of the *Shahnameh* in its mouth (fig. 13). A caption equated participation in the lottery with national duty: "For the completion of the mausoleum of Ferdowsi and for the celebration of his millennium, the Anjoman-e Asar-e Melli invites all Iranians to buy tickets in the lottery as a way of showing gratitude to this reviver of the Persian language."[50]

The cost of the mausoleum was covered by a combination of public and private donations.[51] But before construction could begin, the site of the mausoleum had to be identified and acquired. Keykhosrow Shahrokh accomplished this with help from the governor of Khurasan, in whose province the mausoleum was to be built, and General Jahanbani, a famous military figure.[52] These three members of the society located the site traditionally regarded as Ferdowsi's grave just outside of Tus. The poet Nezami had mentioned the grave's location in a medieval text, and a tomb dating from the early Qajar

FIGURE 13. *Leaflet promoting the reconstruction of the Ferdowsi memorial, 1933. Below a rendering of the mausoleum, the mythical simorgh holds a copy of the* Shahnameh.

period already marked the location. By the time Shahrokh and Jahanbani made their way to the site for the first time in 1927, the Qajar tomb was in a state of extreme disrepair. The society eventually negotiated with the owners of the land on which the grave was located to donate a portion of it to the public in order to make a site large enough for the mausoleum and a surrounding park.[53]

Once the land had been secured, the society had to select a design for the mausoleum and make arrangements for its construction. Sadiq recalled that Teymurtash was adamant that the building be in a neoclassical style, akin to the tomb of Cyrus, which, along with other archaeological sites then being excavated by European and American archaeologists, had become recognized as a significant national monument.[54] The existing Ferdowsi tomb was a typical domed edifice reflecting the Muslim architecture of the Safavid and Qajar periods. In order to create a suitable neoclassical design, the society turned to Ernst Hertzfeld and André Godard. Hertzfeld was a German-born archaeologist who was excavating in Iran under the sponsorship of the Oriental Institute of the University of Chicago. Godard was a French-trained architect who spent almost thirty years in Iran and was intermittently dean of the University of Tehran's Faculty of Arts as well as the first director of Iran's Museum of Antiquities. The two men collaborated with the Iranian architect Karim Taherzadeh in producing the final design, a cubic stone structure approximately thirty feet wide and fifty feet tall with inscriptions from the *Shahnameh* on all sides (fig. 14).[55] The construction took more than two years and was completed just before the beginning of the millennium celebrations.

Among the ceremonies associated with the millennial celebration was the international conference of orientalists that convened at the Dar al-Fonun on October 1–4, 1934 (fig. 15). The conference received wide coverage in the local press and was presented as an affirmation of Iran's national culture by the world.[56] News coverage of the event included announcements made at the conference of official telegrams received from foreign capitals wishing the conveners well. The German and Soviet embassies presented Mohammad 'Ali Forughi, who, as prime minister and president of the Society for National Monuments, had convened the conference, with gifts to commemorate the occasion. The German gift was a special edition of a newly completed work by the German orientalist Fritz Wolf indexing the usage of every word in the *Shahnameh*.[57] The Soviets presented Forughi with an illuminated manuscript copy of the *Shahnameh* from a Russian museum.[58]

Profiles of conference participants were published in the press, as were interviews with attendees, texts of their speeches, and detailed descriptions of the conference itself and the papers presented. The profile of Arthur Christensen (1875–1945), the great Danish scholar of Iranian philology, for example, included an excerpt from a speech in which he lauded Ferdowsi and Iranian national culture: "The acts of aggression which have been perpetrated against the nation of Iran, however great and powerful, have been

FIGURE 14. *The Ferdowsi memorial after its reconstruction.*

FIGURE 15. *Attendees at the Ferdowsi millennium conference in Tehran, 1934.*

unable to diminish Iranians' sense of their distinctiveness."[59] The receipt of telegrams and gifts from foreign capitals and statements such as Christenson's were important parts of the millennial celebration. The press presented an image of Iran as a national culture worthy of respect in the world. Iran's affirmation by foreign capitals and by the words of European orientalists reinforced this feeling of respect and affirmed Reza Shah's national project.

The speeches made at the conference by Mohammad ʿAli Forughi and ʿAli Asghar Hekmat echoed these themes. Forughi gave the opening speech, welcoming the participants and thanking them for making the long journey. He continued in Persian, "You have honored us with your presence, but you have done this rightfully because even though Ferdowsi is of the Iranian people he is also in spirit a child of humanity and, if you will allow me, a father of humanity."[60] Hekmat, then minister of education, next took the stage and, speaking in French, elaborated on Forughi's theme:

> The interest shown in the Millennium celebrations for Ferdowsi in all countries, and the fact that the nations have sent their most noted scholars to this country and to the tomb of the creator of the Persian epic, shows that, despite apparent distinctions, there are no real differences between peoples. . . . It is sometimes said that our century and our world are a century and world of materialism. . . . It is for this reason that we emphatically affirm that where art and science are manifested, the curtain of differences is removed and the one and true reality is made apparent: that is to say, the unity of peoples.[61]

The speeches by Hekmat and Forughi, and the tone of the millennial celebrations in general, reflected this theme of placing the image of Ferdowsi simultaneously in both national and international contexts. The poet was presented as an embodiment of Iranian national identity, a promoter of Iran's language, and a conveyor of national memory. At the same time, the internationalizing of his image and the emphasis placed on having his importance recognized by international arbiters of cultural prestige suggest that Iran's national project was aimed not only at an internal audience. In order for Iranian national identity to be affirmed, the state felt the need to be recognized within the world system. Nationalism in Iran, as in the colonial and semicolonial world more generally, was not only an exercise in internal political consolidation and cultural homogenization; it was also an attempt to project an image outward to the world, declaring a nation's compatibility with and desire to join the new universalism of modernity. The authenticity or worthiness of a national culture was inherently measured in terms of

its status within, or its contribution to, "world civilization." It was this reasoning that made the Indo-European theory so attractive to Iranian nationalists in the nineteenth century and encouraged cultural bureaucrats
during the Reza Shah period to find elements of Iranian tradition that would
be deemed worthy by international standards. The subtext of the millennium celebrations for Ferdowsi, and of the conference in particular, was
the goal of elevating Ferdowsi's status and that of the Iranian nation as a
whole and suggesting Iran's association and compatibility with modern values and standards.

This attempt to affirm Iran's national project to both internal and international audiences culminated with the ceremony at Ferdowsi's tomb on
October 12, 1934, several days after the conclusion of the conference. The dedication ceremony included a speech by Reza Shah in the presence of the
conference participants, who had made the two-day journey by car to the
site. News reports of the event were thick with description, detailing the activities of the participants and embellishing their historic importance for the
public: "Oh, yes, yesterday will be recorded as one of those happy days in
the life of the new Iran," wrote the correspondent for *Ettelaʿat*.[62]

The ceremony began at four o'clock in the afternoon. Staff from the Ministry of Culture and the Ministry of Education, together with members of
the Majles and the cabinet, stood dressed in formal clothing, awaiting Reza
Shah's arrival. With "scholars from both East and West" and other attendees, the audience numbered about two hundred people.[63] They sat in rows
of chairs facing the front of the imposing stone edifice, which at the beginning of the ceremony was draped in the Iranian colors. At the base of the
tomb was a table where Reza Shah was to stand and deliver his dedication
comments. At approximately 4:30 he arrived, ascended the steps leading to
the table,[64] and presented his speech:

> We are very pleased that along with the one-thousandth birthday of Ferdowsi
> we can also accomplish one of the other enduring desires of the Iranian nation,
> that is, the establishment of this structure as a measure of our appreciation
> and gratitude for the pains which Ferdowsi bore to revive the language and
> history of this nation. . . . Although appreciation for this man had not been
> adequately expressed, it was always the case that the people of Iran held the
> *Shahnameh* in their hearts as a memorial to him. . . . However, it was neces-
> sary to take some action and create an adorned structure which in a visual
> way would mark the public gratitude of this nation. It was with this idea that
> We gave the decree to create this historic memorial, this exalted structure,

which will not be harmed by wind, rain, or circumstance. . . . [Ferdowsi] has already immortalized his name, and this ceremony and monument are unnecessary, but appreciation for those who have given service is the moral duty of a nation, and we must not back down from this responsibility.[65]

Reza Shah's comments worked to give the mausoleum meaning and assign a fixed set of associations to the memory of the poet. Ferdowsi thus became, in part, a symbol of Iranian national authenticity, and his mausoleum became a living reminder of the endurance of that authenticity. The shah's comments and the building of the mausoleum itself emphasized, above all, the theme of national continuity. The shah's remark that Iranians had always remembered the *Shahnameh* was partially true. Certainly the practice of reciting the *Shahnameh* from memory had long been part of the premodern oral tradition throughout the Persianate world. More important, however, was the novelty of the way in which this traditional memory was now being used. Ferdowsi and the *Shahnameh* became very public markers of political allegiance. By sponsoring the construction of the monument and hosting the international celebration, Reza Shah and the Pahlavi state associated themselves with the memory of Ferdowsi. National memory and political legitimation went hand in hand through the use of his image.

The ubiquity of references to Ferdowsi in the Pahlavi state's self-representation helps to demonstrate this point. The mausoleum, for example, became one of the most recognizable images of Iranian society and quickly found its way onto the national currency. Statues of Ferdowsi increasingly occupied public spaces in Iranian cities. The first such statue was a gift presented to Iran by the Parsi community of Bombay immediately after the millennial celebrations.[66] The bronze statue was placed in the renamed Ferdowsi Square in Tehran. Later it was moved to the courtyard of the Faculty of Letters at the University of Tehran, and a new, larger statue of the poet was placed in Ferdowsi Square. Streets were also renamed in honor of him immediately after the commemorative celebrations. One of the main thoroughfares leading into Ferdowsi Square was widened, lengthened, and named after Ferdowsi.[67]

Also planned to coincide with the millennial celebrations was the publication of several new editions of the *Shahnameh*. Prior to 1934, printed editions of the epic poem were rare and expensive. During the nineteenth century a growing print industry, mostly in India, had published Persian books including canonized foundational texts such as the *Shahnameh*. But until 1934, no editions of the *Shahnameh* had been produced that circulated on a mass level.

With the millennial celebrations, three new editions appeared, published in Iran with the direct support of the Ministry of Culture. The first was an unabridged, five-volume work edited by Abbas Eqbal.[68] Sa'id Nafisi and Soleyman Hayyim published a similar unabridged edition in 1935.[69] Around the same time, Mohammad 'Ali Forughi edited a one-volume, abridged version containing twenty thousand couplets, or less than half the original text.[70] This edition was inexpensive and allowed the *Shahnameh* for the first time to circulate widely throughout Iranian society.

Magazines, journals, and newspapers also devoted a prolific amount of print to Ferdowsi and the *Shahnameh* after the celebrations. The poet's image appeared in the new medium of cinema as well. In 1936, Abolhoseyn Sepanta completed a sixty-minute film based on Ferdowsi's life, dramatizing the traditional story of Ferdowsi's struggles in composing the poem. Sepanta himself played the role of Ferdowsi. Mahmud Ghaznavi, the tenth-century sultan who was the original patron of Ferdowsi's efforts, was also depicted. The final scene of the black-and-white silent film showed Ferdowsi on his deathbed as he recited lines of his poetry.[71]

Sepanta's biographical film represented one aspect of a much larger pattern of state-sponsored cultural production during the 1930s. The film, the international conference coinciding with Ferdowsi's millennium celebrations, the building of tombs and sites of national memory for Ferdowsi and other poets, and the visit of Rabindranath Tagore were all parts of the state's promotion of a new secular national culture and memory for modern Iran. This promotion was intended to unify Iranians through a common historical memory referencing a common set of national symbols. The new state-sponsored culture was crafted to select values from Iranian tradition that were most compatible with the demands of universal modernity. Elements of Iranian culture that were already recognized by European arbiters of knowledge, such as Persian poetry and Iran's Indo-European identity, were therefore emphasized by state-sponsored culture producers. Finally, the construction of this new secular national culture was intended to build further bonds of loyalty between state and society. By 1941 these bonds had become firmly established. State institutions had produced a uniform infrastructure linking all of Iranian society. The production of a uniform national culture represented the final convergence of state, society, and culture.

CONCLUSION

IN THE SPRING OF 1979, AS THE REVOLUTIONARY DRAMA WAS STILL UNFOLD-
ing in the streets of Iran's major cities, a little-known cleric by the name of
Sadegh Khalkhali (1927–2003) commandeered a bulldozer and headed
toward the tomb of Cyrus at the Pasagradae archaeological site just outside
of Shiraz. As the legend of this event is told and retold—by Iranians living
both inside and outside Iran—Sadegh Khalkhali mounted the bulldozer,
turban-clad, clerical garb blowing behind him, and zealously drove across
the dusty plain toward Cyrus's tomb at the head of a shovel-wielding mob
of antimonarchist revolutionaries. Khalkhali's stated intention was to
destroy the tomb, which he and his Islamist comrades regarded as a symbol of moral decadence associated with the Pahlavi monarchy.

Accounts of what took place next differ. Some remember local villagers
stepping in to confront Khalkhali's bulldozer and saving the monument;
others remember remnants of the old army mobilizing to prevent the tomb's
destruction. Still others suggest that higher authorities in the revolutionary
government ordered a reprieve for the monument and told Khalkhali to
stop his incursion. Despite these conflicting accounts, what is clear is that
the tomb of Cyrus the Great narrowly escaped being destroyed by Iran's
Islamic revolution.

The near destruction of the tomb of Cyrus perfectly encapsulates the
dilemma of Iran's encounter with modernity and its attempt to adopt the
political-cultural form of a modern nation-state. Significantly, it was pre-

cisely at the same site that in 1971 Mohammad Reza Shah Pahlavi made his famous speech commemorating twenty-five hundred years of Iranian monarchy. In that speech the shah tried to associate a certain set of symbols derived from Iran's pre-Islamic history with the cultural and political definition of the Iranian nation. Defining the nation in this way, he was in effect following the rules of nationalism by fixing a stable set of symbols and cultural markers with the notion of Iranianness.

Just as significantly, Khalkhali's aborted attempt to destroy the tomb was, in an inverted way, a tacit acknowledgment of the same rules of nationalism that the shah invoked. With his action Khalkhali was contesting the definition of Iranianness posed by the Pahlavi state and the symbols, markers, and memories that the shah articulated. Yet he was also affirming the idea that nations are defined by a set of clearly delineated cultural symbols and markers. His attempt to destroy the tomb was thus an act born of the culture of modernity and the rules and assumptions that animated the concept of *nation* he and the shah shared. Where the two disagreed was merely over which particular set of symbols, markers, and memories was to define Iranian culture.

The history of Iran in the modern period stemmed from this basic dilemma over how to define the culture of Iran as a modern nation. At the beginning of that period Iran was a weak, semicolonial state under the increasing economic, political, and military influence of the ascendant European powers. Confronted by Iran's position in this international context, Iranian state-builders and reformers sought new models of statecraft to help strengthen their society and negotiate their way into the culture of modernity. A key element in this transformation was the adoption of new models of political community that had become universalized during the course of the nineteenth century. Whether based on the dynastic states of late imperial Europe or on nationalism, these models implied a newly forged congruence between state institutions, social structures, and cultural forms. Their adoption was an important part of Iran's encounter with modernity.

Appropriating new political-cultural forms meant a fundamental transformation of the social, economic, political, and cultural structures that characterized premodern Iranian-Persianate society. In the middle of the nineteenth century, Iranian state and society remained parallel and incongruous social categories with only limited interdependence. Social life was segmented along vertical lines of loyalty linked to tribal, sectarian, and regional identifications. Permanent state institutions were either nonexistent or incapable of extending their authority from the center to the periphery.

Beginning in the late nineteenth century, these premodern patterns of state structure and social organization began to erode under the influence of new models of political community. After 1870, a fundamental transformation took place in Iranian state institutions, social structures, and cultural forms. Most important was a basic transformation of the role of the Iranian state vis-à-vis society. The new model of political community was characterized by a more intimate relationship between state and society. The state was increasingly endowed with a unifying cultural and symbolic ethos, seeing itself as the bearer of an authenticity shared by itself and society. The new model thus demanded a restructuring of state-society relations around a common medium of legitimating symbols that could be uniformly understood by all members of society and could command a common loyalty. Iranian state-builders and reformers began to experiment with new ways of forging a cultural synthesis between state and society.

This experimentation began during the second half of the reign of Naser al-Din Shah. By the 1870s the imperial dynasties of Europe had developed new methods of legitimation grounded in dynastic loyalty and mobilization of the masses in urban ceremonies. The expansion and rebuilding of European cities had produced new urban environments in which state and society could share a repertoire of common symbols. It was this model of political community and its practice of state-managed public legitimation rituals that shaped new legitimation practices in Iran during the late Qajar period. After Naser al-Din Shah's 1873 tour of Europe, urban restructuring in Iran accelerated, and ceremonial forms and legitimating practices began to reflect the late imperial model the shah had observed while abroad. The late Qajar state of Naser al-Din Shah—like the late imperial states of Europe after which it had become patterned—thus sought to forge a newfound unity of state and society grounded primarily in dynastic loyalty.

The late imperial model was only one model for the synthesis of state and society circulating during the second half of the nineteenth century. Equally important was the national model, then just as ubiquitous throughout Europe and other parts of the world. The two models shared much in form but were distinct in ideological content. The late imperial model sought to forge congruence between state and society through dynastic loyalty. Nationalism, too, sought congruence between state institutions, social structures, and cultural forms, but it sought to bring this congruence about through the use of symbols tied to national culture, including symbols of race, geography, language, and historical memory.

The discovery of national culture by Iranian intellectuals and radical reformers posed an important challenge to the late imperial model of political community in place during the late Qajar period. Through the discovery of philological scholarship and European historical writings on pre-Islamic Iran, radical reformers increasingly gained an appreciation for Iran's ancient history. In their attempt to reform Iranian society and negotiate Iran's entry into modernity, the pre-Islamic past became a convenient template on which to reinvent Iranian culture in modern form. The discovery of modern values in the ancient Iranian past became a common literary and philosophical pattern among late-nineteenth- and early-twentieth-century Iranian intellectuals. Decidedly modern benchmarks of progress such as universal education, advanced scientific knowledge, and the equality of women were inscribed into the past as part of the attempt to reform and strengthen Iranian society in accord with the cultural demands of modernity. Nationalist intellectuals agitated to make this version of Iran's past the official culture of the state, a reservoir of symbols to be shared by all Iranians.

After the political disintegration of the post-constitutionalist period, it was Reza Shah and the Pahlavi state of the 1920s and 1930 that successfully institutionalized the nationalist model of political community. The early Pahlavi state borrowed the ideological basis of its legitimation directly from the late-nineteenth- and early-twentieth-century nationalist rearticulation of Iranian culture. By establishing a national system of education and officially sanctioned commemorative practices, the state projected a new set of cultural references and symbols designed to mediate the relationship between state and society.

Looking solely at Iranian political history, the early Pahlavi period seems to have been a moment of disjuncture with the past, marking the beginning of Iran's modern history as a nation-state. In the context of the larger historical transformations of the late nineteenth century, however, elements of continuity with the past seem more striking in understanding the early Pahlavi period, for it grew out of important social, political, and cultural transformations that preceded it. The search for a new model of political community that had begun during the reign of Naser al-Din Shah established the basic framework within which the early Pahlavi state continued to operate. Common to the objectives of both the late Qajar and the early Pahlavi states was the creation of a framework of political community that transcended traditional social bonds of loyalty and replaced them with an allegiance of the masses to the state based on a congruence between state institutions, social structures, and cultural forms. Both the late Qajar and the early Pahlavi states saw a similar role for the state vis-à-vis society, as the bearer of a unifying set of symbols integrating state and society. What distinguished the two periods was the repertoire and ideological content of the symbols each sought to use as the cultural medium to bring about this synthesis.

In understanding the history of nationalism in Iran, the Reza Shah period can therefore be identified not as the time when the modern Iranian nation-state was established but as the culmination of a process of nationalization. That process had its beginnings in the social, economic, political, and cultural transformations of the late nineteenth century, which took place in an international context that demanded basic structural transformations in the relationship between states and societies. Transformations in state structures and notions of statehood, economic transformations and their consequent social dislocations, and new understandings of cultural identity and historical memory cumulatively produced the possibility of a new framework of political community. This framework emerged in Iran not only from the force of internal historical structures but also as a result of models of state-society relations that had become globalized during the late nineteenth and early twentieth centuries. The political discontinuities inside Iran between 1870 and 1940 thus mask a deeper set of historical continuities that unify this period as the transitional phase when modern international structures and models of community found their way permanently into the Iranian context.

Understanding the history of nationalism in Iran in this way is ultimately important for no less a reason than reframing the entire narrative of Iranian modernity. If the late nineteenth and early twentieth centuries are understood as the period of crystallization in which the basic institutional, social, and cultural structures of the Iranian nation took shape, then the subsequent narrative of modern Iran becomes a history of contestation over the ideological *content* that animated the newly crystallized political field—not over the basic dimensions, or *form,* of the political field itself.

The period in which Iran crystallized as a modern nation thus made possible the emergence of modern politics in Iran—whether it was the movement for constitutional government at the beginning of the twentieth century, the mid-century oil nationalization movement of Mohammad Mossadegh, the establishment of an Islamic republic at the end of the century, or the recent political symbolism of the nuclear issue. These movements all used different ideological languages and made reference to different symbols and forms of historical memory. What they shared was a common set of assumptions regarding the political field in which they operated. The boundaries of this commonly understood field took shape as a result of the new model of political community that took hold in Iran during the period considered in this book. The politics of Iran in the twentieth century is therefore the story of rival cultural and symbolic imaginings vying with one another to speak in the name of the same nation. The persistence of this form of politics suggests the success of Iran's appropriation of the national model during the late nineteenth and early twentieth centuries, as well as the continuing durability of that model in contemporary Iranian politics.

The history of Iran in the twentieth century also suggests that a consensus has yet to emerge on the cultural symbols suitable for animating this commonly understood framework of politics. Just as the late imperial model of the Qajar period and the early Pahlavi model represented alternative methods of synthesizing state and society, so in the more recent past has the Islamic Republic posed a means of achieving a similarly conceived synthesis based on yet another repertoire of symbols drawn from premodern history and memory. The inability of all these projects to successfully animate their common political framework suggests that the major failure of Iranian modernity has been the inability of state-builders to construct a common and uniform Iranian culture. While the history of Iran in the twentieth century is one of success in consolidating state institutions and national social structures, the enigma of Iranian modernity continues to be its failure to find a cultural consensus. Given this history, it is safe to assume that until a resolution to the problem of cultural consensus is achieved or the nation form is itself transcended in Iran, politics within the national framework will continue to be characterized by myriad alternative imaginings—ideological, cultural, and symbolic—all claiming to speak on behalf of the nation.

NOTES

INTRODUCTION

1. The European and American press covered the commemoration in great detail. *Newsweek* called it the "Bash of Bashes," *Time* called it the "Show of Shows," *Life* called it "the Shah's Princely Party," and *Vogue* described it as a "Fête for a King." See *Newsweek* 78 (Sept. 27, 1971): 61; *Vogue* 158 (Oct. 15, 1971): 62; *Time* 98 (Oct. 25, 1971): 32–33; and *Life* 71 (Oct. 29, 1971): 22–30.

2. *Time* 98 (Oct. 25, 1971): 32–33.

3. Important discussions of modernization and state-building can be found in the following sources: Ervand Abrahamian, *Iran between Two Revolutions* (Princeton, NJ: Princeton University Press, 1982); Abbas Amanat, *Pivot of the Universe: Nasir al-Din Shah Qajar and the Iranian Monarchy, 1831–1896* (Berkeley: University of California Press, 1997); Amin Banani, *The Modernization of Iran, 1921–1941* (Stanford, CA: Stanford University Press, 1961); Stephanie Cronin, *The Army and the Creation of the Pahlavi State, 1910–1926* (London: I. B. Tauris, 1997); Peter Avery, *Modern Iran* (London: Ernest Benn, 1965); Nikki R. Keddie, *Roots of Revolution: An Interpretive History of Modern Iran* (New Haven, CT: Yale University Press, 1981); Nikki R. Keddie, *Qajar Iran and the Rise of Reza Khan, 1796–1925* (Costa Mesa, CA: Mazda Press, 1999); Shaul Bakhash, *Iran: Monarchy, Bureaucracy, and Reform under the Qajars 1858–1896* (London: Ithaca Press, 1978); and Donald Wilber, *Riza Shah Pahlavi: Resurrection and Reconstruction of Iran* (Hicksville, NY: Exposition Press, 1975).

4. Benedict Anderson, *Imagined Communities: Reflections on the Origin and Spread of Nationalism,* 2nd ed. (London: Verso, 1991), 12.

5. Some of the most evocative descriptions can be found in Jean Chardin, *Voy-*

age de Paris à Ispahan (Paris, 1683); Joannes Feuvrier, *Trois ans a la cour de Perse* (Paris, 1906); John Malcolm, *History of Persia,* 2 vols. (London, 1829); and George Curzon, *Persia and the Persian Question,* 2 vols. (London, 1892).

6. Nineteenth-century Bali, according to Clifford Geertz's description, seems analogous, but the same can be said of the Qajar state's closest neighbor, the Ottoman court. See Clifford Geertz, *Negara: The Theater State in Nineteenth-Century Bali* (Princeton, NJ: Princeton University Press, 1980); and Selim Deringil, *Well-Protected Domains: Ideology and Legitimation of Power in the Ottoman Empire, 1876–1909* (London: I. B. Tauris, 1999).

7. For discussions of Iran's fractured premodern social and economic structures, see especially Abrahamian, *Iran between Two Revolutions* (chap. 1); Nikki Keddie, *Modern Iran: Roots and Results of Revolution* (New Haven, CT: Yale University Press, 2003), chap. 2; Charles Issawi, ed., *The Economic History of Iran, 1800–1914* (Chicago: University of Chicago Press, 1971); and Homa Katouzian, *State and Society in Iran: The Eclipse of the Qajars and the Emergence of the Pahlavis* (London: I. B. Tauris, 2000). For Iran's evolving geographic conceptions, see chapter 1 in Firoozeh Kashani-Sabet, *Frontier Fictions: Shaping of the Iranian Nation, 1804–1946* (Princeton, NJ: Princeton University Press, 1999).

8. Although it is true that ancient texts in Sanskrit and Avestan make reference to "Iran," as does medieval Persianate literature, this philological evidence is far removed from the modern definition of the nation, which presumes a congruence of state institutions, social structures, and cultural identification that became feasible only during the period under review here. For the primordialist argument in Iranian historiography, see Gherardo Gnoli, *The Idea of Iran* (Rome: Instituto Italiano per il Medio ed Estremo Oriente, 1989).

9. John Breuilly, *Nationalism and the State,* 2nd ed. (Chicago: University of Chicago Press, 1992), 1.

10. Ibid.

11. Elie Kedourie, *Nationalism in Asia and Africa* (New York: World Publishing Company, 1970), 28–29.

12. Ibid., 66.

13. Geoff Eley and Ronald Suny make a similar point. See their "Introduction: From the Moment of Social History to the Work of Cultural Representation," in G. Eley and R. G. Suny, eds., *Becoming National: A Reader* (Oxford: Oxford University Press, 1996), 5–6.

14. Quotations are from, respectively, James L. Gelvin, *Divided Loyalties: Nationalism and Mass Politics in Syria at the Close of Empire* (Berkeley: University of California Press, 1998), 51; and Rogers Brubaker, *Nationalism Reframed: Nationhood and the National Question in the New Europe* (Cambridge: Cambridge University Press, 1996), 80.

15. Hobsbawm's equally famous coinage, "the invention of tradition," comes closer to Kedourie's approach in its skepticism and instrumentalist reading of the

phenomenon. Interestingly, Hobsbawm's skepticism came from the Marxian left, whereas Kedourie's came from the Liberal right. Gellner's understanding of the phenomenon was more nuanced. Although, following Kedourie, he acknowledged the invented or fabricated nature of the nation, he nevertheless identified its connection to structural-historical changes of modern industrial society.

16. Anderson, *Imagined Communities,* xiv.

17. Ibid., 6.

18. Ibid.

19. Ibid., 4.

20. Ibid.

21. For the political and intellectual history of nationalism, see, for example, Richard Cottom, *Nationalism in Iran* (Pittsburgh: University of Pittsburgh Press, 1964); and Mangol Bayat, *Mysticism and Dissent: Socioreligious Thought in Qajar Iran* (Syracuse, NY: Syracuse University Press, 1982). For a sophisticated analysis of Iranian nationalism's narrative forms, see Mohamad Tavakoli-Targhi, *Refashioning Iran: Orientalism, Occidentalism and Historiography* (New York: St. Anthony's/Palgrave, 2001).

22. Keddie, *Roots of Revolution,* 170.

1   STAGING THE NATION

1. A large body of primary material exists for the assassination of Naser al-Din Shah. This account is based on the following: Hoseyn La'l, *Qeblah-ye 'Alam: Zendegi-ye Khosusi-ye Naser al-Din Shah* (Tehran: Donya-ye Ketab va Manuchehri, 1993), 655–73; Hasan Morselvand, *Shah Shekar: Bazju'iha-ye Mirza Reza Kermani va Sayerash* (Tabriz: Nashr-e Javanah, 1991), 30–45; 'Ali Khan Zaher al-Dowleh, *Tarikh-e Bidorugh* (Tehran: Entesharat-e Sharq, 1983), 25–58; Yahya Dowlatabadi, *Tarikh-e Mo'aser ya Hayat-e Yahya* (Tehran: Ibn Sina, 1957), 137–47; Mirza 'Ali Khan Amin al-Dowleh, *Khaterat-e Siyasi-ye Mirza 'Ali Khan Amin al-Dowleh* (Tehran: Entesharat-e Daneshgah-e Tehran, 1962), 208–10; Nezam al-Islam Kermani, *Tarikh-e Bidari-ye Iranian* (Tehran: Mu'assaseh-ye Entesharat-e Agah, 1983), 93–99; 'Abdollah Mostowfi, *Sharh-e Zendegani-ye Man,* 2 vols. (Tehran: Chapkhaneh-ye 'Elmi, 1944), vol. 1, 721–23, vol. 2, 3–7; and Nikki R. Keddie, *Sayyid Jamal al-Din "al-Afghani": A Political Biography* (Berkeley: University of California Press, 1972).

2. La'l, *Qeblah-ye 'Alam,* 655.

3. Mursilvand, *Shah Shekar,* 31; Zaher al-Dowleh, *Tarikh-e Bidorugh,* 43; Dowlatabadi, *Tarikh-e Mo'aser,* 137–38; Kermani, *Tarikh-e Bidari-ye Iranian,* 95.

4. For an English-language transcript of Mirza Reza Kermani's interrogation, see Edward Granville Browne, *The Persian Revolution: 1905–1909* (Cambridge, 1910; new edition, Washington, DC: Mage Publishers, 1995), 58–98. See also Keddie, *Sayyid Jamal al-Din,* 404–20.

5. Mursilvand, *Shah Shekar,* 37–39; Zaher al-Dowleh, *Tarikh-e Bidorugh,* 44; La'l, *Qeblah-ye 'Alam,* 667–69; Mostowfi, *Sharh-e Zendegani-ye Man,* vol. 2, 3.

6. Dowlatabadi, *Tarikh-e Mo'aser,* 138; Mostowfi, *Sharh-e Zendegani-ye Man,* vol. 1, 721. Dowlatabadi described the fireworks displays in preparation for the jubilee and the decorative lighting that adorned the main public spaces of the city. Mostowfi described commemorative posters of Naser al-Din Shah prominently displayed on the streets of Tehran.

7. Eric Hobsbawm, *Nations and Nationalism since 1780* (Cambridge: Cambridge University Press, 1990); Eric Hobsbawm and Terence Ranger, eds., *The Invention of Tradition* (Cambridge: Cambridge University Press, 1992); Anderson, *Imagined Communities.* For the non-Western cases, see especially Selim Deringil, "The Invention of Tradition as Public Image in the Late Ottoman Empire, 1808–1908," *Comparative Studies in Society and History* 35, no. 1 (1993): 3–28; T. Fujitani, *Splendid Monarchy: Power and Pageantry in Modern Japan* (Berkeley: University of California Press, 1996); and Carol Gluck, *Japan's Modern Myths: Ideology in the Late Meiji Period* (Princeton, NJ: Princeton University Press, 1985).

8. Eric Hobsbawm, "Mass-Producing Traditions: Europe 1870–1914," in Hobsbawm and Ranger, *Invention of Tradition,* 268.

9. For the effects of Ismail's Paris sojourn on the subsequent reconstruction of Cairo, see Janet Abu-Lughod, *Cairo: 1001 Years of the City Victorious* (Princeton, NJ: Princeton University Press, 1971), especially 103–5; see also Timothy Mitchell, *Colonizing Egypt* (Berkeley: University of California Press, 1991), especially chap. 3, "The Appearance of Order." For a description of the Egyptian exhibition at the 1867 Exposition Universelle, see Charles Edmond, *L'Egypt a l'exposition universelle de 1867* (Paris: Dentu, 1867). Edmond described the elaborate Egyptian displays designed to impress on visitors the equal status of Egypt relative to European states. Iranian participation in the 1867 exhibition was minimal by comparison.

10. For the reconstruction of Istanbul, see Zeynep Çelik, *The Remaking of Istanbul: Portrait of an Ottoman City in the Nineteenth Century* (Seattle: University of Washington Press, 1986), especially 42–48. Çelik states that as early as 1855, just after the Crimean War, the government had established a Commission for the Order of the City to undertake a major infrastructural project in Istanbul for "embellishment," "regularization," and "enlargement," 44.

11. Mostowfi, *Sharh-e Zendegani-ye Man,* vol. 1, 124.

12. Bakhash, *Iran.* Bakhash's work is an important study of nineteenth-century institutional reform based on a careful reading of unpublished Iranian Foreign Ministry documents. The selection of letters and dispatches he includes suggests more than a strict concern with European diplomacy, however. See also Ibrahim Safa'i, ed., *Nameha-ye Tarikhi* (Tehran: Chap-e Sharq, 1969).

13. Military and administrative reforms may have functioned on a similar principle.

14. This "experience of backwardness" remains to be theorized. A slightly different but useful conceptualization of the problem appeared in Tom Nairn's "The Modern Janus," *New Left Review* 94 (Nov.-Dec. 1975): 3–29. Nairn understood periph-

eral and semiperipheral nationalism as a "compensatory ideological mechanism" born out of a "deprivation and impotence suddenly made humiliatingly evident to them by the impact of outside powers" (16).

15. Mirza Hoseyn Khan was something of a fixture in Istanbul's diplomatic circles in the 1860s. He cultivated friendships with important Ottoman Tanzimat reformers such as Fuad Pasha and 'Ali Pasha and frequented the courts of Sultan 'Abdolmajid and Sultan 'Abdolaziz. On at least one occasion he was also asked by European diplomats in residence in Istanbul to mediate the tense relations between the Ottomans and the Greeks. See Mehdi Khan Shaqaqi Momtahen al-Dowleh, *Khaterat-e Momtahen al-Dowleh* (Tehran: Amir Kabir, 1974), 88.

16. For the life and career of Mirza Hoseyn Khan, see Azriel Karny, "Husayn Khan Mushir al-Dauleh and His Atttempts at Reform in Iran, 1871–1873" (PhD dissertation, Department of History, UCLA, 1973); Bakhash, *Iran*, chap. 2; Momtahen al-Dowleh, *Khaterat-e Momtahen al-Dowleh*, 86–89; and Fereydun Adamiyat, *Andishehha-ye Taraqqi va Hokumat-e Qanun* (Tehran: Entesharat-e Khvarazmi, 1972).

17. Hasan 'Ali Khan Garusi (1822–99) held a number of important posts both in Iran and abroad as part of the overseas diplomatic corps. He was chief of the Paris legation from 1858 to 1865 and eventually accompanied Naser al-Din Shah on his 1873 trip to Europe. See Mehdi Khan Shaqaqi Momtahen al-Dowleh, *Rejal-e Vezarat-e Kharejeh* (Tehran: Entesharat-e Asatir, 1986), 65–67.

18. Mohsen Khan Mo'in al-Molk (d. 1900) worked under Garusi in Paris and subsequently became head of the Paris legation in 1865. He also held diplomatic positions in London and was ambassador in Istanbul from 1872 to 1890. His association with Malkom Khan's liberal-constitutionalist newspaper *Qanun* caused his recall to Tehran in 1891. See Momtahen al-Dowleh, *Rejal-e Vezarat-e Kharejeh*, 78–80.

19. Mirza Yusof Khan (d. 1895) held diplomatic posts in St. Petersburg (1862–63), Tiflis (1863–67), and Paris (1867–71). His association with the radical newspapers *Akhtar* and *Qanun* led on more than one occasion to his impisonment. He was most famous for his radical treatise *Yek Kalameh*, published in 1891. See Momtahen al-Dowleh, *Rejal-e Vezarat-e Kharejeh*, 95–97.

20. Adamiyat, *Andishehha-ye Taraqqi*, especially chap. 12; John Gurney, "The Transformation of Tehran in the Later Nineteenth Century," in *Téhéran: Capitale bicentenaire*, ed. Chahryar Adle and Bernard Hourcade (Paris: Institut Français de Recherche en Iran, 1992), 64–67.

21. There is some question about whether Naser al-Din Shah in fact received an official invitation. It is possible that the Iranian diplomats in Paris sought to procure an invitation for the shah upon hearing of similar invitations being sent to his Ottoman and Egyptian counterparts and misled him into believing he had been invited in order to encourage his participation. Bakhash (*Iran*, 49), relying on the Foreign Ministry dispatches sent from the Paris diplomats, assumed that an invitation was in fact issued. Gurney ("Transformation of Tehran," 66) argued that the

invitation was a ruse devised by the progressive Paris diplomats to entice the shah to travel to Paris.

22. As quoted in Bakhash, *Iran*, 49.

23. Naser al-Din Shah had made one previous trip abroad, to the Ottoman Empire in 1870, again at the behest of Mirza Hoseyn Khan. During the 1873 trip to Europe, Mirza Hoseyn Khan accompanied the shah, as he had during his Ottoman trip. For an account of Naser al-Din Shah's 1870 Ottoman journey, see Naser al-Din Shah Qajar, *Safarnameh-ye 'Atabat* (Tehran: Entesharat-e Ferdowsi, 1984); and Mostowfi, *Sharh-e Zendegani-ye Man*, vol. 1, 150–51. For the Eurpean trip, see Mostowfi, 170–73.

24. Hamid Algar, *Religion and State in Iran, 1785–1906: The Role of the Ulama in the Qajar Period* (Berkeley: University of California Press, 1969), 174.

25. The granting of so sweeping a concession to a British subject had upset the delicate balance of interests between the British and the Russians. Naser al-Din's cold reception in St. Petersburg was perhaps indicative of Russian feelings. See Firuz Kazemzadeh, *Russia and Britain in Persia, 1864–1914* (New Haven, CT: Yale University Press, 1968), especially 100–148. See also Ibrahim Timuri, *Asr-e Bikhabari ya Tarikh-e Emtiyazat dar Iran* (Tehran: Eqbal, 1953), especially 96–150.

26. Mostowfi, *Sharh-e Zendegani-ye Man*, vol. 1, 163–66.

27. Amanat, *Pivot of the Universe*, 424–27.

28. See Hobsbawm, "Mass-Producing Traditons"; and G. L. Mosse "Caesarism, Circuses, and Movements," *Journal of Contemporary History* 6, no. 2 (1971): 162–82. For Haussmanization and its affects on the culture of urban life, there is a large literature. See David Pinckney, *Napoleon III and the Rebuilding of Paris* (Princeton: Princeton University Press, 1958); Joan Margaret Chapman and Brian Chapman, *The Life and Times of Baron Haussmann* (London: Weidenfield and Nicolson, 1957); Francoise Choay, *The Modern City: Planning in the Nineteenth Century* (New York: G. Braziller, 1969); David Harvey, *Consciousness and the Urban Experience* (Baltimore, MD: Johns Hopkins University Press, 1985); Mathew Truesdell, *Spectacular Politics: Louis-Napoleon Bonaparte and the Fête Impériale, 1849–1870* (Oxford: Oxford University Press, 1997); and Vanessa R. Schwartz, *Spectacular Realities: Early Mass Culture in Fin-de-Siècle Paris* (Berkeley: Universty of California Press, 1998).

29. As quoted in Adamiyat, *Andishehha-ye Taraqqi*, 241. Malkom Khan was given the responsibility for making most of the arrangements for the European tour.

30. Simmel's important study was "The Metropolis and Mental Life," in George Simmel, *The Sociology of Georg Simmel*, trans. and ed. Kurt H. Wolff (New York, 1950). See also David Frisby, *Fragments of Modernity: Theories of Modernity in the Work of Simmel, Kracauer, and Benjamin* (Cambridge, MA: Polity Press, 1986).

31. Twain's reportage of Naser al-Din Shah's stay in London was originally published in the *New York Herald*: "The Shah," July 4, 1873, 5; "Shah-Doings," July 9, 1873, 3–4; and "Shah'd," July 11, 1873, 3. These articles were later published together as "O'Shah" in Twain's *Europe and Elsewhere* (New York, 1923), 68.

32. Naser al-Din Shah Qajar, *The Diary of His Majesty the Shah of Persia during His Tour through Europe in A.D. 1873,* trans. J. W. Redhouse (London, 1874), 141–42. The Persian original was published in Tehran as *Ruznameh-ye Safar-e Farangestan* (1874). The most recent Persian edition is Naser al-Din Shah Qajar, *Safarnameh* (Esfahan: Entesharat-e Sazman-e Andisheh, 1964), 86.

33. Observers likened the shah's presence to scenes from the "Arabian Nights Entertainments." *Illustrated London News,* June 28, 1873, 598.

34. David Canadine marked the 1870s as an important turning point in the use of public ritual in Victorian England: "From the 1870s onwards, in England as in other western countries, the position of the head of state was ceremonially enhanced. A venerated monarch, conveyed in a splendid state coach along triumphal throughfares, was no longer, as his predecessors had been, just the head of society, but was now seen to be the head of the nation as well." See his "The Context, Performance, and Meaning of Ritual: The British Monarchy and the 'Invention of Tradition', c. 1820–1977," in Hobsbawm and Ranger, *Invention of Tradition,* 133.

35. *Illustrated London News,* July 5, 1873, 18–19.

36. Naser al-Din Shah Qajar, *Diary,* 166.

37. Lord Curzon was the first to document the similarity between the Takyeh Dowlat and the Albert Hall: "The Shah, it is said, having been so impressed with the Albert Hall in London, as to long for a reproduction in Teheran. . . ." See his *Persia and the Persia Question* (London, 1892), vol. 1, 328. The plans for the Takyeh Dowlat, however, predated the shah's first trip to Europe, so the Albert Hall is unlikely to have been a direct influence. See Farrokh Gaffary, "Les lieux de spectacle a Teheran," in Adle and Hourcade, *Téhéran,* 146. It is more likely that Naser al-Din Shah was generally aware of European concert halls through his readings. The presence of French and French-trained Iranian architects at the royal college, the Dar al-Fonun, might have also been a source of influence for the design.

38. Marshall Berman, *All That Is Solid Melts into Air: The Experience of Modernity* (New York: Penguin, 1988), 235–48; see also Patrick Beaver, *The Crystal Palace, 1851–1936: Portrait of a Victorian Enterprise* (London: Hugh Evelyn, 1970).

39. C. H. Gibbs-Smith, *The Great Exhibition of 1851: A Commemorative Album* (London: H. M. Stationary, 1950), 38.

40. Ibid., 26. The encounter with the Crystal Palace was a seminal moment of modernity for many non-Western travelers to London who were engaged in a common project of late-development modernization. Berman cited the effect the Crystal Palace had on visitors from Germany, Russia, India, China, and Japan. Dostoevsky's assessment of the Crystal Palace captured the spirit of his tortured ambivalence toward modernity: "I am afraid of this edifice precisely because it is of crystal and forever indestructible, and it will be impossible to put out one's tongue at it even on the sly." Fyodor Dostoevsky, *Notes from Underground,* translated and annotated by Richard Pevear and Larissa Volokhonsky (New York: Alfred A. Knopf, 1993), 35.

41. *Illustrated London News*, July 12, 1873, 42. A London chronicler wrote, "It was an ordinary shilling admission day, with no particular novelty or specialty in the list of entertainments. The Persian Monarch went on this occasion without his diamonds among the common crowd of English people. He wore a simple tunic, which covered even his sword-belt; not a jewel was to be seen about him."

42. Naser al-Din Shah Qajar, *Diary*, 207; Naser al-Din Shah Qajar, *Safarnameh*, 124.

43. Mitchell, *Colonizing Egypt*, 2.

44. By "sites of national memory," I have in mind Pierre Nora's notion of *lieux de mémoire*. See Pierre Nora, ed., *Realms of Memory: Rethinking the French Past* (New York: Columbia University Press, 1996). For Naser al-Din Shah's visit to the tomb of Napoleon, see *L'Illustration: Journal Universel*, July 19, 1873, 38.

45. Mitchell, *Colonizing Egypt*, 7.

46. Ibid.

47. Naser al-Din Shah Qajar, *Diary*, 204–5; Naser al-Din Shah Qajar, *Safarnameh*, 122.

48. Jean-Marie Mayeur and Medeleine Reberioux, *The Third Republic from Its Origins to the Great War, 1871–1914* (Cambridge: Cambridge University Press, 1984), especially chap. 1, "The End of the Notables."

49. Naser al-Din Shah Qajar, *Diary*, 222; Naser al-Din Shah Qajar, *Safarnameh*, 132.

50. For the mass-ceremonial culture of Napoleon III's Paris, see Truesdell, *Spectacular Politics*.

51. One week before the shah's arrival, on May 24, the center-left Adolphe Thiers had resigned and was replaced by the center-right Marshal MacMahon as the new president of the republic. See Mayeur and Reberieoux, *Third Republic*, 9. The ceremonies welcoming the shah to Paris were among the first public events under MacMahon. His status as the new president was also affirmed in the wide coverage of the shah's visit in the Paris press. See especially *L'Illustration: Journal Universel*, July 12, 1873, and July 19, 1873.

52. *L'Illustration: Journal Universel*, July 19, 1873, 38.

53. Ibid.

54. Ibid., July 12, 1873, 26. The shah's account of the reception at the pavilion recorded shouts of "Vive le Marchal" and "Vive le Shah de Perse."

55. Ibid.

56. Naser al-Din Shah Qajar, *Diary*, 220–21; Naser al-Din Shah Qajar, *Safarnameh*, 131–32.

57. As Anderson wrote, "official nationalisms" were "at bottom . . . *responses* by powerful groups—primarily, but not exclusively, dynastic and aristocratic—threatened with exclusion from, or marginalization in, popular imagined communities." *Imagined Communities*, 109–10.

58. Gurney, "Transformation of Tehran," 64. Mirza Yosuf Mostowfil al-Mamalek,

Mirza 'Isa, and the French supervising architect Boehler prepared the plans; see also Yahya Zoka' and Mohammad Hasan Semsar, eds., *Tehran dar Tasvir*, 2 vols. (Tehran: Sorush, 1997), 7.

59. Amir Hoseyn Zakerzadeh, *Sargozasht-e Tehran* (Tehran: Entesharat-e Qalam, 1994), 15–18; see also Naser Najmi, *Iran-e Qadim va Tehran-e Qadim* (Tehran: Entesharat-e Janzadeh, 1983), 292–93.

60. Ja'far Shahri, *Tarikh-e Ejtema'i-ye Tehran dar Qarn-e Sizdahom* (Tehran: Entesharat-e Esmai'iliyan, 1988), vol. 1, 93–116. Shahri gives the most detailed description of the new gates of the city. See also Zoka' and Semsar, *Tehran dar Tasvir*, 33.

61. Habibollah Zandjani, "Tehran et sa population: Deux siècles d'histoire," in Adle and Hourcade, *Téhéran*, 252; see also Shahri, *Tarikh-e Ejtema'i-ye Tehran*, vol. 1, 7. Zakerzadeh, *Sargozasht-e Tehran*, 203, gives an estimated decade-by-decade population increase for the city.

62. For a description of the royal compound, see Najmi, *Iran-e Qadim*, 235–40, 264–79. See also Yahya Zoka', *Tarikhcheh-ye Sakhtemanha-ye Arg-e Soltani-ye Tehran va Rahnama-ye Kakh-e Golestan* (Tehran: Anjoman-e Asar-e Melli, 1970).

63. Zakerzadeh, *Sargozasht-e Tehran*, 38–40; Najmi, *Iran-e Qadim*, 256–66; Shahri, *Tarikh-e Ejtema'i-ye Tehran*, 355–58. There was also the Meydan-e Mashq, an even larger open space north of the Meydan-e Tupkhaneh, which increasingly came to serve as the parade ground for military maneuvers.

64. Najmi, *Iran-e Qadim*, 329–46.

65. Gurney, "Transformation of Tehran," 70.

66. Curzon, *Persia and the Persian Question*, vol. 1, 306.

67. I do not attempt a discussion of the political philosophy of Iranian monarchy or the dynamism and complexity of Shi'i legal theory. For discussions of these issues, see, for example, Said Amir Arjomand, *The Shadow of God and the Hidden Imam* (Chicago: University of Chicago Press, 1984), 7, 89–100; A. K. S. Lambton, *Theory and Practice in Medieval Persian Government* (London: Variorum Reprints, 1980); Nikki R. Keddie, "The Roots of the Ulama's Power in Modern Iran," in Nikki R. Keddie, ed., *Scholars, Saints, and Sufis: Muslim Religious Institutions in the Middle East since 1500* (Berkeley: University of California Press, 1972), 220–21; and Algar, *Religion and State in Iran.* I am more interested in the way these changing conceptions of political authority affected the public projection of legitimacy.

68. In addition to the sources already named, see Bayat, *Mysticism and Dissent;* and Adamiyat, *Ideolozhi-ye Nehzat-e Mashrutiyat-e Iran.*

69. Anderson discussed this problem for Europe and Japan in *Imagined Communities*, 83–111. For the Ottoman case there is an excellent discussion in Selim Deringil, "Legitimacy Structures in the Ottoman State: The Reign of Abdulhamid II (1876–1909)," *International Journal of Middle Eastern Studies* 23 (1991): 345–59; see also his "The Invention of Tradition as Public Image in the Late Ottoman Empire" and *Well-Protected Domains: Ideology and Legitimation of Power in the Ottoman Empire.* A similar and more self-consciously comparative study is Reinhard Ben-

dix's *Kings or People: Power and the Mandate to Rule* (Berkeley: University of California Press, 1978).

70. Anderson, *Imagined Communities*, 86.

71. The case of Japan and the Ottoman state came after and in emulation of the earlier European programs—in Japan during the Meiji period and in the Ottoman Empire during the reign of 'Abdolhamid II.

72. La'l, *Qeblah-ye 'Alam*, 374.

73. Malcolm, *History of Persia*, vol. 2, 403–4.

74. Zakerzadeh, *Sargozasht-e Tehran*, 273. Zakerzadeh estimated that most royal salaams were attended by seven hundred to eight hundred selected dignitaries.

75. For a list of court ceremonials, see Dust 'Ali Khan Mo'ayyer al-Mamalek, *Yaddashtha-i az Zendegani-ye Khosusi-ye Naser al-Din Shah* (Tehran: Nashr-e Tarikh, 1982), 53.

76. Abbas Manat, *Pivot of the Universe*, plate 17; Government of Iran, *Ruznameh*, no. 472, September 9, 1860, 3–4.

77. Malcolm, *History of Persia*, vol. 2, 399–400.

78. Curzon, *Persian and the Persian Question*, vol. 1, 324–25.

79. See Dust 'Ali Khan Mo'ayyer al-Mamalek, *Yaddashtha-i az Zendegani-ye Khosusi-ye Naser al-Din Shah*, 137, for a photograph of one such ceremony. There are also published photographs of royal salaams in Zoka', *Tarikhcheh-ye Sakhtemanha-ye Arg*, 74 (plate 28), 81 (plate 31), and a description on pp. 76–83.

80. Mostowfi, *Sharh-e Zendegani-ye Man*, vol. 1, 155.

81. General discussions of the Takyeh Dowlat are found in Curzon, *Persia and the Persian Question*, vol. 1, 327–28; Zoka' and Semsar, *Tehran dar Tasvir*, 115; Zoka', *Tarikhcheh-ye Sakhtemanha-ye Arg*, 284–310; and Gaffary, "Les lieux de spectacle à Teheran," 146 (translated by Nikki R. Keddie as "Theatrical Buildings and Performances in Tehran" in her *Qajar Iran*, 102–4).

82. There is a large literature on the ta'ziyeh. For religious and literary interpretations, the most important are the seminal nineteenth-century works. See Ernest Renan, "Les Tézies de la Perse," in his *Nouvelle étude d'histoire religieuse* (Paris: Calmann Lévy, 1884); Mathew Arnold, "A Persian Passion Play," in his *Essays in Criticism* (London: Macmillan, 1889); Edouard Montet, *Le Théâtre en Perse* (Geneva: n.p., 1888); Lewis Pelly, *The Miracle Play of Hasan and Husain*, 2 vols. (London: Wm. H. Allen, 1879); and Edward Granville Browne, *A History of Persian Literature* (Cambridge: Cambridge University Press, 1924), vol. 4, 182–94. The scholarship in Persian has followed the same pattern, emphasizing the literary character of the ta'ziyeh. See Bahram Beyza'i, *Namayesh dar Iran* (Tehran: Chap-e Kaviyan, 1965), vol. 1, 237–38; Jamshid Malekpur, *Adabiyat-e Namayeshi dar Iran* (Tehran: Entesharat-e Tus, 1984), chapter 6; and Sadiq Homayuni, *Ta'ziyeh va Ta'ziyeh-Khani* (Tehran: Entesharat-e Jashn-e Honar, 1971).

83. For an important exception, see Kamran Aghaie, *The Martyrs of Karbala: Shi'i Symbols and Rituals in Modern Iran* (Seattle: University of Washington Press, 2004).

84. See Zoka', *Tarikhche-ye Sakhtemanha-ye Arg-e Soltani-ye Tehran,* 289, for a discussion and photograph of the makeshift theaters.

85. Arthur de Gobineau, "Les Religions et les philosophies dans l'Asie Centrale," in Jean Gaulmier, ed., *Oevres* (Paris: Gallimard, 1983), 678–79. Mostowfi, *Sharh-e Zendegani-ye Man,* vol. 1, 404, makes the same observation.

86. The nineteenth-century vogue for patronizing taʿziyeh performances suggests an encroaching awareness of the ritual's political utility as a legitimating ceremony. Qajar notables such as Mirza ʿAbdolhasan Khan, Mirza Safi Mazanderani, and Haji Mirza Aqasi were among the first to use the taʿziyeh as a political instrument. Naser al-Din Shah's later appropriation of the practice may have been inspired by these earlier precedents. See Jean Calmard, "Le Patronage des taʿziyeh: Eléments pour une étude globale," in Peter J. Chelkowski, ed., *Taʿziyeh: Ritual and Drama in Iran* (New York: New York University Press, 1979), 124–25; see also Jean Calmard, "Le Mécénat des representations de taʿziyeh," in *Le Monde iranian et l'Islam,* vol. 2 (Paris, 1974), 73–126; and Mostowfi, *Sharh-e Zendegani-ye Man,* vol. 1, 402–3.

87. Mostowfi, *Sharh-e Zendegani-ye Man,* vol. 1, 406.

88. Chelkowski, "Taʿziyeh," 1.

89. The person most responsible for carrying out the project was Dust ʿAli Khan Moʿayyer al-Mamalek. See Zakerzadeh, *Sargozasht-e Tehran,* 128.

90. The theater was built on the southern tip of the royal compound, closest to the gate leading to the bazaar. The best descriptions of the Takyeh Dowlat are by European travelers. See Carla Serana, *Hommes et choses en Perse* (Paris: Charpentier, 1883), 172–76; James Bassett, *Persia and the Land of the Imams* (London: Blackie, 1887), 106; Samuel G. W. Benjamin, *Persia and the Persians* (Boston: Ticknor and Co., 1887), 382–86; Curzon, *Persia and the Persian Question,* vol. 1, 327–28; Henry Binder, *Au Kurdistan* (Paris: Maison Quantin, 1887), 406–9; and Joannes Feuvrier, *Trois ans a la cour de Perse* (Paris: Impr. nationale, 1906). See also Zoka', *Tarikhcheh-ye Sakhtemanha-ye Arg,* 293–94.

91. Chelkowski, "Taʿziyeh," 8.

92. Amin al-Dowleh, *Khaterat-e Siyasi-ye Mirza ʿAli Khan Amin al-Dowleh* (Tehran: Entesharat-e Daneshgah-e Tehran, 1962), 215.

93. Zakerzadeh, *Sargozasht-e Tehran,* 128–34. Zakerzadeh also described separate entrances into the theater according to social rank. See also Dust ʿAli Khan Moʿayyer al-Mamalek, *Yaddashtha-i az Zendegani-ye Khosusi-ye Naser al-Din Shah,* 64–68.

94. Benjamin, *Persia and the Persians.* The only detailed description of a taʿziyeh performance at the Takyeh Dowlat I have found in the Persian sources is in Mostowfi, *Sharh-e Zendegani-ye Man,* 396–401. Mostowfi's account is remarkably similar to Benjamin's, suggesting the standardization of the taʿziyeh choreography at the Takyeh Dowlat.

95. Benjamin, *Persia and the Persians,* 365.

96. Ibid., 379.

97. Ibid., 380. Benjamin referred to street battles between procession participants and royal guards.

98. Benjamin's account of the choreography is remarkably similar to accounts
in Zoka', *Tarikhcheh-ye Sakhtemanha-ye Arg,* 298–301, and Mostowfi, *Sharh-e Zendegani-ye Man,* vol. 1, 395–99.

99. 'Abdollah Mostowfi's account highlighted the salute to the shah as central
to the choreography. He also described the sermons to Naser al-Din as the "Shah
of Islam." Mostowfi, *Sharh-e Zendegani-ye Man,* 397.

100. Benjamin, *Persia and the Persians,* 389.

2   NATIONALIZING PRE-ISLAMIC IRAN

1. Biographical information for Taqizadeh is derived from several sources. Most
important is his autobiography: Hasan Taqizadeh, *Zendegi-ye Tufani: Khaterat-e
Sayyed Hasan Taqizadeh,* ed. Iraj Afshar (Tehran: 'Elmi, 1993). Also important is
Mohammad Ali Djamalzadeh, "Taqizadeh, tel que je l'ai connu," in Walter Hen-
ning and Ehsan Yarshater, eds., *A Locust's Leg: Studies in Honor of S. H. Taqizadeh*
(London: Percy Lund, Humphries and Co., 1962), 1–20.

2. Browne, *Persian Revolution,* 332–33.

3. Ibid., 145.

4. Taqizadeh, *Zendegi-ye Tufani,* 59.

5. Ibid., 155.

6. Ibid., 158–73.

7. For these events see Stanford Shaw, *History of the Ottoman Empire and Modern Turkey,* vol. 2 (Cambridge: Cambridge University Press, 1977), 286–96; and Stavro
Skendi, *The Albanian National Awakening, 1878–1912* (Princeton, NJ: Princeton University Press, 1967).

8. Janet Afary, *The Constitutional Revolution of Iran, 1906–1911* (New York:
Columbia University Press, 1996).

9. These articles are suggestive of Taqizadeh's broad awareness of political
trends in the Middle East at that time and the increasing centrality of nationalism
as a political movement. They are "Les Courants politique dans la Turquie con-
temporaine," *Revue du Monde Musulman* 21 (December 1912): 158–221; "Doctrines
et programmes des partis politiques Ottomans," *Revue du Monde Musulman* 22
(March 1913): 151–220; "Les Courants politiques dans le miliue Arabe," *Revue du
Monde Musulman* 25 (December 1913): 236–81; and "La Situation politique de la
Perse," *Revue du Monde Musulman* 27 (June 1914): 238–300.

10. Edward Granville Browne, *The Reign of Terror in Tabriz: England's Responsibility* (London: Luzac, 1912). See also Taqizadeh, *Zendegi-ye Tufani,* 170–71.

11. Taqizadeh, *Zendegi-ye Tufani,* 174–82.

12. Ibid., 184–85. Taqizadeh listed almost twenty Iranian associates who gath-

ered in Berlin to form the Iranian committee. He mentioned other anti-Entente groups supported by the Germans also gathered at Berlin. He paid particular attention to the India Committee, which he recalled was "very friendly towards us." He recalled that the Germans were training the Indians in the use of explosives and preparing them for a clandestine operation in which they would travel through the Ottoman Empire and Iran to engage in anti-British activities in India.

13. Ibid., 185.

14. Anderson, *Imagined Communities,* 11–12.

15. George Mosse, *Crisis of German Ideology* (New York: Grosset and Dunlap, 1964), 67.

16. Anderson, *Imagined Communities,* 72; see also Gerasimos Augustinos, *Consciousness and History: Nationalist Critics of Greek Society, 1897–1914* (Boulder, CO: East European Quarterly, 1977).

17. Prasenjit Duara, *Rescuing History from the Nation: Questioning Narratives of Modern China* (Chicago: University of Chicago Press, 1995), 35.

18. Partha Chatterjee, *The Nation and Its Fragments: Colonial and Postcolonial Histories* (Princeton, NJ: Princeton University Press, 1993), 98.

19. In South Asian historiography this point is made most cogently in Gyan Prakash, *Another Reason: Science and the Imagination of Modern India* (Princeton, NJ: Princeton University Press, 1999). See also his "The Modern Nation's Return in the Archaic," *Critical Inquiry* 23 (Spring 1997): 536–56.

20. Chatterjee described this mediating role as "the subalternity of an elite." *The Nation and Its Fragments,* 37.

21. Ibid., 36.

22. Ibid., 5–6.

23. Jalal al-Din Mirza Qajar, *Nameh-ye Khosravan,* vol. 1 (Tehran, 1869). Two subsequent volumes were published in 1870 and 1871. The *Nameh-ye Khosravan* also circulated in India and was published there in several editions. See Edward Edwards, ed., *A Catalogue of the Persian Printed Books in the British Museum* (London: British Museum, 1922), 263, 309. The edition used here was published as Jalaleddin Mirza, *Nameh-ye Khosravan,* Pahlavi Commemorative Reprint Series (Tehran, 1976).

24. Anderson, *Imagined Communities,* 57–59, 126–27.

25. On the Dar al-Fonun, see Fereydun Adamiyat, *Amir Kabir va Iran* (Tehran: Chap-e Ruz, 1954), 174–90. Jalal al-Din entered the Dar al-Fonun in the mid-1850s. He later dedicated volume one of his *Nameh-ye Khosravan* to his teachers at the college. See Abbas Amanat, "Jalal al-Din Mirza va *Nameh-ye Khosravan,*" *Iran Nameh* 17, no. 1 (1999): 7.

26. Adamiyat, *Amir Kabir va Iran,* 180. The selection of instructors from neutral states was a challenge to British and Russian interests.

27. Ibid., 181.

28. Kamran Arjomand, "The Emergence of Scientific Modernity in Iran: Con-

troversies Surrounding Astrology and Modern Astronomy in the Mid-Nineteenth Century," *Iranian Studies* 30, no. 1–2 (1997): 9, n. 18.

29. Arthur de Gobineau, *Les Religions et les philosophies dans L'Asie Centrale* (Paris: Gallimard, 1933), 129–30. Gobineau was so struck by the eclectic exchange of ideas between students and instructors at the Dar al-Fonun that he wrote from his decidedly imperial perspective: "In this great intellectual swamp some new combustion of principles, of ideas, of pestilential theories will take place, and the poison which it will produce will be transmitted by contact more or less quickly but surely." For Gobineau and Iran, see also Nasih Nateq, *Iran az Negah-e Gubinu* (Tehran: Afshar, 1985), 119–32; and Jean Boissel, *Gobineau, l'orient et l'Iran* (Paris: Klincksieck, 1973), 312–16.

30. Edward Granville Browne, *Press and Poetry in Modern Persia* (Cambridge: Cambridge University Press, 1914), 157–66. See also Peter Avery, "Printing, the Press, and Literature in Modern Iran," in *Cambridge History of Modern Iran*, vol. 7 (Cambridge: Cambridge University Press, 1991), 823. See also Adamiyat, *Amir Kabir va Iran*, 203–7.

31. Amanat, "Jalal al-Din Mirza," 27.

32. Ibid., 17. Later editions of the work placed the sketched images of the coins as an appendix and included drawn portraits of the shahs at the beginnings of chapters.

33. Anderson, *Imagined Communities,* 175. Anderson called this practice of reproducing national imagery "logoization."

34. Adrien de Longpérier, *Essai sur le médailles des rois perses de la dynastie Sassanide* (Paris: F. Didot Frères, 1840); Edward Thomas, *Early Sassanian Inscriptions: Seals and Coins* (London: Trübner, 1868).

35. Amanat, "Jalal al-Din Mirza," 17.

36. A similar set of issues is discussed in a slightly different context in Leonard Barkan, *Unearthing the Past: Archaeology and Aesthetics in the Making of Renaissance Culture* (New Haven, CT: Yale University Press, 1999), 17–27. The relationship between archaeology and romanticism is discussed in Bruce G. Trigger, *A History of Archaeological Thought* (Cambridge: Cambridge University Press, 1989), 65–67.

37. The number of printed editions of the *Shahnameh,* first in India and then in Iran, is striking. See Edwards, *Catalogue,* 247–54. See also Iraj Afshar, *Ketabshenasi-ye Ferdowsi* (Tehran: Anjoman-e Asar-e Melli, 1976), 270–77.

38. J. G. Herder, *Herder on Social and Political Culture,* ed. F. M. Barnard (Cambridge: Cambridge University Press, 1969), 29–32. Herder's conception of literature in relation to the *volk* is also discussed in Robert Ergang, *Herder and the Foundations of German Nationalism* (New York, 1931). For the application of Herder's category "national literature" to the Indian context, see Vinay Dharwadker, "Orientalism and the Study of Indian Literatures," in Carol A. Breckenridge and Peter van der Veer, eds., *Orientalism and the Postcolonial Predicament: Perspectives on South Asia* (Philadelphia: University of Pennsylvania Press, 1993), 164.

39. The *Dasatir* went through several editions in the nineteenth century, as did the *Sharestan*. See Edwards, *Catalogue*, 187.

40. Mohamad Tavakoli-Targhi, "Tarikh-pardazi va Iran-arayi: Bazsazi-ye Huviyat-e Irani dar Gozaresh-e Tarikh," *Iran Nameh* 12, no. 4 (1994): 589. See also his "Contested Memories: Narrative Structures and Allegorical Meanings of Iran's Pre-Islamic History," *Iranian Studies* 29, no. 1–2 (1996): 149–76; and his "Modernity, Herotopia and Homeless Texts," *Comparative Studies of South Asia, Africa, and the Middle East* 18, no. 2 (1998): 2–14. See also his *Refashioning Iran*.

41. Edwards, *Catalogue*, 184.

42. Mary Boyce, "Manekji Limji Hataria in Iran," in *K. R. Cama Oriental Institute Golden Jubilee* (Bombay: Cama Oriental Insitute, 1969), 16–31. There is also a passing reference to Manekji in Edward Granville Browne, *A Year amongst the Persians* (London: A. and C. Black, 1893), 315. Browne, writing in the early 1890s, observed that Manekji had only recently died in Tehran, thus suggesting that Manekji worked in Iran for about forty years. See also T. M. Luhrmann, *The Good Parsi: The Fate of a Colonial Elite in a Postcolonial Society* (Cambridge, MA: Harvard University Press, 1996), 103; Edkehard Kulke, *The Parsis of India: A Minority as Agent of Social Change* (New Delhi: Vikas 1978), 142–43; and Rashna Writer, *Contemporary Zoroastrians: An Unstructured Nation* (Lanham, MD: University Press of America, 1994), 42–45.

43. Susan Stiles Maneck, *The Death of Ahriman: Culture, Identity, and Theological Change among the Parsis of India* (Bombay: K. R. Cama Oriental Institiute, 1997), 160–82.

44. In addition to his Iranian associates, Manekji was acquainted with Rawlinson, Gobineau, and Browne during their stays in Tehran. Gobineau described him as "a learned Parsi from Bombay." He provided Gobineau with informal census data he had collected, which ultimately found its way into *Trois ans en Asie*.

45. Amanat, "Jalal al-din Mirza," 26. See also Fereydun Adamiyat, *Andishehha-ye Mirza Fath 'Ali Akhundzadeh* (Tehran: Entesharat-e Khvarazmi, 1970), 112.

46. Edwards, *Catalogue*, 378.

47. C. A. Storey, *Persian Literature: A Bio-Bibliographical Survey*, vol. 1, part 1 (London: Luzac, 1927), 239. For more on this text see also S. Churchill in *Journal of the Royal Asiatic Society* (London, 1886), 198–99.

48. Edwards, *Catalogue*, 378.

49. Ibid., 92.

50. Storey, *Persian Literature*, 246.

51. Mirza Husain Hamadani, *Tarikh-i Jadid: or New History of Mirza Ali Muhammad the Bab,* trans. E. G. Browne (Cambridge: Cambridge University Press, 1893). Manekji was apparently tireless in his efforts to promote religious and philosophical heterodoxy in Iran. Browne wrote in the introduction to *Tarikh-i Jadid:* "Now it chanced one night that he [Mirza Husain Hamadani] and Mohammad Ismail Khan the Zend . . . were Manekji's guests at supper; and Manekji requested each one of them to write a book (for he was most zealous in book-collecting, and whomsoever

he deemed capable of writing and composing he would urge to write a book or compose a treatise). So on this night he requested Mohammad Ismail Khan to write a history of the kings of Persia, and begged Mirza Husain to compile a history of the Babis." *Tarikh-i Jadid,* xxxviii.

52. Edwards, *Catalogue,* 309.

53. Tavakoli, "Tarikh-pardazi va Iran-arayi," 583.

54. Tavakoli, "Contested Memories," 153. Tavakoli contended that the Persianate creation myth of Kyumars posed the first "man" as an androgyne.

55. The fourth volume would have covered the Qajar period and therefore been politically sensitive, which might also have been a reason he did not complete it. In a letter to Akhundzadeh shortly before his death, Jalal al-Din said as much. See Adamiyat, *Andishehha-ye Mirza Fath 'Ali Akhundzadeh,* 132.

56. As Akhundzadeh commented upon reading the text, "you have completely removed the Arabic words from among the Persian words. I wish that others would follow your example and make our language, which is the sweetest in the world, free from . . . the Arabic. You have freed our language from the domination of Arabic." In Adamiyat, *Andishehha-ye Mirza Fath 'Ali Akhundzadeh,* 130.

57. Amanat, "Jalal al-Din Mirza," 39.

58. Hamid Algar, "Malkom Khan, Akhundzada and the Proposed Reform of the Arabic Alphabet," *Middle Eastern Studies* 5 (1969): 116–30. Interestingly, their proposals for an authentic alphabet did not extend to the adoption of the Middle Persian script.

59. Mirza Fath 'Ali Akhundzadeh, *Maqalat,* ed. Baqer Mo'meni (Tehran: Entesharat-e Ava, 1972), 175–81.

60. Mirza Fath 'Ali Akhundzadeh, *Tamsilat: Sesh Namayesh va Yek Dastan* (Tehran: Entesharat-e Khvarazmi, 1977).

61. Mirza Fath 'Ali Akhundzadeh, *Maktubat-e Mirza Fath 'Ali Akhundzadeh,* ed. M. Subhdam (Düsseldorf, Germany: Mard-i Imruz, 1985).

62. Akhundzadeh, "Biografi," in *Maqalat,* 8–17.

63. Hamid Algar, "Akhundzada," in *Encyclopedia Iranica* (Costa Mesa, CA: Mazda Publishers), 735.

64. Akhundzadeh, "Biografi," 12.

65. Ibid.

66. Adamiyat, *Andishehha-ye Mirza Fath 'Ali Akhundzadeh,* 16.

67. Ibid.

68. For more on Abovian, see Rubina Peroomian, "Commentary: A Comparative Approach to the Jewish and Armenian Enlightenment and Modernization," in Richard Hovannisian and David Myers, eds., *Enlightenment and Diaspora: The Armenian and Jewish Cases* (Atlanta: Scholars Press, 1999), 216–21.

69. Adamiyat, *Andisheh-ye Mirza Fath 'Ali Akhundzadeh,* 17–20.

70. Ibid., 32–40. See also Maryam Sanjabi, "Rereading the Enlightenment: Akhundzadeh and His Voltaire," *Iranian Studies* 28, no. 1–2 (1995): 43.

71. Ernest Renan, *Vie de Jesus* (Paris: Calmann Lévy, 1863). The first French edition sold 100,000 copies in ten months and prompted more than 300 pamphlets by disapproving Catholics written in refutation of the work. The first of ten editions of the Russian translation appeared in 1864. Other translations that likewise appeared almost immediately, and with like numbers of editions, were the German, English, Danish, Spanish, Greek, Dutch, Italian, Hungarian, Portuguese, Swedish, and Czech translations. There was even an Esperanto translation in 1907. See Henri Girard and Henri Moncel, *Bibliographie des oeuvres de Ernest Renan* (Paris: Presses Universitaires de France, 1923), 91–92.

72. Ibid., 31, 46, 97.

73. For Russian oriental scholarship see Kalpana Sahni, *Crucifying the Orient: Russian Orientalism and the Colonization of the Caucasus and Central Asia* (Oslo: Institute for the Comparative Research of Human Culture, 1997).

74. One of Renan's biographers, describing the reaction to *Vie de Jesus,* wrote, "The Catholic greeted the book with howls of rage and calumnies for which Renan thought he had a right to bring legal action for slander." See Lewis Feeman Mott, *Ernest Renan* (New York: D. Appleton, 1921), 234.

75. "Islamic Protestantism" was a recurring theme in Akhundzadeh's writings. In his autobiographical fragment, for example, he discussed the reasons for writing his *Maktubat-e Kamal al-Dowleh:* "In order to change the basis of this religion [Islam] . . . and for the awakening of the peoples of Asia from entrenched sleep and ignorance and for promoting the emergence of Protestantism in Islam, I began work on *Kamal al-Dowleh.*" See Akhundzadeh, "Biografi," 15.

76. Akhundzadeh, *Maktubat,* 138, 156.

77. Ibid., 137–57.

78. Ibid., 150.

79. Ibid., 161.

80. Ibid., 61.

81. Ibid., 161.

82. Ibid., 146.

83. Ibid., 120–34.

84. Ibid., 120.

85. Ibid.

86. Ibid., 20.

87. Ibid.

88. Ibid., 17–18.

89. Ibid.

90. Ibid., 15–16.

91. Ibid.

92. Ibid., 20.

93. Ibid., 31, 32.

94. The implications of Aryanism for European history are best detailed in Léon

Poliakov, *The Aryan Myth: A History of Racist and Nationalist Ideas in Europe* (New York: Barnes and Noble Books, 1996).

95. For William Jones and the early philological discoveries, see Thomas R. Trautmann, *Aryans and British India* (Berkeley: University of California Press, 1997), especially chapter 2, "The Mosaic Ethnology of Asiatick Jones," 28–61.

96. For the popularity of racialism in the nineteenth century, see also Tzetan Todorov, *On Human Diversity: Nationalism, Racism, and Exoticism in French Thought* (Cambridge, MA: Harvard University Press, 1993), especially 106–14. The other great popularizer, especially in France, was of course Renan.

97. Between 1861 and 1886, volume one of *Lectures on the Science of Language* went through fourteen editions.

98. Significantly, Müller's popularization of Aryanism was not itself the source of racialized European chauvinism. Like those of Iranian and some Indian nationalists, Müller's call for an "Aryan brotherhood" was inclusive of a trans-European union that included Indians and Iranians. He even goaded the British, who were averse to admitting a common genealogy with their subject peoples in India, by declaring that "the same blood ran in the veins of English soldiers as in the veins of the dark Bengalese." See Poliakov, *The Aryan Myth*, 209–10.

99. For the Indian case these issues are best elaborated in Chatterjee, *Nation and Its Fragments*, 97; see also Thomas Metcalf, *Ideologies of the Raj* (Cambridge: Cambridge University Press, 1995), 83–91.

100. Many of these tensions are detailed in Afary, *Iranian Constitutional Revolution*, especially chapters 4 and 5.

101. *Kaveh*, January 24, 1916.

102. Ibid.

103. Ibid.

104. This engagement with a Persianate cultural universe is analogous to that described by Prasenjit Duara in his discussion of Chinese and Indian nationalists' engagement with "Chinese culturalism" and "Brahmanic universalism." These premodern cultural forms, which he called "archaic totalizations," were "a mode of consciousness distinct from nationalism," but they nevertheless provided "potent material along which to mobilize the new community." See Prasenjit Duara, *Rescuing History from the Nation*, 55–56.

105. These articles were dated February 15, 1918; March 15, 1918; April 15, 1918; May 15, 1918; and July 15, 1918. Other articles in *Kaveh* also made extensive use of European scholarship on Iran, including a series on German scholarship regarding Ferdowsi and the *Shahnameh*.

106. *Kaveh*, April 15, 1918.

107. Ibid., May 25, 1918.

108. Ibid. He was referring to the important works by these two scholars at the Dar al-Fonun: Zoka' al-Molk's *Tarikh-e Sasanian* and E'temad al-Saltanah's *Tarikh-e Bani Ashkan*. These works were seminal texts in the modern Persian historiogra-

phy of the ancient period. They were both largely derivative of Rawlinson's texts but were not strict translations.

109. Tavakoli called the overlapping assumptions of Iranian nationalism and European orientalism "discursive affinities." *Refashioning Iran,* 4.

110. *Kaveh,* February 15, 1918.

111. Ibid., November 15, 1918.

112. Ibid., January 27, 1920.

113. Ibid.

114. *Iranshahr* 2, no. 11–12 (August 19, 1924), for example, was a special double issue devoted to the position of women in society.

115. *Iranshahr* 4, no. 8–9 (November 23, 1926): 492.

116. Ibid., 494.

117. Ibid., 496.

3   THE PEDAGOGIC STATE

1. *Ettelaʿat,* February 6, 1935; *Salnameh-ye Pars* (Tehran, 1936), 44.

2. ʿAli Asghar Hekmat, *Si Khatereh az ʿAsr-e Farkhondeh-ye Pahlavi* (Tehran: Sazman-e Entesharat-e Vahid, 1976), 338; ʿIsa Sadiq, *Yadegar-e ʿOmr* (Tehran: Amir Kabir, 1966), 98–99.

3. Hekmat, *Si Khatereh,* 340; *Salnameh-ye Pars,* 1936, 44.

4. The relationship between education and reform in the nineteenth century is discussed in Monica Ringer, *Education, Religion, and the Discourse of Cultural Reform in Qajar Iran* (Costa Mesa, CA: Mazda Press, 2001); see also David Menashri, *Education and the Making of Modern Iran* (Ithaca, NY: Cornell University Press, 1992), 46–65; ʿIsa Sadiq, *Tarikh-e Farhang-e Iran* (Tehran: Daneshgah-e Tehran, 1957), 300–332.

5. For the role of American missionaries in Iranian education, see Ahmad Mansoori, "Amercian Missionaries in Iran, 1834-1934" (PhD dissertation, Ball State University, 1986), 100–140; and W. A. Copeland, "American Influence on the Development of Higher Education in Iran" (PhD dissertation, University of Pennsylvania, 1973), 38–45. For the role of French missionaries and the Alliance Française and Alliance Israélite, see Homa Nateq, *Karnameh-ye Farhangi-ye Farangi dar Iran* (Paris: Khavaran, 1996), 83–100.

6. There is a large body of literature on the Dar al-Fonun. For its role in the history of education, see Sadiq, *Tarikh-e Farhang,* 350–55.

7. Ibid., 358–59.

8. Ibid.

9. Ibid., 364-68; The texts of the 1910 and 1911 education laws were published in Reza Arasteh, *Education and Social Awakening in Iran, 1850-1968* (Leiden: E. J. Brill, 1969), 223–32.

10. The sources differ on the number of enrollments. The estimates provided

here are based on *Salnameh-ye Pars,* 1936, 118–19; *Salnameh-ye Pars,* 1932, 87; 'Abbas Khaqani, *Barrasi-ye Tahavvulat-e Amuzesh va Parvaresh-e Iran* (Tehran: Daneshkadeh-ye 'Olum-e Ejtema'i, 1973), 22–23; Menashri, *Education and the Making of Modern Iran,* 110; Arasteh, *Education and Social Awakening in Iran,* 93; Joseph S. Szyliowicz, *Education and Modernization in the Middle East* (Ithaca, NY: Cornell University Press, 1973), 466; and Rudi Mathee, "Transforming Dangerous Nomads into Useful Artisans: Education in the Reza Shah Period," *Iranian Studies* 26, no. 3–4 (1993): 333–34.

11. The classic example of this type of analysis of education is Szyliowicz, *Education and Modernization in the Middle East.* For Iranian historiography, the best example is Banani, *Modernization of Iran.* For a critique of this form of analysis, see Brubaker, *Nationalism Reframed,* 80–81.

12. Hekmat, *Si Khatereh,* 130.

13. Hobsbawm, "Mass-Producing Traditions," 263–64.

14. After 1937 the journal's name was changed to *Amuzesh va Parvaresh,* in order to use words of Persian and not Arabic origin.

15. See, for example, the important series of articles published by Hasan Taqizadeh, 'Isa Sadiq, Mohammad 'Ali Forughi, and others in the 1925 issues of *Ayandeh:* vol. 1, nos. 2, 5, and 7–11.

16. For Kazemzadeh and *Iranshahr,* see Kazem Kazemzadeh-Iranshahr, *Asar va Ahval-e Kazemzadeh Iranshahr* (Tehran: Eqbal, 1971), 174–90.

17. Hoseyn Kazemzadeh, "Ta'lim va Tarbiyat dar Miyan-e Iranian-e Qadim," *Iranshahr* 1, no. 2 (July 26, 1922).

18. Hoseyn Kazemzadeh, "Jang ba Fesad-e Akhlaq," *Iranshahr* 1, no. 5 (October 25, 1922).

19. John Richards, *The Open Road to Persia* (London: Church Missionary Society, 1933), 9; Mansoori, "Amercian Missionaries," 28; Nateq, *Karnameh-ye Farhangi-ye Farangi dar Iran,* 153–54. See also Ahmad Khan Matine-Daftary, *La supression des capitulations en Perse* (Paris: Presses Universitaires de France, 1930), 67–68.

20. Yahya Armajani, "Sam Jordan and the Evangelical Ethic in Iran," in *Religious Ferment in Asia,* ed. Robert J. Miller (Lawrence: University Press of Kansas, 1974), 29, cited in Michael Zirinsky "Render Therefore unto Ceasar the Things Which Are Caesar's: American Presbyterian Educators and Reza Shah," *Iranian Studies* 26, no. 3–4 (1993): 338.

21. Zirinsky, "Render Therefore," 338.

22. Sadiq, *Yadegar-e 'Omr,* 54; Arasteh, *Education and Social Awakening,* 76; Banani, *Modernization of Iran,* 92; 'Ali Pasha Saleh, ed., *Cultural Ties between Iran and the United States* (Tehran, 1976), 192. Boyce wrote that the Ministry of Education wanted the American College of Tehran to change its name to Ferdowsi College. When Dr. Samuel Jordan, the American missionary and founder of the college, refused to change the school's name, it marked the beginning of tension between the college and the ministry. The name Alborz College of Tehran, after the mountain range north of the city that formed the backdrop for the campus, was

settled upon. Boyce wrote that Jordan chose "Alborz" because it would preserve the school's acronym, ACT.

23. Saleh, *Cultural Ties,* 187–92.

24. Ibid.

25. Ibid., 188.

26. Ibid.

27. Cronin, *The Army and the Creation of the Pahlavi State,* 126. The conscription law took effect in 1926.

28. Saleh, *Cultural Ties,* 189.

29. Ibid.

30. Ibid., 191.

31. Ibid.

32. Hekmat, *Si Khatereh,* 301–4. Hekmat also wrote that as the work of the mission schools was legally curtailed, some of them were sold to the Ministry of Education and continued to operate as national schools.

33. Saleh, *Cultural Ties,* 191. Boyce wrote his memoir in 1954.

34. Ibid., 209.

35. Ibid.

36. Hekmat, *Si Khatereh,* 185.

37. 'Isa Sadiq, *Modern Persia and Her Educational System* (New York: Teacher's College of Columbia University, 1931), 53.

38. Sadiq, *Yadegar-e 'Omr,* 317.

39. Hekmat, *Si Khatereh,* 185.

40. Sadiq, *Modern Persia,* 53. There was also a limited attempt during the constitutional period to publish locally produced textbooks. In coordination with the passing of the 1911 Education Law, a committee of constitutionalists had produced a book of "civic lessons" to be distributed to children in middle schools. There is no indication of how widely this text circulated.

41. Nassrollah Nikbin, *Ezhar-e Nazar Dar Bareh-ye Arzesh-e 'Elmi-ye Tarikh-e Moshir al-Dowleh* (Tehran: Dehkhoda, 1968), 182.

42. Ibid., 183.

43. Bastan Parizi, *Talash-e Azadi: Mohit-e Siyasi va Zendegi-ye Moshir al-Dowleh* (Tehran: Mohammad 'Ali 'Elmi, 1968), 10; Nikbin, *Ezhar-e Nazar,* 3.

44. Hasan Pirniya, *Iran-e Qadim* (Tehran: Matba'eh-ye Majles, 1928).

45. Nikbin, *Ezhar-e Nazar,* 184.

46. Ibid.

47. Ibid., 186.

48. Ibid., 184–85.

49. Taqizadeh, *Zendegi-ye Tufani,* 581. Letters between Taqizadeh and Hekmat indicate that Hekmat was perturbed over Taqizadeh's refusal to finish the work. Writing to Taqizadeh in Paris, Hekmat said, "[I]t is hoped that you have not changed your mind regarding the completion of the book" (585). Hekmat did not mention

the issue in his memoir. Nikbin, *Ezhar-e Nazar*, 184, says that the seventy-eight-page text was published in 1936.

50. *Ta'lim va Tarbiyat* 5, no. 5 (Tehran, 1932).

51. Taqizadeh, *Zendegi-ye Tufani*, 257.

52. Ibid.

53. Ibid.

54. Reza Shah in fact ordered all copies of the newspaper and the issue of the journal in which the article had appeared to be confiscated.

55. Taqizadeh, *Zendegi-ye Tufani*, 263. He taught Persian literature at the School of Oriental and African Studies at the University of London.

56. In the acknowledgments page of the book, Pirniya wrote, "This book has been produced at the request of the Ministry of Education for instruction of children in middle school." He also stated that the chapters were arranged to correspond to the weeks of instruction in the school calendar. Pirniya, *Iran-e Qadim*, i.

57. Ibid., 45.

58. Ibid.

59. Ibid.

60. For a discussion of the Kyumars myth, see Tavakoli-Targhi, *Refashioning Iran*, 78–86.

61. Pirniya, *Iran-e Qadim*, 2. His full manuscript, *Iran-e Bastan*, included an even more extensive discussion of the geographical features of Iran.

62. Pirniya, *Iran-e Qadim*, 8.

63. Ibid., 12.

64. Sadiq, *Tarikh-e Farhang*, 374.

65. Ahmad Matin Daftari, *Khaterat-e Yek Nokhost Vazir* (Tehran: Entesharat-e 'Elmi, 1991), 164.

66. *Ganjineh-ye Asnad* 21–22 (1996): 76.

67. Ibid.

68. Mahmud Delfani, ed., *Farhang-e Setizi dar Dowreh-ye Reza Shah: Asnad-e Montasher Nashodeh-ye Sazman-e Parvaresh-e Afkar* (Tehran: Entesharat-e Sazman-e Asnad-e Melli, 1997), 2–3. There is also a brief discussion of the Ministry of Public Enlightenment in Hamid Mowlana, "Journalism in Iran: History and Interpretation" (PhD dissertation, Northwestern University, 1963), 482–87; and L. Elwell-Sutton, *Modern Iran* (London: Routledge, 1944), 147.

69. Matin Daftari, *Khaterat-e Yek Nokhost Vazir*, 164. He described the establishment of a "special school" for writers of newspaper and magazine articles established by the ministry.

70. The establishment of a national distribution network was one of the benefits of having a centralized ministry in charge of circulating magazines and newspapers. Mohammad Hejazi, head of the ministry's publications office, made frequent trips throughout Iran to establish this network. *Ganjineh-ye Asnad* 21–22 (1996): 78.

71. Delfani, *Farhang-e Setizi*, 81.
72. Ibid., 8.
73. Ibid., 35–37.
74. Ibid., 8–9.
75. Ibid.
76. Ibid., 2.
77. Ibid.
78. Ibid., 27.
79. Ibid., 29–30.
80. Ibid., 2.
81. *Etelaʿat*, April 25, 1940.
82. Delfani, *Farhang-e Setizi*, 3.
83. Ibid., 6.
84. Ibid., 27.

4   NATION AND MEMORY

1. *Salnameh-ye Pars*, 1935, 44; Sadiq, *Yadegar-e ʿOmr*, vol. 2, 225.
2. Sadiq, *Yadegar-e ʿOmr*, 227.
3. *Salnameh-ye Pars*, 1935, 45; Sadiq, *Yadegar-e ʿOmr*, 227.
4. *Ettelaʿat*, 28 October, 1934.
5. Nora, *Realms of Memory*, vol. 1, 15.
6. Hobsbawm, "Mass-Producing Traditions," 272.
7. Ibid.
8. Eric Hobsbawm, "Introduction," in *The Invention of Tradition* (Cambridge: Cambridge University Press, 1992), 9.
9. John Gillis, "Introduction," in John Gillis, ed., *Commemorations: The Politics of National Identity* (Princeton, NJ: Princeton University Press, 1994), 8.
10. Ibid.
11. Nora, *Realms of Memory*, 3.
12. George L. Mosse, *The Nationalization of the Masses: Political Symbolism and Mass Movements in Germany from the Napoleonic Wars through the Third Reich* (Ithaca, NY: Cornell University Press, 1975), 14.
13. Ibid., 15.
14. Hobsbawm, "Introduction," 4.
15. Nora, *Realms of Memory*, 2.
16. Mosse, *Nationalization of the Masses*, 42.
17. Anderson, *Imagined Communities*, 12.
18. For the importance of Tagore's life and work, see Krishna Kripalani, *Rabindranath Tagore: A Biography* (London: Oxford University Press, 1980); Krishna Dutta and Andrew Robinson, eds., *Rabindranath Tagore: An Anthology* (London: Picador Press, 1997); Krishna Dutta and Andrew Robinson, eds., *Selected Letters of*

Rabindranath Tagore (London: Cambridge University Press, 1997); and Sisir Kumar Das, ed., *The English Writings of Rabindranath Tagore,* vol. 3 (New Delhi: Sahitya Akademi, 1996).

19. Kripalani, *Rabindranath Tagore,* 239.

20. Ibid., 276–78; Kedar Nath Mukherjee, *The Political Philosophy of Rabindranth Tagore* (New Delhi: S. Chand, 1982), 350–51.

21. Mohit Chakrabarti, *Tagore and Education for Social Change* (New Delhi: Gian Publshing House, 1993). For those reared under the methods of Jeremy Bentham, the Santiniketan Academy was no doubt a curiosity. One observer for the *London Daily Telegraph* commented, with some amusement, that "the boys sit on mats under trees . . . [and] each morning and evening they parade in the school garden, singing hymns." *Daily Telegraph,* February 26, 1914, cited in Kalyan Kundu, ed., *Rabindranath Tagore and the British Press (1912–1941)* (London: Tagore Centre, 1990).

22. Vivek Ranjan Bhattacharya, *Tagore's Vision of a Global Family* (New Delhi: Enkay Publishers, 1987), 143–48.

23. Isaiah Berlin, "Rabindranath Tagore and the Consciousness of Nationality," in his *The Sense of Reality: Studies in Ideas and Their History* (London: Henry Hardy, 1996), 265, quoted in Dutta and Robinson, *Selected Letters,* xxi.

24. Sadiq, *Yadegar-e 'Omr,* 154.

25. A. Aronson, *Rabindranath Tagore through Western Eyes* (Allahabad: Kitabistan, 1943), 12.

26. Sadiq, *Yadegar-e 'Omr,* 154; *Ettela'at,* April 20, 1932.

27. Kripalani, *Rabindranath Tagore,* 384; G. D. Khanolkar, *The Lute and the Plough: A Life of Rabindranath Tagore* (Bombay: Book Centre, 1963), 320.

28. Khanolkar, *The Lute and the Plough,* 320. For the Iran Society of Bombay, see also Kulke, *Parsis of India,* 142–44; and Jesse S. Palsetia, *The Parsis of India: Preservation of Identity in Bombay City* (London: Brill, 2001), 256–57.

29. Ibrahim Pour-e Davoud, *Introduction to the Yashts,* trans. D. J. Irani (Bombay: Iranian Zoroastrian Anjoman and Iran League, 1928), xiii.

30. *Ettela'at,* April 21, 1932.

31. Ibid., April 26, 28, 30, 1932.

32. *Isfahan,* April 25, 1932. Tagore also described his relationship with Hafez in one of his autobiographies. Referring to his boyhood, he wrote that "at night I used to leave my bedroom windows open . . . wrapping myself in a blanket, and sitting up in bed, oblivious of all else, I spent half the night reciting hymns and the verses of Hafez." Mahareshi Devendranath Tagore, *The Autobiography,* trans. Satyendranath Tagore and Indira Devi (London: Macmillan, 1961), 250. For Tagore and Hafez, see also Saleem Ahmed, "Hafiz and Tagore: A Study in Influence," in R. R. Sharma, ed., *Essays on Rabindranath Tagore in Honor of D. M. Gupta* (Ghaziabad: Vimal Prakashan, 1987), 231–82.

33. *Ettela'at,* April 30, 1932.

34. Ibid. For Tagore's visit to the shrines of Saʿdi and Hafez, see also Khanolkar, *The Lute and the Plough*, 320–22.

35. Kripalani, *Rabindranath Tagore*, 385; Khanolkar, *The Lute and the Plough*, 320.

36. Sadiq, *Yadeqar-e 'Omr*, 156. A May 5 article in *Ettelaʿat*, with the headline "The Visage of Tagore," also emphasized his physical appearance.

37. Sadiq, *Yadeqar-e 'Omr*, 156–57.

38. Ibid., 158.

39. Ibid.

40. The chair was established in 1933 at Visva-Bharati University, which was associated with Tagore's Santiniketan Academy. Its first occupant was Ibrahim Purdavud, who was dispatched to India from Germany, where he was pursuing advanced studies in Iranian philology. See Ahmed, "Hafiz and Tagore," 240; and ʿAli Asghar Mostafavi, *Zaman va Zendegi-ye Ostad Purdavud* (Tehran: Mostafavi, 1991), 67.

41. *Ettelaʿat*, May 5, 7, 1932.

42. Ibid., May 7. The poem read in part: "Iran, thy brave sons have brought their priceless gifts of friendship on this birthday of the poet of a faraway shore / for they have known him in their hearts as their own. Iran, crowned with a new glory by the honor from thy hand / this birthday of the poet of a faraway shore finds its fulfillment. / And in return I put this wreath of a verse on thy forehead and cry: 'victory to Iran.'"

43. Iraj Afshar, for example, documented the growth in the number of manuscript, lithographed, and published editions of the *Shahnameh* in the nineteenth century. See his *Kitabshenasi-ye Ferdowsi*, 275–85.

44. Theodor Nöldeke, "Das iranische Nationalepos," in C. Bartholomae et. al., eds., *Grundriss der iranischen Philologie* (Leiden: K. J. Trübner, 1894), vol. 2, 130–211. See also Theodor Nöldeke, *The Iranian National Epic*, trans. L. Bogdanov (Bombay: K. R. Cama Oriental Institute, 1930; reprint, Philadelphia: Porcupine Press, 1979).

45. The *Kaveh* articles by Taqizadeh and Qazvini were later reprinted in *Hezareh-ye Ferdowsi* (Tehran: Vezarat-e Farhang, 1944). Publication of the proceedings of the millennium conference, in which Taqizadeh's Ferdowsi articles were reprinted, was delayed by ten years, because by 1934 Taqizadeh had become persona non grata to Reza Shah, following the controversy over his criticism of the Farhangestan. See also Taqizadeh, *Zendegi-ye Tufani*, 258. It was only in 1944, after Reza Shah's abdication, that ʿIsa Sadiq published the proceedings of the conference; see also Sadiq, *Yadeqar-e 'Omr*, 216–17.

46. For the Anjoman-e Asar-e Melli, see Sadiq, *Yadegar-e 'Omr*, 201–2; Keykhosrow Shahrokh, *Yaddashtha-ye Keykhosrow Shahrokh* (Tehran: n.p., 1977), 160–61; *Salnameh-ye Pars*, 1935, 18–20; Afshar, *Kitabshenasi-ye Ferdowsi* (which includes

numerous original documents from the Anjoman); and Hoseyn Bahr al-'Olumi, *Kar-nameh-ye Anjoman-e Asar-e Melli* (Tehran: Anjoman-e Asar-e Melli, 1976).

47. Sadiq, *Yadegar-e 'Omr,* 201.

48. Ibid., 210.

49. Ibid., 202; Shahrokh, *Yaddashtha,* 164–65.

50. Afshar, *Ketabshenasi-ye Ferdowsi,* 338

51. Sadiq, *Yadegar-e 'Omr,* 210; *Salnameh-ye Pars,* 1935, 19.

52. Shahrokh, *Yaddashtha,* 161–62.

53. Sadiq, *Yadeqar-e 'Omr,* 203; Shahrokh, *Yaddashtha,* 163.

54. Sadiq, *Yadegar-e 'Omr,* 203.

55. Taherzadeh was the first to propose a Ferdowsi monument, in the pages of *Iranshahr;* see the October 23, 1925, issue. For more on the Ferdowsi monument, see also Talinn Grigor, "Recultivating 'Good Taste': The Early Pahlavi Modernists and Their Society for National Heritage," *Iranian Studies* 37, no. 1 (2004): 17–45. See also the important unpublished dissertation by Mina Marefat, "Building to Power: Architecture of Tehran, 1921–1941" (PhD diss., Massachusetts Institute of Technology, 1988). On the design of the mausoleum, see Sadiq, *Yadeqar-e 'Omr,* 203; Shahrokh, *Yaddashtha,* 164–65.

56. The Tehran conference coincided with other Ferdowsi conferences in London, New York, Berlin, and Moscow that had been organized with the help of the Iranian diplomatic corps abroad. The Iranian press took interest in the proceedings of these other conferences as well. See *Ettela'at,* October 2, 6, 1934. The speech of the Iranian ambassador to Nazi Germany, who attended the Berlin conference, was printed in the October 6 issue: "The celebration of the greatest Iranian national poet's millennium . . . which has brought together eminent German orientalists . . . will, it is hoped, affirm the spiritual and intellectual connections between Germans and Iranians."

57. *Ettela'at,* October 4, 1934. *Glossar zu Firdosis Schahname* remains a monumental concordance to the text. See A. Shapur Shabazi, *Ferdowsi: A Critical Biography* (Costa Mesa, CA: Harvard University Center for Middle Eastern Studies/Mazda Press, 1991), 16.

58. *Ettela'at,* October 4, 1934; *Salnameh-ye Pars,* 1935, 28.

59. *Ettela'at,* November 1, 1934.

60. Mohammad 'Ali Forughi, "Opening Remarks," *Hezareh-ye Ferdowsi,* 16.

61. 'Ali Asghar Hekmat, "Opening Remarks," *Hezareh-ye Ferdowsi,* 10.

62. *Ettela'at,* October 13, 1934.

63. Ibid.

64. Ibid.; *Salnameh-ye Pars,* 1935, 22.

65. *Salnameh-ye Pars,* 1935, 54–5; *Ettela'at,* October 13, 1934.

66. Sadiq, *Yadegar-e 'Omr,* 232.

67. Ibid.

68. Ibid., 233; Afshar, *Ketabshenashi-ye Ferdowsi,* 276–77.

69. Ibid.

70. Mohammad 'Ali Forughi, ed., *Kholaseh-ye Shahnameh-ye Ferdowsi* (Tehran: Ibn Sina, 1934).

71. The film itself is not extant. A synopsis of the screenplay and a discussion of the filmmaker are found in Mamad Haghighat, *Histoire du cinéma iranien* (Paris: BPI Centre George Pompidou, 1999), 31–33; and Jamal Omid, *'Abdolhoseyn Sepanta: Zendegi va Sinema* (Tehran: Sherkat-e Tehran Faryab, 1984), 49–54.

BIBLIOGRAPHY

Abrahamian, Ervand. *Iran between Two Revolutions*. Princeton, NJ: Princeton University Press, 1982.

Abu-Lughod, Janet. *Cairo: 1001 Years of the City Victorious*. Princeton, NJ: Princeton University Press, 1971.

Adamiyat, Fereydun. *Amir Kabir va Iran*. Tehran: Chap-e Piruz, 1954.

———. *Andishehha-ye Mirza Fath 'Ali Akhundzadeh*. Tehran: Entesharat-e Khvarazmi, 1970.

———. *Andishehha-ye Taraqqi va Hokumat-e Qanun*. Tehran: Entesharat-e Khvarazmi, 1972.

———. *Ideolozhi-ye Nehzat-e Mashrutiyat-e Iran*. Tehran: Entesharat-e Payam, 1976.

Adle, Chahryar, and Bernard Hourcade, eds. *Téhéran: Capitale bicentenaire*. Paris: Institut Français de Recherche en Iran, 1992.

Afary, Janet. *The Iranian Consitutional Revolution, 1906–1911*. New York: Columbia University Press, 1996.

Afshar, Iraj. *Ketabshenasi-ye Ferdowsi*. Tehran: Anjoman-e Asar-e Melli, 1976.

Aghaie, Kamran. *The Martyrs of Karbala: Shi'i Rituals and Symbols in Modern Iran*. Seattle: University of Washington Press, 2004.

Ahmed, Saleem. "Hafiz and Tagore: A Study in Influence." In *Essays on Rabindranath Tagore in Honor of D. M. Gupta,* ed. R. R. Sharma, pp. 231–82. Ghaziabad: Vimal Prakashan, 1987.

Akhundzadeh, Mirza Fath 'Ali. *Maqalat*. Ed. Baqer Mo'meni. Tehran: Entesharat-e Ava, 1972.

————. *Tamsilat: Shesh Namayesh va Yek Dastan.* Tehran: Entesharat-e Khvarazmi, 1977.

————. *Alefba-ye Jadid va Maktubat.* Ed. Hamid Mohammadzadeh. Tabriz: Nashr-e Ehya, 1978.

————. *Maktubat-e Mirza Fath 'Ali Akhundzadeh.* Ed. M. Sobhdam. Düsseldorf, Germany: Mard-e Emruz, 1985.

Algar, Hamid. "Malkom Khan, Akhundzada and the Proposed Reform of the Arabic Alphabet." *Middle Eastern Studies* 5 (1969): 116–30.

————. *Religion and State in Iran, 1785–1906.* Berkeley: University of California Press, 1969.

Amanat, Abbas. "Jalal al-Din Mirza va *Nameh-ye Khosravan.*" *Iran Nameh* 17, no. 1 (1999): 5–54.

————. *Pivot of the Universe: Nasir al-Din Shah Qajar and the Iranian Monarchy, 1831–1896.* Berkeley: University of California Press, 1997.

Amin al-Dowleh, Mirza 'Ali Khan. *Khaterat-e Siyasi-ye Mirza 'Ali Khan Amin al-Dowleh.* Ed. Hafez Farman Farma'ian. Tehran: Entesharat-e Daneshgah-e Tehran, 1962.

Anderson, Benedict. *Imagined Communities: Reflections on the Origin and Spread of Nationalism.* 2nd ed. London: Verso, 1991.

Arasteh, Reza. *Education and Social Awakening in Iran, 1850–1968.* Leiden: Brill, 1969.

Arjomand, Kamran. "The Emergence of Scientific Modernity in Iran: Controversies Surrounding Astrology and Modern Astronomy in the Mid-Nineteenth Century." *Iranian Studies* 30, no. 1–2 (1997): 5–24.

Arjomand, Said Amir. *The Shadow of God and the Hidden Imam.* Chicago: University of Chicago Press, 1984.

Armajani, Yahya. "Sam Jordan and the Evangelical Ethic in Iran." In *Religious Ferment in Asia,* ed. Robert J. Miller, pp. 23–36. Lawrence: University Press of Kansas, 1974.

Arnold, Mathew. *Essays in Criticism.* London: Macmillan, 1889.

Aronson, A. *Rabindranath Tagore through Western Eyes.* Allahabad: Kitabistan, 1943.

Augustinos, Gerasimos. *Consciousness and History: Nationalist Critics of Greek Society, 1897–1914.* Boulder, CO: East European Quarterly, 1977.

Avery, Peter. *Modern Iran.* London: Ernest Benn, 1965.

————. "Printing, the Press, and Literature in Modern Iran." In *Cambridge History of Modern Iran,* vol. 7, pp. 815–69. Cambridge: Cambridge University Press, 1991.

Bahr al-'Olumi, Hoseyn. *Karnameh-ye Anjoman-e Asar-e Melli.* Tehran: Anjoman-e Asar-e Melli, 1976.

Bakhash, Shaul. *Iran: Monarchy, Bureaucracy, and Reform under the Qajars, 1858–1896.* London: Ithaca Press, 1978.

Banani, Amin. *The Modernization of Iran, 1921–1941.* Stanford, CA: Stanford University Press, 1961.

Barkan, Leonard. *Unearthing the Past: Archaeology and Aesthetics in the Making of Renaissance Culture.* New Haven, CT: Yale University Press, 1999.

Basri, 'Ali. *Yaddashtha-ye Reza Shah keh be Qalam-e Khudash Neveshteh.* Tehran, n.d..

Bassett, James. *Persia and the Land of the Imams.* London: Backie, 1887.

Bayat, Mangol. *Mysticism and Dissent: Socioreligious Thought in Qajar Iran.* Syracuse, NY: Syracuse University Press, 1982.

Beaver, Patrick. *The Crystal Palace, 1851–1936: Portrait of a Victorian Enterprise.* London: Hugh Evelyn, 1970.

Bendix, Reinhard. *Kings or People: Power and the Mandate to Rule.* Berkeley: University of California Press, 1978.

Benjamin, Samuel. *Persia and the Persians.* Boston: Ticknor, 1887.

Berberian, Houri. *The Love of Freedom Has No Fatherland: Armenians and the Iranian Constitutional Revolution of 1905–1911.* Boulder, CO: Westview Press, 2001.

Berkes, Niyazi. *The Development of Secularism in Turkey.* Montreal: McGill University Press, 1964.

Berman, Marshall. *All That Is Solid Melts into Air: The Experience of Modernity.* New York: Penguin Books, 1988.

Beyza'i, Bahram. *Namayesh dar Iran: Yek Motale'eh ba Shast Tasvir va Tarh va Yek Vazhehnameh.* Tehran: Chap-e Kaviyan, 1965.

Bhattacharya, Vivek Ranjan. *Tagore's Vision of a Global Family.* New Delhi: Enkay Publishers, 1987.

Binder, Henry. *Au Kurdistan.* Paris: Maison Quanton, 1887.

Blue, Gregory. "Gobineau on China: Race Theory, the 'Yellow Peril,' and the Critique of Modernity." *Journal of World History* 10, no. 1 (1999): 93–139.

Boissel, Jean. *Gobineau, l'orient et l'Iran.* Paris: Klincksieck, 1973.

Boyce, Mary. "Manekji Limji Hataria in Iran." In *K. R. Cama Oriental Institute Golden Jubilee,* pp. 16–31. Bombay: Cama Oriental Institute, 1969.

Breuilly, John. *Nationalism and the State.* 2nd ed. Chicago: University of Chicago Press, 1992.

Browne, Edward Granville. *A History of Persian Literature.* 4 vols. Cambridge: Cambridge University Press, 1924.

———. *The Persian Revolution: 1905–1909.* Cambridge, 1910; new edition, Washington, DC: Mage Publishers, 1995.

———. *Press and Poetry in Modern Persia.* Cambridge: Cambridge University Press, 1914.

———. *The Reign of Terror in Tabriz: England's Responsibility.* London: Luzac, 1912.

———. *A Year amongst the Persians.* London: A. and C. Black, 1893.

Brubaker, Rogers. *Nationalism Reframed: Nationhood and the National Question in the New Europe.* Cambridge: Cambridge University Press, 1996.

Calmard, Jean. "Le mécénat des representations de ta'ziyeh." In *Le monde iranian et l'Islam,* vol 2, pp. 73–126. Paris, 1974.

———. "Le patronage des ta'ziyeh: Eléments pour une étude globale." In *Ta'ziyeh: Ritual and Drama in Iran,* ed. Peter J. Chelkowski, pp. 121–30. New York: New York University Press, 1979.

Canadine, David. "The Context, Performance, and Meaning of Ritual: The British Monarchy and the 'Invention of Tradition', c. 1820–1977." In *The Invention of Tradition,* ed. Eric Hobsbawm and Terence Ranger, pp. 101–164. Cambridge: Cambridge University Press, 1992.

Çelik, Zeynep. *The Remaking of Istanbul: Portrait of an Ottoman City in the Nineteenth Century.* Seattle: University of Washington Press, 1986.

Chakrabarti, Mohit. *Tagore and Education for Social Change.* New Delhi: Gian Publishing House, 1993.

Chapman, Joan Margaret, and Brian Chapman. *The Life and Times of Baron Haussmann.* London: Weidenfield and Nicholson, 1957.

Chardin, Jean. *Voyage de Paris à Ispahan.* Paris, 1683.

Chatterjee, Partha. *The Nation and Its Fragments: Colonial and Postcolonial Histories.* Princeton, NJ: Princeton University Press, 1993.

Chaudhuri, Nirad C. *Scholar Extraordinary: The Life of Professor the Rt. Hon. Friedrich Max Müller, P.C.* London: Chatto and Windus, 1974.

Chehabi, Houchang. "Staging the Emperor's New Clothes: Dress Codes and Nation-Building under Reza Shah." *Iranian Studies* 26, nos. 3–4 (1993): 209–33.

———. "From Revolutionary Tasnif to Patriotic Surud: Music and Nation-Building in Pre-World War II Iran." *Iran* 37 (1999): 143–54.

Chelkowski, Peter J. "Ta'ziyeh: Indigenous Avant-Garde Theatre of Iran." In *Ta'ziyeh: Ritual and Drama in Iran,* ed. Peter Chelkowski, pp. 1–11. New York: New York University Press, 1979.

Chevalier, Nicole. *Une mission en Perse, 1897–1912: Les dossiers du musée du Louvre.* Paris: Réunion des Musées Nationaux, 1997.

Choay, Françoise. *The Modern City: Planning in the Nineteenth Century.* New York: G. Braziller, 1969.

Copeland, W. A. "American Influence on the Development of Higher Education in Iran." PhD dissertation, University of Pennsylvania, 1973.

Cottam, Richard. *Nationalism in Iran.* Pittsburgh: University of Pittsburgh Press, 1964.

Cronin, Stephanie. *The Army and the Creation of the Pahlavi State, 1910–1926.* London: I. B. Tauris, 1997.

Curzon, George. *Persia and the Persian Question.* 2 vols. London, 1892.

Das, Sisir Kumar, ed. *The English Writings of Rabindranath Tagore.* Vol. 3, Miscellany. New Delhi: Sahitya Akademi, 1996.

Dehbashi, 'Ali. *Yadnameh-ye 'Allameh Mohammad Qazvini*. Tehran: Entesharat-e Ketab va Farhang, 1999.

Deldam, Eskandar. *Zendegi-ye Por Majera-ye Reza Shah*. Tehran: Nashr-e Golfam, 1991.

Delfani, Mahmud, ed. *Farhang-e Setizi dar Dowreh-ye Reza Shah: Asnad-e Montasher Nashodeh-ye Sazman-e Parvaresh-e Afkar*. Tehran: Entesharat-e Sazman-e Asnad-e Melli, 1997.

Deringil, Selim. "Legitimacy Structures in the Ottoman State: The Reign of Abdulhamid II (1876–1909)." *International Journal of Middle Eastern Studies* 23 (1991): 345–59.

———. "The Invention of Tradition as Public Image in the Late Ottoman Empire, 1808–1908." *Comparative Studies in Society and History* 35, no. 1 (1993): 3–28.

———. *Well-Protected Domains: Ideology and Legitimation of Power in the Ottoman Empire, 1876–1909*. London: I. B. Tauris, 1999.

Dharwadker, Vinay. "Orientalism and the Study of Indian Literatures." In *Orientalism and the Postcolonial Predicament: Perspectives on South Asia*, ed. Carol A. Breckenridge and Peter van der Veer, pp. 158–85. Philadelphia: University of Pennsylvania Press, 1993.

Djamalzadeh, Mohammad 'Ali. "Taqizadeh, tel que je l'ai connu." In *A Locust's Leg: Studies in Honor of S. H. Taqizadeh*, eds. Walter Henning and Ehsan Yarshater, pp. 1–20. London: Percy Lund, Humphries and Co., 1962.

Dostoevsky, Fyodor. *Notes from the Underground*. Translated and annotated by Richard Pevear and Larissa Volokhonsky. New York: Alfred A. Knopf, 1993.

Dowlatabadi, Yahya. *Tarikh-e Mo'aser ya Hayat-e Yahya*. Tehran: Ibn Sina, 1957.

Duara, Prasenjit. *Rescuing History from the Nation: Questioning Narratives of Modern China*. Chicago: University of Chicago Press, 1995.

Dutta, Krishna, and Andrew Robinson, eds. *Rabindranath Tagore: An Anthology*. London: Picador Press, 1997.

———. *Selected Letters of Rabindranath Tagore*. Cambridge: Cambridge University Press, 1997.

Edmond, Charles. *L'Egypt a l'exposition universelle de 1867*. Paris: Dentu, 1867.

Edwards, Edward, ed. *A Catalogue of the Persian Printed Books in the British Museum*. London: British Museum, 1922.

Eley, Geoff, and Ronald Grigor Suny. "Introduction: From the Moment of Social History to the Work of Cultural Representation." In *Becoming National: A Reader*, eds. Geoff Eley and Ronald Suny, pp. 3–37. Oxford: Oxford University Press, 1996.

Elwell-Sutton, L. P. *Modern Iran*. London: Routledge, 1944.

Eqbal, 'Abbas. *Tarikh-e Moghul*. Tehran: Amir Kabir, 1986.

Ergang, Robert. *Herder and the Foundations of German Nationalism*. New York, 1931.

Farmanfarmayan, Hafez. "The Forces of Modernization in Nineteenth-Century Iran." In *Beginnings of Modernization in the Middle East: The Nineteenth Century*, eds. William Polk and Richard Chambers, pp. 115–51. Chicago: University of Chicago Press, 1968.

Feuvrier, Joannes. *Trois ans a la cour de Perse*. Paris: Impr. nationale, 1906.

Floor, William. "Change and Development in the Judicial System of Qajar Iran (1800–1925)." In *Qajar Iran: Political, Social, and Cultural Change, 1800–1925*, eds. Edmond Bosworth and Carole Hillenbrand, pp. 113–47. Costa Mesa, CA: Mazda Press, 1992.

Foran, John. *Fagile Resistance: Social Transformation in Iran from 1500 to the Revolution*. Boulder, CO: Westview Press, 1993.

Forughi, Mohammad 'Ali, ed. *Kholaseh-ye Shahnameh-ye Ferdowsi*. Tehran: Ibn Sina, 1934.

Frisby, David. *Fragments of Modernity: Theories of Modernity in the Work of Simmel, Kracauer, and Benjamin*. Cambridge, MA: Polity Press, 1986.

Fujitani, T. *Splendid Monarchy: Power and Pageantry in Modern Japan*. Berkeley: University of California Press, 1996.

Gaffary, Farrokh. "Les lieux de spectacle a Teheran." In *Téhéran: Capitale bicentenaire*, ed. Chahryar Adle and Bernard Hourcade, pp. 141–54. Paris: Institut Français de Recherche en Iran, 1992.

Galibar, Gad G. "Demographic Developments in Late Qajar Iran, 1870–1906." *Asian and African Studies* 11, no. 2 (1976): 125–56.

Geertz, Clifford. *Negara: The Theater State in Nineteenth-Century Bali*. Princeton, NJ: Princeton University Press, 1980.

Gelvin, James L. *Divided Loyalties: Nationalism and Mass Politics in Syria at the Close of Empire*. Berkeley: University of California Press, 1998.

Ghani, Cyrus. *Iran and the Rise of Reza Shah: From Qajar Collapse to Pahlavi Power*. London: I. B. Tauris, 1998.

Ghods, M. Reza. "Iranian Nationalism and Reza Shah." *Middle Eastern Studies* 27 (1991): 35–45.

Gibbs-Smith, C. H. *The Great Exhibition of 1851: A Commemorative Album*. London: H. M. Stationary, 1950.

Gillis, John, ed. *Commemorations: The Politics of National Identity*. Princeton, NJ: Princeton University Press, 1994.

Girard, Henri, and Henri Moncel. *Bibliographie des oeuvres de Ernest Renan*. Paris: Les Presses Universitaires de France, 1923.

Gluck, Carol. *Japan's Modern Myths: Ideology in the Late Meiji Period*. Princeton, NJ: Princeton University Press, 1985.

Gluck, Jay, and Noel Silver, eds. *Surveyors of Persian Art: A Documentary Biography of Arthur Upham Pope and Phyllis Ackerman*. Costa Mesa, CA: Mazda Press, 1996.

Gnoli, Gherardo. *The Idea of Iran*. Rome: Instituto Italiano per il Medio ed Estremo Oriente, 1989.

Gobineau, Arthur de. *Oevres*. Ed. Jean Gaulmier. Paris: Gallimard, 1983.

———. *Les religions et les philosophies dans l'Asie Centrale*. Paris: Gallimard, 1933.

Gurney, John. "The Transformation of Tehran in the Later Nineteenth Century." In *Téhéran: Capitale bicentenaire*, ed. Chahryar Adle and Bernard Hourcade, pp. 51–72. Paris: Institut Français de Recherche en Iran, 1992.

Haghighat, Mamad. *Histoire du cinéma iranien: 1900–1999*. Paris: BPI Centre George Pompidou, 1999.

Hakimian, Hasan. "Wage Labor and Migration: Persian Workers in Southern Russia, 1880–1914." *International Journal of Middle East Studies* 17, no. 4 (1985): 443–62.

Hamadani, Mirza Husain. *Tarikh-i Jadid, or New History of Mirza 'Ali Moham-mad the Bab*. Trans. E. G. Browne. Cambridge: Cambridge University Press, 1893.

Harvey, David. *Consciousness and the Urban Experience*. Baltimore, MD: Johns Hopkins University Press, 1985.

Hejazi, Mohammad. *Mihan-e Ma*. Tehran: Entesharat-e Vezarat-e Farhang, 1959.

Hekmat, 'Ali Asghar. *Si Khatereh az 'Asr-e Farkhondeh-ye Pahlavi*. Tehran: Sazman-e Entesharat-e Vahid, 1976.

Herder, J. G. *Herder on Social and Political Culture*. Ed. F. M. Barnard. Cambridge: Cambridge University Press, 1969.

Heydari, Gholam. *Filmshenakht-e Iran: Filmshenasi-ye sinema-ye Iran, 1309–1340*. Tehran: Daftar-e Pazhuheshha-ye Farhangi, 1994.

Hobsbawm, Eric. *Nations and Nationalism since 1780*. Cambridge: Cambridge University Press, 1990.

Hobsbawm, Eric, and Terence Ranger, eds. *The Invention of Tradition*. Cambridge: Cambridge University Press, 1992.

Homayuni, Sadiq. *Ta'ziyeh va Ta'ziyeh-Khani*. Tehran: Entesharat-e Jashn-e Honar, 1971.

Hovannisian, Richard, and David Myers, eds. *Enlightenment and Diaspora: The Armenian and Jewish Cases*. Atlanta: Scholars Press, 1999.

Issawi, Charles. "The Tabriz-Trabzon Trade: 1830–1900: The Rise and Decline of a Route." *International Journal of Middle East Studies* 1 (1970): 18–27.

———, ed. *The Economic History of Iran, 1800–1914*. Chicago: University of Chicago Press, 1971.

Karny, Azriel. "Husayn Khan Mushir al-Dowleh and His Atttempts at Reform in Iran, 1871–1873." PhD dissertation, University of California at Los Angeles, 1973.

Kashani-Sabet, Firoozeh. *Frontier Fictions: Shaping of the Iranian Nation, 1804–1946*. Princeton, NJ: Princeton University Press, 1999.

Kasravi, Ahmad. *Zendegani-ye Man.* Tehran: n.p., 1944.

Katouzian, Homa. *State and Society in Iran: The Eclipse of the Qajars and the Emergence of the Pahlavis.* London: I. B. Tauris, 2000.

Kazemzadeh, Firuz. "The Origin and Early Development of the Persian Cossack Brigade." *American Slavic and East European Review* 15 (Oct. 1956): 351–63.

———. *Russia and Britain in Iran, 1864–1914: A Study in Imperialism.* New Haven, CT: Yale University Press, 1968.

Kazemzadeh-Iranshahr, Kazem. *Asar va Ahval-e Kazemzadeh Iranshahr.* Tehran: Eqbal, 1971.

Keddie, Nikki R. *Iran: Religion, Politics, and Society.* London: Frank Cass, 1980.

———. *Modern Iran: Roots and Results of Revolution.* New Haven, CT: Yale University Press, 2003.

———. *Qajar Iran and the Rise of Reza Khan, 1796–1925.* Costa Mesa, CA: Mazda Press, 1999.

———. *Religion and Rebellion in Iran: The Tobacco Protest of 1891–1892.* London: Frank Cass, 1966.

———. *Roots of Revolution: An Interpretive History of Modern Iran.* New Haven, CT: Yale University Press, 1981.

———. "The Roots of the Ulama's Power in Modern Iran." In *Scholars, Saints, and Sufis: Muslim Religious Institutions in the Middle East since 1500,* ed. Nikki R. Keddie, pp. 211–30. Berkeley: University of California Press, 1972.

———. *Sayyid Jamal al-Din "al-Afghani": A Political Biography.* Berkeley: University of California Press, 1972.

———. "Thoughts on the Twentieth Anniversary of *Orientalism* and the Rise of Postmodernism." Unpublished conference paper, 1998.

Kedourie, Elie. *Nationalism in Asia and Africa.* New York: World Publishing Company, 1970.

Kermani, Nezam al-Islam. *Tarikh-e Bidari-ye Iranian.* Ed. Sa'id Sirjani. Tehran: Mu'assaseh-ye Entesharat-e Agah, 1983.

Khanolkar, G. D. *The Lute and the Plough: A Life of Rabindranath Tagore.* Bombay: Book Centre, 1963.

Khaqani, 'Abbas. *Barrasi-ye Tahavvulat-e Amuzesh va Parvaresh-e Iran.* Tehran: Daneshkadeh-ye 'Olum-e Ejtema'i, 1973.

Kripalani, Krishna. *Rabindranath Tagore: A Biography.* Oxford: Oxford University Press, 1980.

Kulke, Edkehard. *The Parsis of India: A Minority as Agent of Social Change.* New Delhi: Vikas Publishing House, 1978.

Kundu, Kalyan, ed. *Rabindranath Tagore and the British Press, 1912–1941.* London: Tagore Centre, 1990.

La'l, Hoseyn. *Qeblah-ye 'Alam: Zendegi-ye Khosusi-ye Naser al-Din Shah.* Tehran: Donya-ye Ketab va Manuchehri, 1993.

Lambton, Ann K. S. "Social Change in Persia in the Nineteenth Century." In *The*

Modern Middle East, ed. Albert Hourani, Phillip Khoury, and Mary Wilson, pp. 145–68. Berkeley: University of California Press, 1993).

———. *Theory and Practice in Medieval Persian Government.* London: Variorum Reprints, 1980.

———. "The Tobacco Régie: Prelude to Revolution." *Studia Islamica* 22 (1965): 119–57.

Leopold, Joan. "The Aryan Theory of Race." *Indian Economic and Social History Review* 7, no. 2 (1970): 271–97.

———. "British Applications of the Aryan Theory of Race to India, 1850–1870." *English Historical Review* 89 (1974): 578–603.

Lewis, Bernard. *The Emergence of Modern Turkey.* Oxford: Oxford University Press, 1961.

Longpérier, Adrien de. *Essai sur le médailles des rois Perses de la dynastie Sassanide.* Paris: F. Didot Frères, 1840.

Luhrmann, T. M. *The Good Parsi: The Fate of a Colonial Elite in a Postcolonial Society.* Cambridge, MA: Harvard University Press, 1996.

Mahbubi Ardakani, Hoseyn. *Tarikh-e Mu'assesat-e Tamaddoni-ye Jadid dar Iran,* vol. 1. Tehran: Entesharat-e Anjoman-e Daneshjuyan-e Daneshgah-e Tehran, 1975.

Makki, Hoseyn. *Tarikh-e Bist Saleh-ye Iran.* 6 vols. Tehran: Nashr-e Nashir, 1983.

Malcolm, John. *History of Persia.* 2 vols. London, 1829.

Malekpur, Jamshid. *Adabiyat-e Namayeshi dar Iran.* Tehran: Entesharat-e Tus, 1984.

Maneck, Susan Stiles. *The Death of Ahriman: Culture, Identity, and Theological Change among the Parsis of India.* Bombay: K. R. Cama Oriental Institute, 1997.

Mansoori, Ahmad. "Amercian Missionaries in Iran, 1834–1934." PhD dissertation, Ball State University, 1986.

Marefat, Mina. "The Protagonists Who Shaped Modern Tehran." In *Téhéran: Capitale bicentenaire,* ed. Chahryar Adle and Bernard Hourcade, pp. 95–125. Paris: Institut Français de Recherche en Iran, 1992.

Ma'sumi, Qolam Reza. *Bastanshenasi-ye Iran az 2407 ta 2535 Shahanshahi.* Tehran: Artesh, 1976.

Mas'udi, 'Abbas. *Ettela'at dar Yek Rob' Qarn.* Tehran: Ruznameh-ye Ettela'at, 1951.

Mathee, Rudi. "Transforming Dangerous Nomads into Useful Artisans: Education in the Reza Shah Period." *Iranian Studies* 26, no. 3–4 (1993): 313–36.

Matin Daftari, Ahmad. *Khaterat-e Yek Nokhost Vazir.* Tehran: Entesharat-e 'Elmi, 1991.

———. *La supression des capitulations en Perse.* Paris: Presses Universitaires de France, 1930.

Mayeur, Jean-Marie, and Madeleine Reberioux. *The Third Republic from Its Origins to the Great War, 1871–1914.* Cambridge: Cambridge University Press, 1984.

Menashri, David. *Education and the Making of Modern Iran.* Ithaca, NY: Cornell University Press, 1992.

Metcalf, Thomas. *Ideologies of the Raj.* Cambridge: Cambridge University Press, 1995.

Mirjafari, J. "The Haydari-Naymati Conflicts in Iran." *Iranian Studies* 12 (1979): 135–62.

Mitchell, Timothy. *Colonizing Egypt.* Berkeley: University of California Press, 1991.

Mo'ayyer al-Mamalek, Dust 'Ali Khan. *Yaddashtha-i az Zendegani-ye Khosusi-ye Naser al-Din Shah.* Tehran: Nashr-e Tarikh, 1982.

Momtahen al-Dowleh, Mehdi Khan Shaqaqi. *Khaterat-e Momtahen al-Dowleh.* Ed. Hoseyn Qoli Khan Shaqaqi. Tehran: Amir Kabir, 1974.

———. *Rejal-e Vezarat-e Kharejeh.* Edited by Iraj Afshar and Hoseyn Qoli Khan Shaqaqi. Tehran: Entesharat-e Asatir, 1986.

Montet, Edouard. *Le théâtre en Perse.* Geneva: n.p., 1888.

Morselvand, Hasan. *Shah Shekar: Bazju'iha-ye Mirza Reza Kermani va Sayerash.* Tabriz: Nashr-e Javanah, 1991.

Mosse, George. "Caesarism, Circuses, and Movements." *Journal of Contemporary History* 6, no. 2 (1971): 162–82.

———. *Crisis of German Ideology.* New York: Grosset and Dunlap, 1964.

———. *The Nationalization of the Masses: Political Symbolism and Mass Movements in Germany from the Napoleonic Wars through the Third Reich.* Ithaca, NY: Cornell University Press, 1975.

Mostafavi, 'Ali Asghar. *Zaman va Zendegi-ye Ostad Purdavud.* Tehran: Mostafavi, 1991.

Mostowfi, 'Abdollah. *Sharh-e Zendegani-ye Man.* 2 vols. Tehran: Chapkhaneh-ye 'Elmi, 1944.

Motia-Esfahani, Sadreddin. "Sayyid Hasan Taqizadeh: The Emergence of Modern Iran." PhD dissertation, New York University, 1981.

Mott, Lewis Feeman. *Ernest Renan.* New York: D. Appleton, 1921.

Mowlana, Hamid. "Journalism in Iran: History and Interpretation." PhD dissertation, Northwestern University, 1963.

Mukherjee, Kedar Nath. *The Political Philosophy of Rabindranth Tagore.* New Delhi: S. Chand, 1982.

Müller, Friedrich Max. *Lectures on the Science of Language.* New York: Charles Scribner, 1865.

Nafisi, Sa'id. *Tarikh-e Ejtema'i va Siyasi-ye Iran,* vol. 1. Tehran: Entesharat-e Bonyad, 1965.

Nairn, Tom. "The Modern Janus." *New Left Review* 94 (Nov.-Dec. 1975): 3–29.

Najmi, Naser. *Iran-e Qadim va Tehran-e Qadim.* Tehran: Entesharat-e Janzadeh, 1983.

Nashat, Guity. *The Origins of Modern Reform in Iran: 1870–1880.* Urbana: University of Illinois Press, 1982.

Nateq, Homa. *Karnameh-ye Farhangi-ye Farangi dar Iran.* Paris: Khavaran, 1996.
———, ed. *Qanun.* Tehran, 1976.

Nateq, Nasih. *Iran az Negah-e Gubinu.* Tehran: Afshar, 1985.

Nejand, Sa'id. *Muzeha-ye Jahan va Asar-e Honari-ye Iran.* Tehran: n.p., 1971.

Nikbin, Nassrollah. *Ezhar-e Nazar Dar Bareh-ye Arzesh-e 'Elmi-ye Tarikh-e Moshir al-Dowleh.* Tehran: Dehkhoda, 1968.

Niya, Ja'far Mehdi. *Zendegi-ye Siyasi-ye Mohammad 'Ali Forughi.* Tehran: Entesharat-e Panus, 1992.

Nöldeke, Theodor. *The Iranian National Epic.* Trans. L. Bogdanov. Bombay: K. R. Cama Oriental Institute, 1930; reprint, Philadelphia: Porcupine Press, 1979.
———. "Das iranische Nationalepos." In *Grundriss de iranischen Philologie,* eds. C. Bartholamae et al., vol. 2, pp. 130–211. Leiden: K. J. Krübner, 1894.

Nora, Pierre, ed. *Realms of Memory: Rethinking the French Past.* New York: Columbia University Press, 1996.

Omid, Jamal. *'Abdolhoseyn Sepanta: Zendegi va Sinema.* Tehran: Sherkat-e Tehran Faryab, 1984.

Pahlavi, Reza Shah. *Ejmali az Tarikh-e Dowreh-ye Zamamdari-ye Reza Shah-e Kabir.* Tehran: Qesmat-e Tablighat va Entesharat, 1950.

Palsetia, Jesse S. *The Parsis of India: Preservation of Identity in Bombay City.* London: E. J. Brill, 2001.

Parizi, Bastan. *Talash-e Azadi: Mohit-e Siyasi va Zendegi-ye Moshir al-Dowleh.* Tehran: Mohammad 'Ali 'Elmi, 1968.

Parsinejad, Iraj. *Mirza Fath 'Ali Akhundzadeh: A Literary Critic.* Piedmont, CA: Jahan Book Co., 1990.
———. *Mirza Fath 'Ali Akhundzadeh and Literary Criticism.* Tokyo: Institute for the Study of Languages and Cultures of Asia and Africa, 1988.

Pelly, Lewis. *The Miracle Play of Hasan and Husain.* 2 vols. London: Wm. H. Allen, 1879.

Peroomian, Rubina. "Commentary: A Comparative Approach to the Jewish and Armenian Enlightenment and Modernization." In *Enlightenment and Diaspora: The Armenian and Jewish Cases,* ed. Richard Hovannisian and David Myers. Atlanta: Scholars Press, 1999.

Pesyan, Najafqoli. *Az Savad Kuh ta Zhuhanesburg.* Tehran: Nashr-e Sales, 1998.

Pinckney, David. *Napoleon III and the Rebuilding of Paris.* Princeton: Princeton University Press, 1958.

Pirniya, Hasan. *Iran-e Qadim.* Tehran: Matba'eh-ye Majles, 1928.

Pistor-Hatam, Anja. "Iran and the Reform Movement in the Ottoman Empire: Persian Travelers, Exiles and Newsmen under the Impact of the Tanzimat." In *Proceedings of the Second European Conference of Iranian Studies,* pp. 561–79. Rome: Instituto Italiano per il Medio ed Estremo Oriente, 1995.

Poliakov, Léon. *The Aryan Myth: A History of Racist and Nationalist Ideas in Europe.* New York: Barnes and Noble Books, 1996.

Pour-e Davoud, Ibrahim. *Introduction to the Yashts.* Trans. D. J. Irani. Bombay: Iranian Zoroastrian Anjuman and Iran League, 1928.

Prakash, Gyan. *Another Reason: Science and the Imagination of Modern India.* Princeton, NJ: Princeton University Press, 1999.

———. "The Modern Nation's Return in the Archaic." *Critical Inquiry* 23 (1997): 536–56.

Qajar, Jalal al-Din Mirza. *Nameh-ye Khosravan,* vol. 1. Tehran: Pahlavi Commemorative Reprint Series, 1976.

Qajar, Naser al-Din Shah. *The Diary of His Majesty the Shah of Persia during His Tour through Europe in* A.D. *1873.* Trans. J. W. Redhouse. London, 1874.

———. *Ruznameh-ye Safar-e Farangestan.* Tehran, 1874.

———. *Safarnameh.* Esfehan: Sazman-e Entesharat-e Andisheh, 1964.

———. *Safarnameh-ye ʿAtabat.* Ed. Iraj Afshar. Tehran: Entesharat-e Ferdowsi, 1984.

Ramazani, R. K. *The Foreign Policy of Iran, 1500–1914.* Charlottesville: University of Virginia Press, 1966.

Renan, Ernest. *Nouvelle étude d'histoire religieuse.* Paris: Calmann Lévy, 1884.

———. *Vie de Jesus.* Paris: Calmann Lévy, 1863.

Richards, John. *The Open Road to Persia.* London: Church Missionary Society, 1933.

Ringer, Monica. *Education, Religion, and the Discourse of Cultural Reform in Qajar Iran.* Costa Mesa, CA: Mazda Press, 2001.

Rosul, Morteza. "Vezarat-e Farhang-e Diruz: Az Zaban-e ʿAli Akbar Kusari." *Tarikh-e Moʿaser-i Iran* 4, no. 13–14 (2000): 345–474.

Sadiq, ʿIsa. "Cheguneh Aramgah-e Ferdowsi bevojud Amad." In *Ferdowsi va Adabiyat-e Hamasi: Majmuʿeh-ye Sokhanraniha-ye Nokhostin Jashn-e Tus,* pp. 204–7. Tehran: Entesharat-e Sorush, 1976.

———. *Modern Persia and Her Educational System.* New York: Teacher's College of Columbia University, 1931.

———. *Tarikh-e Farhang-e Iran.* Tehran: Daneshgah-e Tehran, 1957.

———. *Yadegar-e ʿOmr.* Tehran: Amir Kabir, 1966.

Sadiqipur, ʿAbdolreza, ed. *Yadegar-e Gozashteh: Majmuʿeh-ye Sokhanraniha-ye Reza Shah.* Tehran: Sazman-e Chap va Entesharat-e Javidan, 1967.

Safaʾi, Ibrahim, ed. *Nameha-ye Tarikhi.* Tehran: Chap-e Sharq, 1969.

Safavi, Ibrahim, ed. *Reza Shah-e Kabir dar Aʾineh-ye Khaterat.* Los Anjeles: n.p., 1986.

Sahni, Kalpana. *Crucifying the Orient: Russian Orientalism and the Colonization of the Caucasus and Central Asia.* Oslo: Institute for the Comparative Research of Human Culture, 1997.

Saleh, ʿAli Pasha, ed. *Cultural Ties between Iran and the United States.* Tehran: Sherkat-e Chapkhaneh Bistopanj-e Shahrivar, 1976.

Sanjabi, Maryam. "Rereading the Enlightenment: Akhundzadeh and His Voltaire." *Iranian Studies* 28, no. 1–2 (1995): 39–60.

Schwartz, Vanessa R. *Spectacular Realities: Early Mass Culture in Fin-de-Siècle Paris*. Berkeley: University of California Press, 1998.

Serana, Carla. *Hommes et choses en Perse*. Paris: Charpentier, 1883.

Seyf, Ahmad. "The Commercialization of Agriculture: Production and Trade of Opium in Persia, 1850–1906." *International Journal of Middle East Studies* 16, no. 2 (1984): 233–50.

Shahbazi, A. Shapour. *Ferdowsi: A Critical Biography*. Costa Mesa, CA: Harvard University Center for Middle Eastern Studies/Mazda Press, 1991.

Shahri, Ja'far. *Tarikh-e Ejtema'i-ye Tehran dar Qarn-e Sizdahom*. Tehran: Entesharat-e Esma'iliyan, 1988.

Shahrokh, Keykhosrow. *Yaddashtha-ye Keykhosrow Shahrokh*. Tehran: n.p., 1977.

Shaw, Stanford. *History of the Ottoman Empire and Modern Turkey*. 2 vols. Cambridge: Cambridge University Press, 1977.

Sheikholislami, A. Reza. *The Structure of Central Authority in Qajar Iran, 1871–1896*. Atlanta: Scholars Press, 1997.

Sheil, J. *Glimpses of Life and Manners in Persia*. London, 1856.

Simmel, George. *The Sociology of Georg Simmel*. Trans. and ed. Kurt H. Wolff. New York, 1950.

Skendi, Stavro. *The Albanian National Awakening, 1878–1912*. Princeton, NJ: Princeton University Press, 1967.

Storey, C. A. *Persian Literature: A Bio-Bibliographical Survey*, vol. 1, part 1. London: Luzac, 1927.

Suny, Ronald Grigor. *The Baku Commune, 1917–1918*. Princeton, NJ: Princeton University Press, 1972.

———, ed. *Transcaucasia, Nationalism, and Social Change: Essays in the History of Armenia, Azerbaijan, and Georgia*. Ann Arbor: University of Michigan Press, 1983.

Szyliowicz, Joseph S. *Education and Modernization in the Middle East*. Ithaca, NY: Cornell University Press, 1973.

Tagore, Mahareshi Devendranath. *The Autobiography*. Trans. Satyendranath Tagore and Indira Devi. London: Macmillan, 1961.

Taqizadeh, Hasan. *Zendegi-ye Tufani: Khaterat-e Sayyed Hasan Taqizadeh*. Ed. Iraj Afshar. Tehran: 'Elmi, 1993.

———. *Maqalat*. Ed. Iraj Afshar. Tehran: Sherkat-e Sahami Afsat, 1972.

Tavakoli-Targhi, Mohamad. "Contested Memories: Narrative Structures and Allegorical Meanings of Iran's Pre-Islamic History." *Iranian Studies* 29, no. 1–2 (1996): 149–76.

———. "Modernity, Herotopia and Homeless Texts." *Comparative Studies of South Asia, Africa, and the Middle East* 18, no. 2 (1998): 2–14.

———. *Refashioning Iran: Orientalism, Occidentalism and Historiography*. New York: St. Anthony's/Palgrave, 2001.

————. "Tarikh-pardazi va Iran-arayi: Bazsazi-ye Huviyat-e Irani dar Gozaresh-e Tarikh." *Iran Nameh* 12, no. 4 (1994): 583–628.

Timuri, Ibrahim. *'Asr-e Bikhabari ya Tarikh-e Emtiyazat dar Iran.* Tehran: Eqbal, 1953.

Thomas, Edward. *Early Sassanian Inscriptions: Seals and Coins.* London: Trübner, 1868.

Todorov, Tzetan. *On Human Diversity: Nationalism, Racism, and Exoticism in French Thought.* Cambridge, MA: Harvard University Press, 1993.

Trautmann, Thomas R. *Aryans and British India.* Berkeley: University of California Press, 1997.

Trigger, Bruce G. *A History of Archaeological Thought.* Cambridge: Cambridge University Press, 1989.

Truesdell, Mathew. *Spectacular Politics: Louis-Napoleon Bonaparte and the Fête Impériale, 1849–1870.* Oxford: Oxford University Press, 1997.

Twain, Mark. *Europe and Elsewhere.* New York, 1923.

van der Veer, Peter. "Hindus: A Superior Race." *Nations and Nationalism* 5, no. 3 (1999): 419–30.

Vatandoust, Gholamreza. "Sayyid Hasan Taqizadah and *Kaveh:* Modernism in Post-Constitutional Iran (1916–1921)." PhD dissertation, University of Washington, 1977.

Vaziri, Mostafa. *Iran as Imagined Nation: The Construction of National Identity.* New York: Paragon House, 1993.

Wilber, Donald. *Reza Shah Pahlavi: Resurrection and Reconstruction of Iran.* Hicksville, NY: Exposition Press, 1975.

Writer, Rashna. *Contemporary Zoroastrians: An Unstructured Nation.* Lanham, MD: University Press of America, 1994.

Zaher al-Dowleh, 'Ali Khan. *Tarikh-e Bidorugh.* Tehran: Entesharat-e Sharq, 1983.

Zakerzadeh, Amir Hoseyn. *Sargozasht-e Tehran.* Tehran: Entesharat-e Qalam, 1994.

Zandjani, Habibullah. "Tehran et sa population: Deux siècles d'histoire." In *Téhéran: Capitale bicentenaire,* ed. Chahryar Adle and Bernard Hourcade, pp. 251–66. Paris: Institut Français de Recherche en Iran, 1992.

Zirinsky, Michael. "Render Therefore unto Caesar the Things Which Are Caesar's: American Presbyterian Educators and Reza Shah." *Iranian Studies* 26, no. 3–4 (1993): 337–56.

Zoka', Yahya. *Tarikhcheh-ye Sakhtemanha-ye Arg-e Soltani-ye Tehran va Rahnama-ye Kakh-e Golestan.* Tehran: Anjoman-e Asar-e Melli, 1970.

Zoka', Yahya, and Mohammad Hasan Semsar, eds. *Tehran dar Tasvir.* 2 vols. Tehran: Sorush, 1997.

INDEX